DAVY CROCKETT'S OWN STORY

DAVY CROCKETT'S

OWN STORY

As written by himself

The Autobiography of America's Great Folk Hero

KONECKY&KONECKY

Konecky & Konecky
72 Ayers Point Rd.
Old Saybrook, CT 06475

ISBN: 1-56852-243-6

Printed and bound in the USA

PUBLISHER'S NOTE

Davy Crockett's Own Story consists of three volumes of autobiographical writings: *A Narrative of the Life of David
Crockett . . . Written by Himself,* published in 1834; *An
Account of Col. Crockett's Tour to the North and Down East,*
published in 1834, and *Col. Crockett's Exploits and Adventures in Texas,* published posthumously in 1836.

Some question has arisen as to the authenticity of these
autobiographical writings. It has been claimed that Davy
Crockett lacked the education to produce these books, and
that the "literary style . . . is clearly such to have been out of
Crockett's compass." (J. D. Wade, "The Authorship of David
Crockett's *Autobiography,*" *Georgia Historical Quarterly,* vol.
VI, pp. 265-68.)

It is true, as Crockett points out in his preface, that he had
a friend "go over" his writing to correct the spelling and
grammar. However, one has but to read the speeches delivered by Crockett in Congress, several of which are repro-
duced in this book, to conclude that he was quite capable of
producing these autobiographical accounts. As for his spelling and grammar, they were not much worse than those of
many of Crockett's contemporaries whose writings were published.

In order to preserve the flavor of Davy Crockett's style, the
present edition retains the spelling and punctuation of the
original. Explanatory notes and chapter titles have been especially prepared.

ed and established in conformity with the laws of Tennessee, or by agreement between the respective occupants. Nor in any event where surveys have been made, and returned by the surveyor of a district, shall it be necessary to re-survey; but entries may be made upon said surveys, as made and returned.

"SEC. 3. *And be it further enacted,* That every person applying to make any such entry, shall, before making the same, prove, to the satisfaction of the said principal surveyor, that he or she was in the actual occupation and possession of the land by him or her proposed to be entered on the said first day of April, one thousand eight hundred and twenty-nine; and that the improvements thereon were made by him or herself, or by their procurement, or that he or she had peaceably acquired the possession thereof, by the consent of the person making the same; and that the land is considered vacant.

"SEC. 4. *And be it further enacted,* That all the right, title, and claim, of the United States to the land which may be so entered and granted, shall vest in the grantees, and their heirs, forever : *Provided,* That such grants shall only operate as relinquishments of the title of the United States to the lands contained therein; nor will the United States, in any manner, be accountable to the grantees under this act, for any lands, or the value thereof, in case a better title should be in any other person."

This amendment having been read, and the question thereon having been stated from the Chair—

Mr. CROCKETT said that he had offered to the House the foregoing amendment to the bill, with the confident hope that, if he could succeed in convincing the House that this could not prove a precedent for its action in relation to other States, and that the land it proposed to give away would, if retained, be of no use or value to the General Government, they would adopt the amendment, and pass the bill. He regretted, on this subject, to be under the necessity of differing from his respectable colleague,* [Mr. POLK] but the House would remember that his colleague and himself were very differently situated. They had received instructions from the Legislature of their State to ask Congress for a general grant of all the public lands remaining unpatented within its bounds for the purposes of education; and, having no prior obligation to conflict with those instructions, they were, of course, bound to obey them. He, it was true, as one of the Representatives of the State of Tennessee, was included within these instructions; but he had a higher authority, to which it was his duty and his pride ever to bow—his last instructions were from his own constituents, and these, in his estimation, took precedence of all others. The people who had honored him by making him their Representative, conceived that they were fairly entitled to the lands for which they had instructed him to ask this House, and which it was the object of his amendment to confer upon them. He asked this, however, not on the ground of strict legal right; he presented nothing in the shape of a demand; but he presented such a case as he believed and trusted would not fail to awaken the sympathies of this House, and effectually command its liberality. The persons in whose behalf he pleaded were the hardy sons of the soil; men who had entered the country when it lay in a state of native wildness; men who had broken the cane, and opened in the wilderness a home for their wives and children. The most of these enterprising and industrious settlers had once possessed other and better homes than they now enjoyed; they had entered on fertile lands, under titles which they believed to be good, and were successfully pushing their humble but independent fortune, when they were unexpectedly driven from their improvements by the appearance of a stranger, bringing a warrant of older date than theirs. Some of them had suffered this cruel disappointment more than once; they had been driven from improvement to

improvement, and from home to home, till, in despair of ever realizing their early hopes, they had settled on lands that nobody would claim—on scraps and refuse fragments of the soil, which remained after all that was valuable had been first selected and occupied. The country where their humble homes were situated had been thrown open to warrant holders for eight years; floods of warrants had been issued, and armies of their holders had overspread the soil, picking and culling out all the good land as long as any was to be found; and it was the fractions, the odds and ends, the refuse which remained, in shapeless fragments, between the boundary lines of other tracts, that they now asked of Congress. The land was of poor quality, and of little value in itself; but it was dear to them, because it held their home, and was their all. The country thus situated formed but a small portion of the State, embracing the Congressional district from which he came, and part of another from which came his colleague on his right, [Mr. POLK.] The great mass of it lay in his own district, and, in fact, made up the whole of that district.

The House would, therefore, perceive how he was situated, and would appreciate the obligations under which he lay to press this amendment. It was impossible that the grant of fractions of land thus situated could ever operate as a precedent for grants in those States where the public lands were regularly laid out in townships and sections, by lines at right angles. This country had never been laid out at all. The General Government had never had a surveyor within its boundaries. It was thrown open in a mass for the satisfaction of the North Carolina warrants; and every man who had a warrant hunted out the best land he could find; and, in fixing his boundary lines, had respect only to the quality of the soil, and the quantity he had a right to take; and thus the tracts located were of every conceivable shape. On the intervals between these lines, the people for whom he was pleading had fixed their little homes. They had mingled the sweat of their brows with the soil they occupied, and by the hand of hard and persevering toil had earned the little comforts they possessed. Was it fair for the General Government to take away these humble cottages from them, and make a donation of the whole to the Legislature of the State, for the purpose of raising up schools for the children of the rich? I ask the House [said Mr. C.] if to do this will be an act of charity to the poor? It is asked by the State as charity: will it be so in practical effect? I ask some of it, but not for the State—not for the sons of the wealthy; but for the poor and industrious men who have given it all its value by their toil. Give it to them, and you will bind them to their Government by an indissoluble tie. Nothing makes a people love their Government like such acts of parental kindness. Sir, these people, though poor, are of inestimable value in a free republic. They are the bone and sinew of the land; they are its strength and its bulwark; they are its main reliance in the hour of danger, and the first to breast the onset of an enemy. Will you take away their little all and give it to the Legislature to speculate upon? Or will you make to each of these meritorious citizens the donation of his humble piece of land, where he has at last found a refuge from the pursuit of more successful warrant holders?- It is dear to him, however humble; his children were born upon it; and there he has lived in peace and contentment. I ask you to give it him, and I ask with the confident hope that you will do it. Sir, my people think that those who live northeast of the dividing line have already made enough out of them. My district has had to pay one hundred thousand dollars towards the erection of colleges in the northeast part of the State. I think this is quite enough, but still more is now demanded, and I find myself under the necessity of defending one poor district against all the rest of the State of Tennes-

Davy Crockett's eloquent defense in Congress of the rights of the small farmers to own the land they occupied is reported in

see. I shall do it; for I am dependent upon them for my station here; and so long as I hold a seat upon this floor I shall take their part against all who would exact upon them. Three hundred and five thousand acres of the best land in the district have already gone to satisfy warrants which I never believed to be just in principle. The compromise between the States of Tennessee and North Carolina required, indeed, the satisfying of these warrants, but they had been issued to Revolutionary soldiers, who were dead, and had no heirs living, and I ever viewed the arrangement as unjust and oppressive. When the measure was debated in the Legislature of my State, I opposed it to the best of my poor ability, but we were overruled and had to submit. According to that arrangement, the Colleges got sixty thousand acres of our land, The University of North Carolina got one hundred and forty thousand acres more of it. After a little while, the demand for ninety-six thousand acres more was made. They demanded that this amount should be provided for and secured: that I also opposed. I could not, in my conscience, consent to it, because I did not think it right in principle. The measure, however, went into effect; and in a little while the ninety-six thousand acres had swelled to one hundred and five thousand. Yes, one hundred and five thousand acres taken out of one little district! You can readily believe that such a draught as that, made in twenty-five acre warrants, cut us up at an awful rate. The grant for the support of colleges drained us of fifty-two thousand five hundred dollars in cash. Ay, sir, in hard cash, wrung from the hands of poor men, who live by the sweat of their brow. I repeat, that I was utterly opposed to this: not because I am the enemy of education, but because the benefits of education are not to be dispensed with an equal hand. This College system went into practice to draw a line of demarcation between the two classes of society—it separated the children of the rich from the children of the poor. The children of my people never saw the inside of a college in their lives, and never are likely to do so. Those who passed the act well knew that we never should derive any good from it: but they insisted that the land should be given up, and they sent State surveyors to survey it. The expenses of that survey pressed heavily on my constituents—it drove some of them to their wit's end. Sir, I have seen the last blanket of a poor, but honest and industrious family, sold under the hammer of the sheriff, to pay for that survey. Ay, sir, the little furniture they had saved from better days, or earned by long and honorable toil, was torn from them to pay the fees of those surveyors. Exactions like these were made on men whose whole worldly estate consisted of some twenty or thirty acres of the poorest land. Sir, it is for such men that I plead. I ask, in my place, as their advocate and Representative, that you will make them a donation of that little property. Let it be their own. While they bedew it with the sweat of their faces, let them at least have the consolation of knowing that they may leave it to their own children, and not have it squandered on the sons of a stranger. Such fragments of miserable soil can be of no use or value to this Government. You will never insist on retaining it in your own hands. You will never sell it, for it will never bear the expense of surveying. You must do something with it. Will you not bestow it as a boon upon the unfortunate people who have nothing else in the world? There they are living in peace—they can there make shift to bring up their children. Some of them are widows, whose husbands fell while fighting your battles on the frontiers. None of them are rich, but they are an honest, industrious, hardy, persevering, kind-hearted people. I know them—I know their situation. I have shared the hospitality of their cottages, and been honored by their confidence with a seat in this assembly; and base and ungrateful, indeed, must I be, when I cease to remember it. No,

sir, I cannot forget it: and if their little all is to be wrested from them, for the purposes of State speculation; if a swindling machine is to be set up to strip them of what little the surveyors, and the colleges, and the warrant holders, have left them, it shall never be said that I sat by in silence, and refused, however humbly, to advocate their cause.

Mr. POLK rose, and said he did not differ so much from his colleague as he imagined. The Legislature of the State of Tennessee, in anticipation of the relinquishment which they expected to obtain from Congress, had already provided that, when the relinquishment should be obtained, the actual occupants should have a preference of entry. He was confident, therefore, if the relinquishment was made, that the constituents of his colleague would not be molested in their possessions by the Legislature, but would have a preference of entry. He had prepared an amendment, however, to the original bill, (which, when it should be in order, he would offer) which provided, in substance, that the Legislature, in appropriating these lands, should, as they had already by their acts avowed their intention to do, give a preference of entry to the actual settlers. This, it occurred to him, would embrace all the objects his colleague asked. He would ask how the object of his colleague was to be effected by the amendment which he proposed? How could the United States patent these lands without first establishing a land office in the country and surveying them? We know the United States never had a land officer in the State; no Federal officer had ever surveyed them; and without first doing so, how could they ascertain what lands were vacant, and what were not? The lands that remained vacant were in detached parcels and scattered pieces, and were the refuse lands. All the lands that had ever been granted in the State had been granted by State authority, and by State officers—by State surveyors, by State registers, and by the Governor of the State. All the records in reference to these lands were in the archives of the State. The Government of the United States had none of them; they had no power or control over the State officers. Would not the amendment, therefore, be a nullity, unless Federal officers, over whom Congress had power and control, are appointed to carry it into effect? He said he was as friendly to these settlers as any one, but preferred leaving their interests to the State, who had never failed to provide for others similarly situated. He read the amendment which he proposed to offer, for the information of the House.

The SPEAKER said it was then in order to offer it.

Mr. POLK accordingly offered the following as an additional section to the original bill:

"Sec. 3. *And be it further enacted,* That the State of Tennessee, in appropriating said lands as a condition on which the cession herein contained is made, shall grant a preference of entry to all persons who shall have made improvements on, or shall be in the actual occupation or possession of, any of the vacant lands herein ceded, on or before the first day of April next, or their lawful assignees, by transfer or otherwise, for a quantity of such vacant land, not exceeding, each, one hundred and sixty acres; which shall, in all cases, include their improvements or settlements: *Provided,* That, when two or more persons are settled on vacant lands so contiguous to each other as not to allow the grant of one hundred and sixty acres each, the surveys shall be made in such a manner as to give an equal proportion to each, quantity and quality being considered, unless the settlers shall agree on a dividing line; in which case, the surveys shall be made in conformity to such agreement."

On motion of Mr. WICKLIFFE, this amendment was amended, by adding, after the words "preference of entry," the words, 'without charge.'

Gales & Seaton's *Register of Debates in Congress.* For excerpts from this speech, *see* pp. 283-84.

Here is an excerpt from one of Davy Crockett's own letters with the spelling and grammar unaltered. The original is in the Tennessee Historical Society.

Washington City 27th January, 1829.
My Dear Brother
    I received your favour of the 11th inst and parused its contents with great Pleasure all except that part whare it Relats to the disagreeable situation of friends Differeing it is is certainly the worst of all furiz I Received a letter on yesterday from John which affected my feelings a great deal that was in consequence of the Death of our Poor Dear little neece Rebecca ann Burgin. . . . I thought almost as much of her as one of my own I hope she is this day in eternal happiness whare I am endeavouring to make my way. . . .
    I have a fine sted horse at home a packlet which I would like to Breed from that mare and would like much if Father & brother Could Bring her out this I wish you to informe them I wish you to tender my kindest friendship to all my connection also except to your self & Family my warmest esteem I must conclude with a hope that the protecting hand of the almighty may Bless guard & protect you and all our Connection is the Prayer of your affectionate Brother Farwell
                                                    David Crockett

P.S. Pleas write imediately on the Receipt of these lines let me know how all is.
                                                    D.C.

How I Came to Be a Writer

In the following pages I have endeavored to give the reader a plain, honest, homespun account of my state in life, and some few of the difficulties which have attended me along its journey, down to this time. I am perfectly aware, that I have related many small and, as I fear, uninteresting circumstances; but if so, my apology is, that it was rendered necessary by a desire to link the different periods of my life togther, as they have passed, from my childhood onward, and thereby to enable the reader to select such parts of it as he may relish most, if, indeed, there is anything in it which may suit his palate.

I have also been operated on by another consideration. It is this:—I know, that obscure as I am, my name is making a considerable deal of fuss in the world. I can't tell why it is, nor in what it is to end. Go where I will, everybody seems anxious to get a peep at me; and it would be hard to tell which would have the advantage, if I, and the "Government," and "Black Hawk," and a great eternal big caravan of *wild varmints* were all to be showed at the same time in four different parts of any of the big cities in the nation. I am not so sure that I shouldn't get the most custom of any of the crew. There must therefore be something in me, or about me, that attracts attention, which is even mysterious to myself. I can't understand it, and I therefore put all the facts down, leaving the reader free to take his choice of them.

On the subject of my style, it is bad enough, in all conscience, to please critics, if that is what they are after. They are a sort of vermin, though, that I sha'n't even so much as stop to brush off. If they want to work on my book, just let them go ahead; and after they are done, they had better blot out all their criticisms, than to know what opinion I would express of *them*, and by what sort of a curious name I would call *them*, if I was standing near them, and looking over their shoulders. They will, at most, have only their trouble for their pay. But I rather expect I shall have them on my side.

But I don't know of anything in my book to be criticised on by honorable men. Is it on my spelling?—that's not my trade. Is it on my grammar?—I hadn't time to learn it, and make no pretensions to it. Is it on the order and arrangement of my book?—I never wrote one before, and never read very many; and, of course, know mighty little about that. Will it be on the authorship of the book?— this I claim, and I'll hang on to it like a wax plaster. The whole book is my own, and every sentiment and sentence in it. I would not be such a fool, or knave either, as to deny that I have had it run hastily over by a friend or so, and that some little alterations have been made in the spelling and grammar; and I am not so sure that it is not the worse of even that, for I despise this way of spelling contrary to nature. And as for grammar, it's pretty much a thing of nothing at last, after all the fuss that's made about it. In some places, I wouldn't suffer either the spelling, or grammar, or anything else to be touched; and therefore it will be found in my own way.

But if anybody complains that I have had it looked over, I can only say to him, her, or them—as the case may be—that while critics were learning grammar, and learning to spell, I and "Doctor Jackson, LL.D." were fighting in the wars; and if our books, and messages, and proclamations, and cabinet writings, and so forth, and so on, should need a little looking over, and a little correcting of the spelling and the grammar to make them fit for use, its just nobody's business. Big men have more important matters to attend to than crossing their *t*'s—and dotting their *i*'s—, and such like small things. But the "Government's" name is to the proclamation, and my name's to the book; and if I didn't write the book, the "Government" didn't write the proclamation, which no man *dares to deny!*

But just read for yourself, and my ears for a heel tap, if before you get through you don't say, with many a good-natured smile and hearty laugh, "This is truly the very thing itself—the exact image of its Author,

DAVID CROCKETT."

Contents

DAVY CROCKETT'S OWN STORY

CHAPTER ONE

I Come Into the World

As the public seem to feel some interest in the history of an individual so humble as I am, and as that history can be so well known to no person living as to myself, I have, after so long a time, and under many pressing solicitations from my friends and acquaintances, at last determined to put my own hand to it, and lay before the world a narrative on which they may at least rely as being true. And seeking no ornament or coloring for a plain, simple tale of truth, I throw aside all hypocritical and fawning apologies, and according to my own maxim, just *"go ahead."* Where I am not known, I might, perhaps, gain some little credit by having thrown around this volume some of the flowers of learning; but where I am known, the vile cheatery would soon be detected, and like the foolish jackdaw, that with *borrowed* tail attempted to play the peacock, I should be justly robbed of my pilfered ornaments, and sent forth to strut without a tail for the balance of my time. I shall commence my book with what little I have learned of the history of my father, as all *great men* rest many, if not most, of their hopes on their noble ancestry. Mine was poor, but I hope honest, and even that is as much as many a man can say. But to my subject.

My father's name was John Crockett, and he was of Irish descent. He was either born in Ireland or on a passage from that country to America across the Atlantic. He was by profession a farmer, and spent the early part of his life in the State of Pennsylvania. The name of my mother was Rebecca Hawkins. She was an American woman, born in the State of Maryland, between York and Baltimore. It is likely I may have heard where they were married, but if so, I have forgotten. It is, however, certain that they were, or else the public would never have been troubled with the history of David Crockett, their son.

I have an imperfect recollection of the part which I have understood my father took in the revolutionary war. I personally know nothing about it, for it happened to be a little before my day; but from himself, and many others who were well acquainted with its troubles and afflictions, I have learned that he was a soldier in the revolutionary war, and took part in that bloody struggle. He fought, according to my information, in the battle of King's Mountain, against the British and tories, and in some other engagements, of which my remembrance is too imperfect to enable me to speak with any certainty. At some time, though I cannot say certainly when, my father, as I have understood, lived in Lincoln county, in the State of North Carolina. How long I don't know. But when he removed from there, he settled in that district of country which is now embraced in the east division of Tennessee, though it was not then erected into a State.

He settled there under dangerous circumstances, both to himself and his family, as the country was full of Indians, who were at that time very troublesome. By the Creeks, my grandfather and grandmother Crockett were both murdered in their own house, and on the very spot of ground where Rogersville, in Hawkins county, now stands. At the same time, the Indians wounded Joseph Crockett, a brother to my father, by a ball, which broke his arm; and took James a prisoner, who was still a younger brother than Joseph, and who, from natural defects, was less able to make his escape, as he was both deaf and dumb. He remained with them for seventeen years and nine months, when he was discovered and recollected by my father and his eldest brother, William Crockett; and was purchased by them from an Indian trader, at a price which I do not now remember; but so it was, that he was delivered up to them, and they returned him to his relatives. He now lives in Cumberland county, in the State of Kentucky, though I have not seen him for many years.

My father and mother had six sons and three daughters. I was the fifth son. What a pity I hadn't been the seventh! For then I might have been, by *common consent,* called *doctor,* as a heap of people get to be great men. But, like many of them, I stood no chance to become great in any other way than by accident. As my father was very poor, and living as he did, *far back in the back woods,* he had neither the means nor the opportunity to give me, or any of the rest of his children, any learning.

But before I get on the subject of my own troubles, and a great many very funny things that have happened to me, like all other historians and biographers, I should inform the public that I was born, myself, as well as other folks, and that this important event took place, according to the best information I have received on the subject, on the 17th of August, in the year 1786; whether by day or night, I believe I never heard, but if I did, I have forgotten. I suppose, however, it is not very material to my present purpose, nor to the world, as the more important fact is well attested, that I was born; and, indeed, it might be inferred, from my present size and appearance, that I was pretty *well born,* though I have never yet attached myself to that numerous and worthy society.

At the time my father lived at the mouth of Lime Stone, on the Nolachucky river; and for the purpose not only of showing what sort of a man I now am, but also to show how soon I began to be a *sort of a little man,* I have endeavored to take the *back track* of life, in order to fix on the first thing that I can remember. But even then, as now, so many things were happening, that, as Major Jack Downing would say,* they are all in "a pretty considerable of a snarl," and I find it "kinder hard" to fix on that thing, among them all, which really happened first. But I think it likely I have hit on the outside line of my recollection; as one thing happened at which I was so badly scared, that it seems to me I could not have forgotten it, if it had happened a little time only after I was born. Therefore it furnishes me with no certain

* Major Jack Downing was the name used over the letters of Seba Smith of the Portland (Maine) *Courier.* They were outstanding examples of newpaper humor and political satire of the day and were widely reprinted.

evidence of my age at the time; but I know one thing very well, and that is, that when it happened I had no knowledge of the use of breeches, for I had never had any nor worn any.

But the circumstance was this: My four elder brothers, and a well-grown boy of about fifteen years old, by the name of Campbell, and myself, were all playing on the river's side, when all the rest of them got into my father's canoe, and put out to amuse themselves on the water, leaving me on the shore alone.

Just a little distance below them, there was a fall in the river, which went slap-right straight down. My brothers, though they were little fellows, had been used to paddling the canoe, and could have carried it safely anywhere about there; but this fellow Campbell wouldn't let them have the paddle, but, fool like, undertook to manage it himself. I reckon he had never seen a water craft before; and it went just any way but the way he wanted it. There he paddled, and paddled, and paddled—all the while going wrong, until, in a short time, here they were all going, straight forward, stern foremost, right plump to the falls; and if they had only a fair shake, they would have gone over as slick as a whistle. It wasn't this, though, that scared me, for I was so infernal mad that they had left me on the shore, that I had as soon have seen them all go over the falls a bit, as any other way. But their danger was seen by a man by the name of Kendall, but I'll be shot if it was Amos, for I believe I would know him yet if I was to see him. This man Kendall was working in a field on the bank, and knowing there was no time to lose, he started full tilt, and here he come like a cane brake afire; and as he ran he threw off his coat, and then his jacket, and then his shirt, for I know when he got to the water he had nothing on but his breeches. But seeing him in such a hurry, and tearing off his clothes as he went, I had no doubt but that the devil, or something else was after him—and close on him, too—as he was running within an inch of his life. This alarmed me, and I screamed out like a young painter. But Kendall didn't stop for this. He went ahead with all might, and as full bent on saving the boys, as Amos was on moving the deposites. When he came to the water, he plunged in, and where it was too deep to wade, he would swim, and where it was shallow enough he went bolting on; and by such exertion as I never saw at any other time in my life, he reached the canoe, when it was within twenty or thirty feet of the falls; and so great was the suck and so swift the current, that poor Kendall had a hard time of it to stop them at last, as Amos will to stop the mouths of the people about his stockjobbing. But he hung on to the canoe, till he got it stopp'd, and then draw'd it out of danger. When they got out, I found the boys were more scared than I had been, and the only thing that comforted me was the belief that it was a punishment on them for leaving me on shore.

Shortly after this, my father removed and settled in the same county, about ten miles above Greenville.

There, another circumstance happened, which made a lasting impression on my memory, though I was but a small child. Joseph Hawkins, who was a brother to my mother, was in the woods hunting for deer. He was passing near a thicket of brush, in which one of our neighbors was gathering some grapes, as it was in the fall of the year, and the grape season. The body of the man was hid by the brush, and it was only as he would raise his hand to pull the bunches, that any part of him could be seen. It was a likely place for deer, and my uncle, having no suspicion that it was any human being, but supposing the raising of the hand to be an occasional twitch of a deer's ear, fired at the lump, and as the devil would have it, unfortunately shot the man through the body. I saw my father draw a silk handkerchief through the bullet hole, and entirely through his body; yet after a while he got well, as little as any one would have thought it. What become of him, or whether he is dead or alive, I don't know; but I reckon he didn't fancy the business of gathering grapes in an out-of-the-way thicket soon again.

The next move my father made was to the mouth of Cove creek, where he and a man by the name of Thomas Galbreath undertook to build a mill in partnership. They went on very well with their work until it was nigh done, when there came a second epistle to Noah's freshet, and away went their mill, shot, lock, and barrel. I remember the water rose so high, that it got up into the house we lived in, and my father moved us out of it to keep us from being drowned. I was now about seven or eight years old, and have a pretty distinct recollection of everything that was going on. From his bad luck in that business, and being ready to wash out from mill building, my father again removed, and this time, settled in Jefferson county, now in the State of Tennessee, where he opened a tavern on the road from Abbingdon to Knoxville.

His tavern was on a small scale, as he was poor; and the principal accommodations which he kept were for the wagoners who traveled the road. Here I remained with him until I was twelve years old; and about that time, you may guess, if you belong to Yankee land, or reckon, if like me you belong to the back-woods, that I began to make up my acquaintance with hard times, and a plenty of them.

An old Dutchman, by the name of Jacob Siler, who was moving from Knox county to Rockbridge, in the State of Virginia, in passing, made a stop at my father's house. He had a large stock of cattle, that he was carrying on with him, and I suppose, made some proposition to my father to hire some one to assist him.

Being hard run every way, and having no thought, as I believe, that I was cut out for a Congressman, or the like, young as I was, and as little as I knew about traveling or being from home, he hired me to the old Dutchman to go four hundred miles on foot, with a perfect stranger that I had never seen until the evening before. I set out with a heavy heart, it is true, but I went ahead until we arrived at the place, which was three miles from what is called the Natural Bridge, and made a stop at the house of a Mr. Hartley, who was father-in-law to Mr. Siler, who had hired me. My Dutch master was very kind to me, and gave me five or six dollars, being pleased, as he said, with my services.

This, however, I think was a bait for me, as he persuaded me to stay with him, and not return any more to my father. I had been taught so many lessons of obedience by my father, that I at first supposed I was bound to obey this man, or at least I was afraid openly to disobey him; and I therefore staid with him, and tried to put on a look of perfect contentment until I got the family all to believe I was fully satisfied. I had been there about four or five weeks, when one day myself and two other boys were playing on the roadside, some distance from the house. There came along three wagons. One belonged to an old man by the name of Dunn, and the others to two of his sons. They had each of them a good team, and were all bound for Knoxville. They had been in the habit of stopping at my father's as they passed the road, and I knew them. I made myself known to the old gentleman, and informed him of my situation; I expressed a wish to get back to my father and mother, if they could fix any plan for me to do so. They told me that they would stay that night at a tavern seven miles from there, and that if I could get to them before day the next morning, they would take me home; and if I was pursued, they would protect me. This was a Sunday evening; I went back to the good old Dutchman's house, and as good fortune would have it, he and the family were out on a visit. I gathered my clothes and what little money I had, and put them all together under the head of my bed. I went to bed early that night, but sleep seemed to be a stranger to me. For though I was a wild boy, yet I dearly loved my father and mother, and their images appeared to be so deeply fixed in my mind, that I could not sleep for thinking of them. And then the fear that when I should attempt to go out, I should be discovered and called to a halt, filled me with anxiety; and between my childish love of home, on the one hand, and the fears of which I have spoken, on the other, I felt mighty queer.

But so it was, about three hours before day in the morning, I got up to make my start. When I got out, I found it was snowing fast, and that the snow was then on the ground about eight inches deep. I had not even the advantage of moonlight, and the whole sky was hid by the falling snow, so that I had to guess at my way to the big road, which was about a half mile from the house. I, however, pushed ahead, and soon got to it, and then pursued it in the direction to the wagons.

I could not have pursued the road if I had not guided myself by the opening it made between the timber, as the snow was too deep to leave any part of it to be known by either seeing or feeling.

Before I overtook the wagons, the earth was covered about as deep as my knees; and my tracks filled so briskly after me, that by daylight my Dutch master would have seen no trace which I left.

I got to the place about an hour before day. I found the wagoners already stirring, and engaged in feeding and preparing their horses for a start. Mr. Dunn took me in and treated me with great kindness. My heart was more deeply impressed by meeting with such a friend and "at such a time," than by wading the snow-storm by night, or all the other sufferings which my mind had endured. I warmed myself by the fire, for I was very cold, and after an early breakfast, we set out on our journey. The thoughts of home now began to take the entire possession of my mind, and I almost numbered the sluggish turns of the wheels, and much more certainly the miles of our travel, which appeared to me to count mighty slow. I continued with my kind protectors until we got to the house of a Mr. John Cole, on Roanoke, when my impatience became so great, that I determined to set out on foot and go ahead by myself, as I could travel twice as fast in that way as the wagons could.

Mr. Dunn seemed very sorry to part with me, and used many arguments to prevent me from leaving him.

But home, poor as it was, again rushed on my memory, and it seemed ten times as dear to me as it ever had before. The reason was, that my parents were there, and all that I had been accustomed to in the hours of child- hood and infancy was there; and there my anxious little heart panted also to be. We remained at Mr. Cole's that night, and early in the morning I felt that I could not stay; so, taking leave of my friends, the wagoners, I went forward on foot, until I was fortunately overtaken by a gentleman, who was returning from market, to which he had been with a drove of horses. He had a led horse, with a bridle and saddle on him, and he kindly offered to let me get on his horse and ride him. I did so, and was glad of the chance, for I was tired, and was, moreover, near the first crossing of Roanoke, which I would have been com- pelled to wade, cold as the water was, if I had not fortu- nately met this good man. I travelled with him in this way, without anything turning up worth recording until we got within fifteen miles of my father's house. There we parted, and he went on to Kentucky, and I trudged on homeward, which place I reached that evening. The name of this kind gentleman I have entirely forgotten, and I am sorry for it; for it deserves a high place in my little book. A remembrance of his kindness to a little straggling boy, and a stranger to him, has, however, a resting place in my heart, and there it will remain as long as I live.

CHAPTER TWO

I Run Away from Home

Having gotten home, as I have just related, I remained with my father until the next fall, at which time he took it into his head to send me to a little country school, which was kept in the neighborhood by a man whose name was Benjamin Kitchen; though I believe he was no way connected with the cabinet. I went four days and had just began to learn my letters a little, when I had an unfortunate falling out with one of the scholars,—a boy much larger and older than myself. I knew well enough that though the school-house might do for a still hunt, it wouldn't do for *a drive*, and so I concluded to wait until I could get him out, and then I was determined to give him salt and vinegar. I waited till in the evening, and when the larger scholars were spelling I slipp'd out, and going some distance along his road, I lay by the way-side in the bushes, waiting for him to come along. After awhile, he and his company came on sure enough, and I pitched out from the bushes and set on him like a wild cat. I scratched his face all to a flitter jig, and soon made him cry out for quarters in good earnest. The fight being over, I went on home, and the next morning was started again to school; but do you think I went? No, indeed. I was very clear of it; for I expected the master would lick me up as bad as I had the boy. So, instead of going to the school-house, I laid out in the woods all day until in the evening the scholars were dismissed, and my brothers, who were also going to school, came along, returning home. I wanted to conceal this whole business from my father, and I persuaded them not to tell on me, which they agreed to.

Things went on in this way for several days; I starting with them to school in the morning, and returning with them in the evening, but lying out in the woods all day. At last, however, the master wrote a note to my father, inquiring why I was not sent to school. When he read this note he called me up, and I knew very well that I was in a devil of a hobble, for my father had been taking a few *horns*, and was in a good condition to make the fur fly. He called on me to know why I had not been at school. I told him I was afraid to go, and that the master would whip me, for I knew quite well if I was turned over to this old Kitchen, I should be cooked up to a cracklin' in little or no time. But I soon found that I was not to expect a much better fate at home; for my father told me, in a very angry manner, that he would whip me an eternal sight worse than the master if I didn't start immediately to the school. I tried again to beg off, but nothing would do but to go to the school. Finding me rather too slow about starting, he gathered about a two year old hickory, and broke after me. I put out with all my might, and soon we were both up to the top of our speed. We had a tolerable tough race for about a mile; but mind me, not on the school-house road, for I was trying to get as far the t'other way as possible. And I yet believe, if my father and the schoolmaster could both have levied on me about that time, I should never have been called on to sit in the councils of the nation, for I think they would have used me up. But fortunately for me, about this time I saw just before me a hill, over which I made headway, like a young steamboat. As soon as I had passed over it, I turned to one side, and hid myself in the bushes. Here I waited until the old gentleman passed by, puffing and blowing, as though his steam was high enough to burst his boilers. I waited until he gave up the hunt, and passed back again: I then cut out, and went to the house of an acquaintance a few miles off, who was just about to start with a drove. His name was Jesse Cheek, and I hired myself to go with him, determining not to return home, as home and the school-house had both become too hot for me. I had an elder brother, who also hired to go with the same drove. We set out and went on through Abbingdon, and the county seat of Withe county, in the State of Virginia; and then through Lynchburgh, by Orange court-house, and Charlottesville, passing through what was called Chester Gap, on to a town called Front Royal, where my employer sold out his drove to a man by the name of Vanmetre; and I was started homeward again, in company with a brother of the first owner of the drove, with one horse between us; having left my brother to come on with the balance of the company.

I traveled on with my new comrade about three days'

journey; but much to his discredit, as I then thought, and still think, he took care all the time to ride, but never to tie; at last I told him to go ahead, and I would come when I got ready. He gave me four dollars to bear my expenses upwards of four hundred miles, and then cut out and left me.

I purchased some provisions, and went on slowly, until at length I fell in with a wagoner, with whom I was disposed to scrape up a hasty acquaintance. I inquired where he lived, and where he was going, and all about his affairs. He informed me that he lived in Greenville, Tennessee, and was on his way to a place called Gerards-town, fifteen miles below Winchester. He also said, that after he should make his journey to that place, he would immediately return to Tennessee. His name was Adam Myers, and a jolly good fellow he seemed to be. On a little reflection, I determined to turn back and go with him, which I did; and we journeyed on slowly, as wagons commonly do, but merrily enough. I often thought of home, and, indeed, wished bad enough to be there; but, when I thought of the school-house, and Kitchen, my master, and the race with my father, and the big hickory he carried, and of the fierceness of the storm of wrath that I had left him in, I was afraid to venture back; for I knew my father's nature so well, that I was certain his anger would hang on to him, like a turkle does to a fisher-man's toe, and that, if I went back in a hurry, he would give me the devil in three or four ways. But I and the wagoner had traveled two days when we met my brother, who, I before stated, I had left behind when the drove was sold out. He persuaded me to go home, but I refused. He pressed me hard, and brought up a great many mighty strong arguments to induce me to turn back again. He pictured the pleasure of meeting my mother, and my sisters, who all loved me dearly, and told me what uneasiness they had already suffered about me. I could not help shedding tears, which I did not often do, and my affections all pointed back to those dearest friends, and as I thought, nearly the only ones I had in the world; but then the promised whipping—that was the thing. It came right slap down on every thought of home; and I finally determined that make or break, hit or miss, I would just hang on to my journey, and go ahead with the wagoner. My brother was much grieved at our parting, but he went his way, and so did I. We went on until at last we got to Gerardstown, where the wagoner tried to get a back load, but he could not without going to Alexandria. He engaged to go there, and I concluded that I would wait until he returned. I set in to work for a man by the name of John Gray, at twenty-five cents per day. My labor, however, was light, such as ploughing in some small grain, in which I succeeded in pleasing the old man very well. I continued working for him until the wagoner got back, and for a good long time afterwards, as he continued to run his team back and forward, hauling to and from Baltimore. In the next spring, from the proceeds of my daily labor, small as it was, I was able to get me some decent clothes, and concluded I would make a trip with the wagoner to Baltimore, and see what sort of a place that was, and what sort of folks lived there. I gave him the balance of what money I had for safe keeping, which, as well as I recollect, was about seven dollars. We got on well enough until we came near Ellicott's Mills. Our load consisted of flour in barrels. Here I got into the wagon for the purpose of changing my clothing, not thinking that I was in any danger; but, while I was in there, we were met by some wheelbarrow men, who were working on the road, and the horses took a scare and away they went, like they had seen a ghost. They made a sudden wheel around, and broke the wagon tongue slap, short off, as a pipe-stem; and snap went both of the axletrees at the same time, and of all devilish flouncing about of flour barrels that ever was seen, I reckon this took the beat. Even *a rat* would have stood a bad chance in a *straight* race among them, and not much better in a crooked one; for he would have been in a good way to be ground up as fine as ginger by their rolling over him. But this proved to me, that if a fellow is born to be hung, he will never be drowned; and, further, that if he is born for a seat in Congress, even flour barrels can't make a mash of him. All these dangers I escaped unhurt, though, like most of the office-holders of these times, for a while I was afraid to say my soul was my own; for I didn't know how soon I should be knocked into a cocked hat, and get my walking papers for another country.

We put our load into another wagon, and hauled ours to a workman's shop in Baltimore, having delivered the flour, and there we intended to remain two or three days, which time was necessary to repair the runaway wagon. While I was there, I went one day, down to the wharf, and was much delighted to see the big ships, and their sails all flying, for I had never seen such things before, and, indeed, I didn't believe there were any such things in all nature. After a short time, my curiosity induced me to step aboard of one, where I was met by the captain, who asked me if I didn't wish to take a voyage to London? I told him I did, for by this time I had become pretty well weaned from home, and I cared but little where I was, or where I went, or what became of me. He said he wanted just such a boy as I was, which I was glad to hear. I told him I would go and get my clothes and go with him. He enquired about my parents, where they lived, and all about them. I let him know that they lived in Tennessee, many hundred miles off. We soon agreed about my intended voyage, and I went back to my friend, the wagoner, and informed him that I was going to London, and wanted my money and my clothes. He refused to let me have either, and swore that he would confine me, and take me back to Tennessee. I took it to heart very much, but he kept so close and constant watch over me, that I found it impossible to escape from him, until he had started homeward, and made several days journey on the road. He was, during this time, very ill to me, and threatened me with his wagon-whip on several occasions. At length I resolved to leave him at all hazards; and so, before day, one morning, I got my clothes out of his wagon, and cut out, on foot, without a farthing of money to bear my expenses. For, all other friends having failed, I determined then to throw myself on Providence, and see how that would use me. I had gone, however, only a few miles, when I came up with another wagoner, and such was my situation, that I felt more than ever the necessity of endeavoring to find a friend. I therefore concluded I would seek for one in him. He was going westwardly, and very kindly enquired of me where I was traveling? My youthful resolution, which had brooked almost everything else, rather gave way at this inquiry; for it brought the loneliness of my situation, and everything else that was calculated to oppress me, directly to view. My first answer to his questions was in a sprinkle of tears, for if the world had been given to me, I could not, at that moment have helped crying. As soon as the storm of feeling was over, I told him how I had been treated by the wagoner but a little before, who kept what little money I had, and left me without a copper to buy even a morsel of food.

He became exceedingly angry, and swore that he would make the other wagoner give up my money, pronouncing him a scoundrel, and many other hard names.

I told him I was afraid to see him, for he had threatened me with his wagon-whip, and I believed he would injure me. But my new friend was a very large, stout-looking man, and as resolute as a tiger. He bid me not to be afraid, still swearing he would have my money, or whip it out of the wretch who had it.

We turned, and went back about two miles, when we reached the place where he was. I went reluctantly; but I depended on my friend for protection. When we got there, I had but little to say; but, approaching the wagoner, my friend said to him, "You damn'd rascal, you have treated this boy badly." To which he replied it was my fault. He was then asked if he did not get seven dollars of my money, which he confessed. It was then demanded of him; but he declared most solemnly that he had not that amount in the world; that he had spent my money, and intended paying it back to me when we got to Tennessee. I then felt reconciled, and persuaded my friend to let him alone, and we returned to his wagon, geared up, and started. His name I shall never forget while my memory lasts; it was Henry Myers. He lived in Pennsylvania, and I found him what he professed to be, a faithful friend, and a clever fellow.

We traveled together for several days, but at length I concluded to endeavor to make my way homeward; and for that purpose, set out again on foot, and alone. But one thing I must not omit. The last night I staid with Mr. Myers was at a place where several wagoners also staid. He told them before we parted, that I was a poor little straggling boy, and how I had been treated, and that I was without money, though I had a long journey before me, through a land of strangers, where it was not even a wilderness.

They were good enough to contribute a sort of money-purse, and presented me with three dollars. On this amount I traveled as far as Montgomery court-house, in the State of Virginia, where it gave out. I set in to work for a man by the name of James Caldwell, a month, for five dollars, which was about a shilling a day. When this time was out, I bound myself to a man by the name of Elijah Griffith, by trade a hatter, agreeing to work for him for four years. I remained with him about eighteen months, when he found himself so involved in debt, that he broke up and left the country. For this time, I had received nothing, and was, of course, left without money, and with but very few clothes, and them very indifferent ones. I, however, set in again, and worked about as I could catch employment, until I got a little money and some clothing, and once more cut out for home. When I reached New River, at the mouth of a small stream called Little River, the white caps were flying, so that I couldn't get anybody to attempt to put me across. I argued the case as well as I could, but they told me there was great danger of being capsized and drowned, if I attempted to cross. I told them if I could get a canoe I would venture, caps or no caps. They tried to persuade me out of it; but finding they could not, they agreed I might take a canoe, and so I did, and put off. I tied my clothes to the rope of the canoe to have them safe, whatever might happen. But I found it a mighty ticklish business, I tell you. When I got out fairly on the river, I would have given the world, if it had belonged to me, to have been back on shore. But there was no time to lose now, so I just determined to do the best I could, and the devil take the hindmost. I turned the canoe across the waves, to do which, I had to turn it nearly up the river, as the wind came from that way; and I went about two miles before I could land. When I struck land, my canoe was about half full of water, and I was as wet as a drowned rat. But I was so much rejoiced that I scarcely felt the cold, though my clothes were frozen on me; and, in this situation, I had to go above three miles before I could find any house or fire to warm at. I, however, made out to get to one at last, and then I thought I would warm the inside a little, as well as the outside, that there might be no grumbling.

So I took "a leetle of the creater,"—that warmer of the cold, and cooler of the hot—and it made me feel so good, that I concluded it was like the negro's rabbit, "good any way." I passed on until I arrived in Sullivan county, in the State of Tennessee, and there I met with my brother, who had gone with me when I started from home with the cattle drove.

I staid with him a few weeks, and then went on to my father's, which place I reached late in the evening. Several wagons were there for the night, and considerable company about the house. I enquired if I could stay all night, for I did not intend to make myself known until I saw whether any of the family would find me out. I was told that I could stay, and went in, but had mighty little to say to anybody. I had been gone so long, and had grown so much, that the family did not at first know me. And another, and perhaps a stronger reason was, they had no thought or expectation of me, for they all had long given me up for finally lost.

After a while, we were all called to supper. I went with the rest. We had sat down to the table and begun to eat, when my eldest sister recollected me; she sprung up, ran and seized me around the neck, and exclaimed, "Here is my lost brother."

My feelings at this time it would be vain and foolish for me to attempt to describe. I had often thought I felt before, and I suppose I had, but sure I am, I never had felt as I then did. The joy of my sisters and my mother, and, indeed, of all the family, was such, that it humbled me, and made me sorry that I hadn't submitted to a hundred whippings, sooner than cause so much affliction as they had suffered on my account. I found the family had never heard a word of me from the time my brother left me. I was now almost fifteen years old; and my increased age and size, together with the joy of my father occasioned by my unexpected return, I was sure would secure me against my long dreaded whipping;

and so they did. But it will be a source of astonishment to many, who reflect that I am now a member of the American Congress—the most enlightened body of men in the world—that at so advanced an age, the age of fifteen, I did not know the first letter in the book.

CHAPTER THREE

I Fall in Love and Get Jilted

I had remained for some short time at home with my father, when he informed me that he owed a man, whose name was Abraham Wilson, the sum of thirty-six dollars, and that if I would set in and work out the note, so as to lift it for him, he would discharge me from his service, and I might go free. I agreed to do this, and went immediately to the man who held my father's note, and contracted with him to work six months for it. I set in, and worked with all my might, not losing a single day in the six months. When my time was out, I got my father's note, and then declined working with the man any longer, though he wanted to hire me mighty bad. The reason was, it was a place where a heap of bad company met to drink and gamble, and I wanted to get away from them, for I know'd very well if I staid there, I should get a bad name, as nobody could be respectable that would live there. I therefore returned to my father and gave him up his paper, which seemed to please him mightily, for though he was poor, he was an honest man, and always tried mighty hard to pay off his debts.

I next went to the house of an honest old Quaker, by the name of John Kennedy, who had removed from North Carolina, and proposed to hire myself to him, at two shillings a day. He agreed to take me a week on trial; at the end of which he appeared pleased with my work, and informed me that he held a note on my father for forty dollars, and that he would give me that note if I would work for him six months. I was certain enough that I should never get any part of the note; but then I remembered it was my father that owed it, and I concluded it was my duty as a child to help him along, and ease his lot as much as I could. I told the Quaker I would take him up at his offer, and immediately went to work. I never visited my father's house during the whole time of this engagement, though he lived only fifteen miles off. But when it was finished, and I had got the note, I borrowed one of my employer's horses, and, on a Sunday evening, went to pay my parents a visit. Some time after I got there, I pulled out the note and handed it to my father, who supposed Mr. Kennedy had sent it for collection. The old man looked mighty sorry, and said to me he had not the money to pay it, and didn't know what he should do. I then told him I had paid it for him, and it was then his own; that it was not presented for collection, but as a present from me. At this he shed a heap of tears; and as soon as he got a little over it, he said he was sorry he could not give me anything, but he was not able, he was too poor.

The next day I went back to my old friend, the Quaker, and set in to work for him for some clothes; for I had now worked a year without getting any money at all, and my clothes were nearly all worn out, and what few I had left were mighty indifferent. I worked in this way for about two months; and in that time a young woman from North Carolina, who was the Quaker's niece, came on a visit to his house. And now I am just getting on a part of my history that I know I never can forget. For though I have heard people talk about hard loving, yet I reckon no poor devil in this world was ever cursed with such hard love as mine has always been, when it came on me. I soon found myself head over heels in love with this girl, whose name the public could make no use of; and I thought that if all the hills about there were pure chink, and all belonged to me, I would give them if I could just talk to her as I wanted to: but I was afraid to begin, for when I would think of saying anything to her, my heart would begin to flutter like a duck in a puddle; and if I tried to outdo it and speak, it would get right smack up in my throat, and choke me like a cold potato. It bore on my mind in this way, till at last I concluded I must die if I didn't broach the subject; and so I determined to begin and hang on a trying to speak, till my heart would get out of my throat one way or t'other. And so one day at it I went, and after several trials I could say a little. I told her how well I loved her; that she was the darling object of my soul and body; and I must have her, or else I should pine down to nothing, and just die away with the consumption.

I found my talk was not disagreeable to her; but she was an honest girl, and didn't want to deceive nobody. She told me she was engaged to her cousin, a son of the old Quaker. This news was worse to me than war, pestilence, or famine; but still I knowed I could not help myself. I saw quick enough my cake was dough, and I tried to cool off as fast as possible; but I had hardly safety pipes enough, as my love was so hot as mighty nigh to burst my boilers. But I didn't press my claims any more, seeing there was no chance to do anything.

I began now to think that all my misfortunes growed out of my want of learning. I had never been to school but four days, as the reader has already seen, and did not yet know a letter.

I thought I would try to go to school some, and as the Quaker had a married son who was living about a mile and a half from him, and keeping a school, I proposed to him that I would go to school four days in the week, and work for him the other two, to pay my board and schooling. He agreed I might come on these terms; and so at it I went, learning and working, backwards and forwards, until I had been with him nigh on to six months. In this time, I learned to read a little in my primer, to write my own name, and to cypher some in the first three rules in figures. And this was all the schooling I ever had in my life, up to this day. I should have continued longer, if it hadn't been that I concluded I couldn't go any longer without a wife; and so I cut out to hunt me one.

I found a family of very pretty little girls that I had known when very young. They had lived in the same neighborhood with me, and I had thought very well of them. I made an offer to one of them, whose name is nobody's business, no more than the Quaker girl's was, and I found she took it very well. I still continued paying my respects to her, until I got to love her as bad as I had the Quaker's niece; and I would have agreed to fight a whole regiment of wild cats if she would only have said she would have me. Several months passed in this way, during all of which time she continued very kind and friendly. At last, the son of the old Quaker and my first girl had concluded to bring their matter to a close, and my little queen and myself were called on to wait on them. We went on the day, and performed our duty as attendants. This made me worse than ever; and after it was over, I pressed my claim very hard on her, but she would still give me a sort of evasive answer. However, I gave her mighty little peace, till she told me at last she would have me. I thought this was glorification enough, even without spectacles. I was then about eighteen years old. We fixed the time to be married; and I thought if that day come, I should be the happiest man in the created world, or in the moon, or anywhere else.

I had by this time got to be mighty fond of the rifle, and had bought a capital one. I most generally carried her with me wherever I went, and though I had got back to the old Quaker's to live, who was a very particular man, I would sometimes slip out and attend the shooting matches, where they shot for beef; I always tried, though, to keep it a secret from him. He had, at the same time, a bound boy living with him, who I had gotten into almost as great a notion of the girls as myself. He was about my own age, and was deeply smitten with the sister to my intended wife. I know'd it was in vain to try to get the leave of the old man for my young associate to go with me on any of my courting frolics; but I thought I could fix a plan to have him along, which would not injure the Quaker, as we had no notion that he should ever know it.

We commonly slept up stairs, and at the gable end of the house there was a window. So, one Sunday, when the old man and his family were all gone to meeting, we went out and cut a long pole, and taking it to the house, we set it up on end in the corner, reaching up the chimney as high as the window. After this we would go up stairs to bed, and then putting on our Sunday clothes, would go out at the window, and climb down the pole, take a horse a-piece, and ride about ten miles to where his sweetheart lived, and the girl I claimed as my wife. I was always mighty careful to be back before day, so as to escape being found out; and in this way I continued my attentions very closely, until a few days before I was to be married, or at least thought I was, for I had no fear that anything was about to go wrong.

Just now I heard of a shooting-match in the neighborhood, right between where I lived and my girl's house; and I determined to kill two birds with one stone—to go to the shooting-match first, and then to see her. I therefore made the Quaker believe I was going to hunt for deer, as they were pretty plenty about in those parts; but, instead of hunting them, I went straight on to the shooting-match, where I joined in with a partner, and we put in several shots for the beef. I was mighty lucky, and when the match was over, I had won the whole beef. This was on a Saturday, and my success had put me in the finest humor in the world. So I sold my part of the beef for five dollars in the real grit, for I believe that was before bank-notes was invented; at least, I had never heard of any. I now started on to ask for my wife; for, though the next Thursday was our wedding-day, I had never said a word to her parents about it. I had always dreaded the undertaking so bad, that I had put the evil hour off as long as possible; and, indeed, I calculated they knowed me so well, they wouldn't raise any objection to having me for their son-in-law. I had a great deal better opinion of myself, I found, than other people had of me; but I moved on with a light heart, and my five dollars jingling in my pocket, thinking all the time there was but few greater men in the world than myself.

In this flow of good humor, I went ahead till I got within about two miles of the place, when I concluded I would stop awhile at the house of the girl's uncle, where I might enquire about the family, and so forth, and so on. I was, indeed, just about ready to consider her uncle my uncle; and her affairs, my affairs. When I went in, tho', I found her sister there. I asked how all was at home? In a minute I found from her countenance something was wrong. She looked mortified, and didn't answer as quick as I thought she ought, being it was her *brother-in-law* talking to her. However, I asked her again. She then burst into tears, and told me her sister was going to deceive me; and that she was to be married to another man the next day. This was as sudden to me as a clap of thunder of a bright, sunshiny day. It was the capstone of all the afflictions I had ever met with; and it seemed to me that it was more than any human creature could endure. It struck me perfectly speechless for some time, and made me feel so weak that I thought I should sink down. I, however, recovered from my shock after a little, and rose and started without any ceremony, or even bidding anybody good-bye. The young woman followed me out to the gate, and entreated me to go on to her father's, and said she would go with me. She said the young man who was going to marry her sister, had got his license and asked for her; but she assured me her father and mother both preferred me to him; and that she had no doubt but that, if I would go on, I could break off the match. But I found that I could go no further. My heart was bruised, and my spirits were broken down; so I bid her farewell, and turned my lonesome and miserable steps back again homeward, concluding that I was only born for hardships, misery, and disappointment. I now began to think that, in making me, it was entirely forgotten to make my mate; that I was born odd, and should always remain so, and that nobody would have me.

But all these reflections did not satisfy my mind, for I had no peace day nor night for several weeks. My appetite failed me, and I grew daily worse and worse. They all thought I was sick; and so I was. And it was the worst kind of sickness,—a sickness of the heart, and all the tender parts, produced by disappointed love.

CHAPTER FOUR

I Get Married

I continued in this down-spirited situation for a good long time, until one day I took my rifle and started a-hunting. While out, I made a call at the house of a Dutch widow, who had a daughter that was well enough as to smartness, but she was as ugly as a stone fence. She was, however, quite talkative, and soon began to laugh at me about my disappointment.

She seemed disposed, though, to comfort me as much as she could; and, for that purpose, told me to keep in good heart, that "there was as good fish in the sea as had ever been caught out of it." I doubted this very much; but whether or not, I was certain that she was not one of them, for she was so homely that it almost gave me a pain in the eyes to look at her.

But I couldn't help thinking that she had intended what she had said as a banter for me to court her!!!—

the last thing in creation I could have thought of doing. I felt little inclined to talk on the subject, it is true; but, to pass off the time, I told her I thought I was born odd, and that no fellow to me could be found. She protested against this, and said if I would come to their reaping, which was not far off, she would show me one of the prettiest little girls there I had ever seen. She added that the one who had deceived me was nothing to be compared with her. I didn't believe a word of all this, for I had thought that such a piece of flesh and blood as she was had never been manufactured, and never would again. I agreed with her, though, that the little varment had treated me so bad, that I ought to forget her, and yet I couldn't do it. I concluded the best way to accomplish it was to cut out again, and see if I could find any other that would answer me; and so I told the Dutch girl that I would be at the reaping, and would bring as many as I could with me.

I employed my time pretty generally in giving information of it, as far as I could, until the day came; and I then offered to work for my old friend, the Quaker, two days, if he would let his bound boy go with me one to the reaping. He refused, and reproved me pretty considerable roughly for my proposition; and said, if he was in my place he wouldn't go; that there would be a great deal of bad company there; and that I had been so good a boy, he would be sorry for me to get a bad name. But I knowed my promise to the Dutch girl, and I was resolved to fulfil it; so I shouldered my rifle, and started by myself. When I got to the place, I found a large company of men and women, and among them an old Irish woman, who had a great deal to say. I soon found out from my Dutch girl, that this old lady was the mother of the little girl she had promised me, though I had not yet seen her. She was in an out-house with some other youngsters, and had not yet made her appearance. Her mamma, however, was no way bashful. She came up to me, and began to praise my red cheeks, and said she had a sweetheart for me. I had no doubt she had been told what I come for, and all about it. In the evening I was introduced to her daughter, and I must confess I was plaguy well pleased with her from the word go. She had a good countenance, and was very pretty, and I was full bent on making up an acquaintance with her.

It was not long before the dancing commenced, and I asked her to join me in a reel. She very readily consented to do so; and after we had finished our dance, I took a seat alongside of her, and entered into a talk. I found her very interesting; while I was sitting by her, making as good a use of my time as I could, her mother came to us, and very jocularly called me her son-in-law. This rather confused me, but I looked on it as a joke of the old lady, and tried to turn it off as well as I could; but I took care to pay as much attention to her through the evening as I could. I went on the old saying, of salting the cow to catch the calf. I soon become so much pleased with this little girl, that I began to think the Dutch girl had told me the truth, when she said there was still good fish in the sea.

We continued our frolic till near day, when we joined in some plays, calculated to amuse youngsters. I had not often spent a more agreeable night. In the morning, however, we all had to part; and I found my mind had become much better reconciled than it had been for a long time. I went home to the Quaker's, and made a bargain to work

with his son for a low-priced horse. He was the first one
I had ever owned, and I was to work six months for him.
I had been engaged very closely five or six weeks, when
this little girl run in my mind so, that I concluded I must
go and see her, and find out what sort of people they were
at home. I mounted my horse and away I went to where
she lived, and when I got there I found her father a very
clever old man, and the old woman as talkative as ever.
She wanted badly to find out all about me, and as I
thought, to see how I would do for her girl. I had not yet
seen her about, and I began to feel some anxiety to know
where she was.

In a short time, however, my impatience was relieved,
as she arrived at home from a meeting to which she had
been. There was a young man with her, who I soon found
was disposed to set up claim to her, as he was so attentive
to her that I could hardly get to slip in a word edgeways.
I began to think I was barking up the wrong tree again;
but I was determined to stand up to my rack, fodder or
no fodder. And so, to know her mind a little on the subject, I began to talk about starting, as I knowed she would
then show some sign, from which I could understand
which way the wind blowed. It was then near night,
and my distance was fifteen miles home. At this my little
girl soon began to indicate to the other gentleman that
his room would be the better part of his company. At
length she left him, and came to me, and insisted mighty
hard that I should not go that evening; and, indeed, from
all her actions and the attempts she made to get rid of
him, I saw that she preferred me all holler. But it wasn't
long before I found trouble enough in another quarter.
Her mother was deeply enlisted for my rival, and I had

to fight against her influence as well as his. But the girl herself was the prize I was fighting for; and as she welcomed me, I was determined to lay siege to her, let what would happen. I commenced a close courtship, having cornered her from her old beau; while he set off, looking on, like a poor man at a country frolic, and all the time almost gritting his teeth with pure disappointment. But he didn't dare to attempt anything more, for now I had gotten a start, and I looked at him every once in a while as fierce as a wild-cat. I staid with her until Monday morning, and then I put out for home.

It was about two weeks after this that I was sent for to engage in a wolf hunt, where a great number of men were to meet, with their dogs and guns, and where the best sort of sport was expected. I went as large as life, but I had to hunt in strange woods, and in a part of the country which was very thinly inhabited. While I was out it clouded up, and I began to get scared; and in a little while I was so much so, that I didn't know which way home was, nor anything about it. I set out the way I thought it was, but it turned out with me, as it always does with a lost man, I was wrong, and took exactly the contrary direction from the right one. And for the information of young hunters, I will just say, in this place, that whenever a fellow gets bad lost, the way home is just the way he don't think it is. This rule will hit nine times out of ten. I went ahead, though, about six or seven miles, when I found night was coming on fast; but at this distressing time I saw a little woman streaking it along through the woods like all wrath, and so I cut on too, for I was determined I wouldn't lose sight of her that night any more. I run on till she saw me, and she stopped; for she was as glad to see me as I was to see her, as she was lost as well as me. When I came up to her, who should she be but my little girl, that I had been paying my respects to? She had been out hunting her father's horses, and had missed her way, and had no knowledge where she was, or how far it was to any house, or what way would take us there. She had been traveling all day, and was mighty tired; and I would have taken her up, and toated her, if it hadn't been that I wanted her just where I could see her all the time, for I thought she looked sweeter than sugar; and by this time I loved her almost well enough to eat her.

At last I came to a path, that I know'd must go somewhere, and so we followed it, till we came to a house, at about dark. Here we staid all night. I sat up all night courting, and in the morning we parted. She went to her home, from which we were distant about seven miles, and I to mine, which was ten miles off.

I now turned in to work again; and it was about four weeks before I went back to see her. I continued to go occasionally, until I had worked long enough to pay for my horse, by putting in my gun with my work, to the man I had purchased from; and then I began to count whether I was to be deceived again or not. At our next meeting, we set the day for our wedding; and I went to my father's to make arrangements for an infair, and returned to ask her parents for her. When I got there, the old lady appeared to be mighty wrathy; and when I broached the subject, she looked at me as savage as a meat axe. The old man appeared quite willing, and treated me very clever. But I hadn't been there long, before the old woman as good as ordered me out of her house. I thought

I would put her in mind of old times, and see how that would go with her. I told her she had called me her son-in-law before I had attempted to call her my mother-in-law, and I thought she ought to cool off. But her Irish was up too high to do anything with her, and so I quit trying. All I cared for, was to have her daughter on my side, which I knowed was the case then; but how soon some other fellow might knock my nose out of joint again, I couldn't tell. I, however, felt rather insulted at the old lady, and I thought I wouldn't get married in her house. And so I told her girl, that I would come the next Thursday, and bring a horse, bridle, and saddle for her, and she must be ready to go. Her mother declared I shouldn't have her; but I know'd I should, if somebody else didn't get her before Thursday. I then started, bidding them good day, and went by the house of a justice of the peace, who lived on the way to my father's, and made a bargain with him to marry me.

When Thursday came, all necessary arrangements were made at my father's to receive my wife; and so I took my eldest brother and his wife, and another brother, and a single sister that I had, and two other young men with me, and cut out to her father's house to get her. We went on, until we got within two miles of the place, where we met a large company that had heard of the wedding, and were waiting. Some of that company went on with my brother and sister, and the young man I had picked out to wait on me. When they got there, they found the old lady as wrathy as ever. However, the old man filled their bottle, and the young men returned in a hurry. I then went on with my company, and when I arrived I never pretended to dismount from my horse, but rode up to the door, and asked the girl if she was ready; and she said she was. I then told her to light on the horse I was leading; and she did so. Her father, though, had gone out to the gate, and when I started, he commenced persuading me to stay and marry there; that he was entirely willing to the match, and that his wife, like most women, had entirely too much tongue; but that I oughtn't to mind her. I told him if she would ask me to stay and marry at her house, I would do so. With that he sent for her, and after they had talked for some time out by themselves, she came to me and looked at me mighty good, and asked my pardon for what she had said, and invited me to stay. She said it was the first child she ever had to marry; and she couldn't bear to see her go off in that way; that if I would light, she would do the best she could for us. I couldn't stand everything, and so I agreed, and we got down, and went in. I sent off then for my parson, and got married in a short time; for I was afraid to wait long, for fear of another defeat. We had as good treatment as could be expected; and that night all went on well. The next day we cut out for my father's, where we met a large company of people, that had been waiting a day and a night for our arrival. We passed the time quite merrily, until the company broke up; and having gotten my wife, I thought I was completely made up, and needed nothing more in the whole world. But I soon found this was all a mistake —for now having a wife, I wanted everything else; and, worse than all, I had nothing to give for it.

I remained a few days at my father's, and then went back to my new father-in-law's, where, to my surprise, I found my old Irish mother in the finest humor in the world.

She gave us two likely cows and calves, which, though it was a small marriage portion, was still better than I had expected, and, indeed, it was about all I ever got. I rented a small farm and cabin, and went to work; but I had much trouble to find out a plan to get anything to put in my house. At this time, my good old friend the Quaker came forward to my assistance, and gave me an order to a store for fifteen dollars' worth of such things as my little wife might choose. With this, we fixed up pretty grand, as we thought, and allowed to get on very well. My wife had a good wheel, and know'd exactly how to use it. She was also a good weaver, as most of the Irish are, whether men or women; and being very industrious with her wheel, she had, in a little or no time, a fine web of cloth, ready to make up; and she was good at that, too, and at almost anything else that a woman could do.

We worked on for some years, renting ground and paying high rent, until I found it wasn't the thing it was cracked up to be, and that I couldn't make a fortune at it just at all. So I concluded to quit it, and cut out for some new country. In this time we had two sons, and I found I was better at increasing my family than my fortune. It was, therefore, the more necessary that I should hunt some better place to get along; and as I knowed I would have to move at some time, I thought it was better to do it before my family got too large, that I might have less to carry.

The Duck and Elk river country was just beginning to settle, and I determined to try that. I had now one old horse, and a couple of two year old colts. They were both broke to the halter, and my father-in-law proposed, that if I went, he would go with me, and take one horse to help me move. So we all fixed up, and I packed my two colts with as many of my things as they could bear; and away we went across the mountains. We got on well enough, and arrived safely in Lincoln county, on the head of the Mulberry fork of Elk river. I found this a very rich country, and so new that game of different sorts was very plenty. It was here that I began to distinguish myself as a hunter, and to lay the foundation for all my future greatness; but mighty little did I know of what sort it was going to be. Of deer and smaller game I killed abundance; but the bear had been much hunted in those parts before, and were not so plenty as I could have wished. I lived here in the years 1809 and '10, to the best of my recollection, and then I moved to Franklin county, and settled on Beans creek, where I remained till after the close of the last war.

CHAPTER FIVE

I Join Andrew Jackson's Army

I was living ten miles below Winchester when the Creek war commenced:* and as military men are making so much fuss in the world at this time, I must give an account of the part I took in the defence of the country. If it should make me President, why I can't help it; such things will sometimes happen, and my pluck is, never to "seek nor decline office."

It is true, I had a little rather not; but yet, if the government can't get on without taking another President from Tennessee, to finish the work of "retrenchment and reform," why, then I reckon I must go in for it. But I

---

* The Creek Indians lived in Georgia, Alabama and Florida. Their outstanding leader was Tecumseh who caused them to rebel and massacre the white settlers in that region in 1813. On August 30, 1813, Fort Mimms was attacked and the inhabitants massacred. Andrew Jackson was sent to stop the uprising.

must begin about the war, and leave the other matter for the people to begin on.

The Creek Indians had commenced their open hostilities by a most bloody butchery at Fort Mimms. There had been no war among us for so long, that but few who were not too old to bear arms, knew anything about the business. I, for one, had often thought about war, and had often heard it described; and I did verily believe in my own mind, that I couldn't fight in that way at all; but my after experience convinced me that this was all a notion. For, when I heard of the mischief which was done at the fort, I instantly felt like going, and I had none of the dread of dying that I expected to feel. In a few days, a general meeting of the militia was called, for the purpose of raising volunteers; and when the day arrived for that meeting, my wife, who had heard me say I meant to go to the war, began to beg me not to turn out. She said she was a stranger in the parts where we lived, had no connections living near her, and that she and our little children would be left in a lonesome and unhappy situation if I went away. It was mighty hard to go against such arguments as these; but my countrymen had been murdered, and I knew that the next thing would be that the Indians would be scalping the women and children all about there, if we didn't put a stop to it. I reasoned the case with her as well as I could, and told her that if every man would wait till his wife got willing for him to go to war, there would be no fighting done, until we would all be killed in our own houses; that I was as able to go as any man in the world, and that I believed it was a duty I owed to my country. Whether she was satisfied with this reasoning or not, she did not tell me, but seeing I was bent on it, all she did was to cry a little, and turn about to her work. The truth is, my dander was up, and nothing but war could bring it right again.

I went to Winchester, where the muster was to be, and a great many people had collected, for there was as much fuss among the people about the war as there is now about moving the deposites. When the men were paraded, a lawyer by the name of Jones addressed us, and closed by turning out himself, and enquiring at the same time, who among us felt like we could fight the Indians? This was the same Mr. Jones who afterwards served in Congress, from the State of Tennessee. He informed us he wished to raise a company, and that then the men should meet and elect their own officers. I believe I was about the second or third man that stepp'd out; but on marching up and down the regiment a few times, we found we had a large company. We volunteered for sixty days, as it was supposed our services would not be longer wanted. A day or two after this, we met and elected Mr. Jones our captain, and also elected our other officers. We then received orders to start on the next Monday week; before which time I had fixed as well as I could to go, and my wife had equipp'd me as well as she was able for the camp. The time arrived; I took a parting farewell of my wife and my little boys, mounted my horse, and set sail to join my company. Expecting to be gone only a short time, I took no more clothing with me than I supposed would be necessary, so that if I got into an Indian battle, I might not be pestered with any unnecessary plunder to prevent my having a fair shake with them. We all met and went ahead, till we passed Huntsville, and camped at a large spring called Beaty's spring. Here we staid for several days, in which time the troops began to collect from all quarters. At last we mustered about thirteen hundred strong, all mounted volunteers, and all determined to fight, judging from myself, for I felt wolfish all over. I verily believe the whole army was of the real grit. Our captain didn't want any other sort: and to try them he several times told his men that if any of them wanted to go back home, they might do so at any time before they were regularly mustered into the service. But he had the honor to command all his men from first to last, as not one of them left him.

General Jackson had not yet left Nashville with his old foot volunteers, that had gone with him to Natchez in 1812, the year before. While we remained at the spring, a Major Gibson came, and wanted some volunteers to go with him across the Tennessee river and into the Creek nation, to find out the movements of the Indians. He came to my captain, and asked for two of his best woodsmen, and such as were best with a rifle. The captain pointed me out to him, and said he would be security that I would go as far as the major would himself, or any other man. I willingly engaged to go with him, and asked him to let me choose my own mate to go with me, which he said I might do. I chose a young man by the name of George Russel, a son of old Major Russel, of Tennessee. I called him up, but Major Gibson said he thought he hadn't beard enough to please him,—he wanted men, and not boys. I must confess I was a little nettled at this; for I know'd George Russel, and I know'd there was no mistake in him; and I didn't think that courage ought to be measured by the beard, for fear a goat would have the preference over a man. I told the major he was on the wrong scent; that Russel could go as far as he could, and I must have him along. He saw I was a little wrathy, and said I had the best chance of knowing, and agreed that it should be as I wanted it. He told us to be ready early in the morning for a start; and so we were. We took our camp equipage, mounted our horses, and thirteen in number, including the major, we cut out. We went on and crossed the Tennessee river at a place called Ditto's Landing; and then travelled about seven miles further, and took up camp for the night. Here a man by the name of John Haynes overtook us. He had been an Indian trader in that part of the nation, and was well acquainted with it. He went with us as a pilot. The next morning, however, Major Gibson and myself concluded we should separate and take different directions to see what discoveries we could make; so he took seven of the men, and I five, making thirteen in all, including myself. He was to go by the house of a Cherokee Indian, named Dick Brown, and I was to go by Dick's father's; and getting all the information we could, we were to meet that evening where the roads came together, fifteen miles the other side of Brown's. At old Mr. Brown's I got a half blood Cherokee to agree to go with me, whose name was Jack Thompson. He was not then ready to start, but was to fix that evening, and overtake us at the fork road where I was to meet Major Gibson. I know'd it wouldn't be safe to camp right at the road; and so I told Jack, that when he got to the fork he must holler like an owl, and I would answer him in the same way; for I know'd it would be night before he got there. I and my men then started, and went on to the place of meeting, but Major Gibson was not there. We waited till almost dark but still he didn't come. We then left the Indian trace a little distance and turning into the head of a hollow, we struck up camp. It was about ten o'clock at night when I heard my owl, and I answered him. Jack soon found us, and we determined to rest there during the night. We staid also next morning till after breakfast: but in vain, for the major didn't still come.

I told the men we had set out to hunt a fight, and I wouldn't go back in that way; that we must go ahead, and see what the red men were at. We started and went to a Cherokee town about twenty miles off; and after a short stay there, we pushed on to the house of a man by the name of Radcliff. He was a white man, but had married a Creek woman, and lived just in the edge of the Creek nation. He had two sons, large likely fellows, and a great deal of potatoes and corn, and, indeed, almost every thing else to go on; so we fed our horses and got dinner with him, and seemed to be doing mighty well. But he was bad scared all the time. He told us that there had been ten painted warriors at his house only an hour before, and if we were discovered there, they would kill us and his family with us. I replied to him, that my business was to hunt for just such fellows as he had described, and I was determined not to go back unti. I had done it. Our dinner being over, we saddled up our horses, and made ready to start. But some of my small company I found were disposed to return. I told them, if we were to go back then, we should never hear the last of it: and I was determined to go ahead. I knowed some of them would go with me, and that the rest were afraid to go back by themselves; and so we pushed on to the camp of some friendly Creeks, which was distant about eight miles. The moon was about the full, and the night was clear; we therefore had the benefit of her light from night to morning, and I knew if we were placed in such danger as to make a retreat necessary, we could travel by night as well as in the day time.

We had not got very far when we met two negroes, well mounted on Indian ponies, and each with a good rifle. They had been taken from their owners by the Indians, and were running away from them, and trying to get back to their masters again. They were brothers, both very large and likely: and could talk Indian as well as English. One of them I sent on to Ditto's Landing, the other I took back with me. It was after dark when we got to the camp, where we found about forty men, women, and children.

They had bows and arrows, and I turned in to shooting with their boys by a pine light. In this way we amused ourselves very well for a while, but at last the negro, who had been talking to the Indians, came to me and told me they were very much alarmed, for the "red sticks," as they called the war party of the Creeks, would come and find us there; and, if so, we should all be killed. I directed him to tell them that I would watch, and if one would come that night, I would carry the skin of his head home to make me a moccasin. When he made this communication, the Indians laughed aloud. At about ten o'clock at night we all concluded to try to sleep a little; but that our horses might be ready for use, as the treasurer said of the drafts on the United States' bank, on certain "con-

tingencies," we tied them up with our saddles on them,
and every thing to our hand, if in the night our quarters
should get uncomfortable. We lay down with our guns
in our arms, and I had just gotten into a doze of sleep,
when I heard the sharpest scream that ever escaped the
throat of a human creature. It was more like a wrathy
painter than any thing else. The negro understood it, and
he sprang to me; for tho' I heard the noise well enough,
yet I wasn't wide awake enough to get up. So the negro
caught me, and said the red sticks was coming. I rose
quicker then, and asked what was the matter? Our negro
had gone and talked with the Indian who had just fetched
the scream, as he came into camp, and learned from him,
that the war party had been crossing the Coosa river all
day at the Ten Islands; and were going on to meet Jackson, and this Indian had come as a runner. This news
very much alarmed the friendly Indians in camp, and
they were all off in a few minutes. I felt bound to make
this intelligence known as soon as possible to the army
we had left at the landing; and so we all mounted our
horses, and put out in a long lope to make our way back
to that place. We were about sixty-five miles off. We went
on to the same Cherokee town we had visited on our way
out, having first called at Radcliff's who was off with his
family; and at the town we found large fires burning, but
not a single Indian was to be seen. They were all gone.
These circumstances were calculated to lay our dander a
little, as it appeared we must be in great danger; though
we could easily have licked any force of not more than
five to one. But we expected the whole nation would be
on us, and against such fearful odds we were not so
rampant for a fight.

We therefore staid only a short time in the light of the fires about the town, preferring the light of the moon and the shade of the woods. We pushed on till we got again to old Mr. Brown's, which was still about thirty miles from where we had left the main army. When we got there, the chickens were just at the first crowing for day. We fed our horses, got a morsel to eat ourselves, and again cut out. About ten o'clock in the morning we reached the camp, and I reported to Col. Coffee the news. He didn't seem to mind my report a bit, and this raised my dander higher than ever; but I knowed I had to be on my best behaviour, and so I kept it all to myself; though I was so mad that I was burning inside like a tar-kiln, and I wonder that the smoke hadn't been pouring out of me at all points.

Major Gibson hadn't yet returned, and we all began to think he was killed; and that night they put out a double guard. The next day the Major got in, and brought a worse tale than I had, though he stated the same facts so far as I went. This seemed to put our colonel all in a fidget; and it convinced me, clearly, of one of the hateful ways of the world. When I made my report, it wasn't believed, because I was no officer; I was no great man, but just a poor soldier. But when the same thing was reported by Major Gibson! ! why, then it was all as true as preaching, and the colonel believed it every word.

He, therefore, ordered breastworks to be thrown up near a quarter of a mile long, and sent an express to Fayetteville, where General Jackson and his troops was, requesting them to push on like the very mischief, for fear we should all be cooked up to a cracklin before they

could get there. Old Hickory-face made a forced march
on getting the news; and on the next day, he and his
men got into camp, with their feet all blistered from the
effects of their swift journey. The volunteers, therefore,
stood guard altogether, to let them rest.

CHAPTER SIX

My Adventures in the Creek War

About eight hundred of the volunteers, and of that number I was one, were now sent back, crossing the Tennessee river, and on through Huntsville, so as to cross the river again at another place, and to get on the Indians in another direction.* After we passed Huntsville, we struck on the river at Muscle Shoals, and at a place on them called Melton's Bluff. This river is here about two miles wide, and a rough bottom; so much so, indeed, in many places, as to be dangerous; and in fording it this time, we left several of the horses belonging to our men, with their feet fast in the crevices of the rocks. The men, whose horses were thus left, went ahead on foot. We pushed on till we got to what was called the Black Warrior's town, which stood near the very spot where Tuscaloosa now

* This was in November, 1813. The detachment was commanded by General Coffee.

stands, which is the seat of government for the State of Alabama.

This Indian town was a large one; but when we arrived we found the Indians had all left it. There was a large field of corn standing out, and a pretty good supply in some cribs. There was also a fine quantity of dried beans, which were very acceptable to us; and without delay we secured them as well as the corn, and then burned the town to ashes; after which we left the place.

In the field where we gathered the corn we saw plenty of fresh Indian tracks, and we had no doubt they had been scared off by our arrival.

We then went on to meet the main army at the fork road, where I was first to have met Major Gibson. We got that evening as far back as the encampment we had made the night before we reached the Black Warrior's town, which we had just destroyed. The next day we were entirely out of meat. I went to Col. Coffee, who was then in command of us, and asked his leave to hunt as we marched. He gave me leave, but told me to take mighty good care of myself. I turned aside to hunt, and had not gone far when I found a deer that had just been killed and skinned, and his flesh was still warm and smoking. From this I was sure that the Indian who had killed it had been gone only a very few minutes; and though I was never much in favor of one hunter stealing from another, yet meat was so scarce in camp, that I thought I must go in for it. So I just took up the deer on my horse before me, and carried it on till night. I could have sold it for almost any price I would have asked; but this wasn't my rule, neither in peace nor war. Whenever I had anything, and saw a fellow-being suffering, I was more anxious to relieve him than to benefit myself. And this is one of the true secrets of my being a poor man to this day. But it is my way; and while it has often left me with an empty purse, which is as near the devil as anything else I have seen, yet it has never left my heart empty of consolations which money couldn't buy, the consolation of having sometimes fed the hungry and covered the naked.

I gave all my deer away, except a small part I kept for myself, and just sufficient to make a good supper for my mess; for meat was getting to be a rarity to us all. We had to live mostly on parched corn. The next day we marched on, and at night took up camp near a large cane brake. While here, I told my mess I would again try for some meat; so I took my rifle and cut out, but hadn't gone far, when I discovered a large gang of hogs. I shot one of them down in his tracks, and the rest broke directly towards the camp. In a few minutes the guns began to roar, as bad as if the whole army had been in an Indian battle, and the hogs to squeal as bad as the pigs did, when the devil turned barber. I shouldered my hog, and went on to the camp; and when I got there I found they had killed a good many of the hogs, and a fine fat cow into the bargain, that had broke out of the cane brake. We did very well that night, and the next morning marched on to a Cherokee town, where our officers stopp'd, and gave the inhabitants an order on Uncle Sam for their cow, and the hogs we had killed. The next day we met the main army having had, as we thought, hard times, and a plenty of them, though we had yet seen hardly the beginning of trouble.

After our meeting we went on to Radcliff's, where I

had been before, while out as a spy; and when we got there, we found he had hid all his provisions. We also got into the secret, that he was the very rascal who had sent the runner to the Indian camp, with the news that the "red sticks" were crossing at the Ten Islands; and that his object was to scare me and my men away, and send us back with a false alarm.

To make some atonement for this, we took the old scoundrel's two big sons with us, and made them serve in the war.

We then marched to a place which we called Camp Wills; and here it was that Captain Cannon was promoted to a colonel, and Colonel Coffee to a general. We then marched to the Ten Islands, on the Coosa river, where we established a fort, and our spy companies were sent out. They soon made prisoners of Bob Catala and his warriors, and, in a few days afterwards, we heard of some Indians in a town about eight miles off. So we mounted our horses, and put out for that town, under the direction of two friendly Creeks we had taken for pilots. We had also a Cherokee colonel, Dick Brown, and some of his men with us. When we got near the town we divided; one of our pilots going with each division. And so we passed on each side of the town, keeping near to it, until our lines met on the far side. We then closed up at both ends, so as to surround it completely; and then we sent Captain Hammond's company of rangers to bring on the affray. He had advanced near the town, when the Indians saw him, and they raised the yell, and came running at him like so many red devils. The main army was now formed in a hollow square around the town, and they pursued Hammond till they came in reach of us. We then gave them a fire, and they returned it, and then ran back into their town. We began to close on the town by making our files closer and closer, and the Indians soon saw they were our property. So most of them wanted us to take them prisoners; and their squaws and all would run and take hold of any of us they could, and give themselves up. I saw seven squaws have hold of one man, which made me think of the Scriptures. So I hollered out the Scriptures was fulfilling; that there was seven women holding to one man's coat tail. But I believe it was a hunting-shirt all the time. We took them all prisoners that came out to us in this way; but I saw some warriors run into a house until I counted forty-six of them. We pursued them until we got near the house, when we saw a squaw sitting in the door, and she placed her feet against the bow she had in her hand, and then took an arrow, and, raising her feet, she drew with all her might, and let fly at us, and she killed a man, whose name, I believe, was Moore. He was a lieutenant, and his death so enraged us all, that she was fired on, and had at least twenty balls blown through her. This was the first man I ever saw killed with a bow and arrow. We now shot them like dogs; and then set the house on fire, and burned it up with the forty-six warriors in it. I recollect seeing a boy who was shot down near the house. His arm and thigh was broken, and he was so near the burning house that the grease was stewing out of him. In this situation he was still trying to crawl along; but not a murmur escaped him, though he was only about twelve years old. So sullen is the Indian, when his dander is up, that he had sooner die than make a noise, or ask for quarters.*

* This battle is generally called the battle of Tallushatchee.

The number that we took prisoners, being added to the number we killed, amounted to one hundred and eighty-six; though I don't remember the exact number of either. We had five of our men killed. We then returned to our camp, at which our fort was erected, and known by the name of Fort Strother.* No provisions had yet reached us, and we had now been for several days on half rations. However, we went back to our Indian town on the next day, when many of the carcasses of the Indians were still to be seen. They looked very awful, for the burning had not entirely consumed them, but given them a terrible appearance, at least what remained of them. It was, somehow or other, found out that the house had a potato cellar under it, and an immediate examination was made, for we were all as hungry as wolves. We found a fine chance of potatoes in it, and hunger compelled us to eat them, though I had a little rather not, if I could have helped it, for the oil of the Indians we had burned up on the day before, had run down on them, and they looked like they had been stewed with fat meat. We then again returned to the army, and remained there for several days, almost starving, as all our beef was gone. We commenced eating the beef-hides, and continued to eat every scrap we could lay our hands on. At length an Indian came to our guard one night, and hollered, and said he wanted to see "Captain Jackson." He was conducted to the general's markee, into which he entered, and in a few minutes we received orders to prepare for marching.

In an hour we were all ready, and took up the line of march. We crossed the Coosa river, and went on in the direction to Fort Taladega. When we arrived near the

* This is the Fort at Ten Islands, referred to before.

place, we met eleven hundred painted warriors, the very choice of the Creek nation. They encamped near the fort, and had informed the friendly Indians who were in it, that if they didn't come out, and fight with them against the whites, they would take their fort and all their ammunition and provision. The friendly party asked three days to consider of it, and agreed that if on the third day they didn't come out ready to fight with them, they might take their fort. Thus they put them off. They then immediately started their runner to General Jackson, and he and the army pushed over, as I have just before stated.

The camp of warriors had their spies out and discovered us coming some time before we got to the fort. They then went to the friendly Indians, and told them Captain Jackson was coming, and had a great many fine horses, and blankets, and guns and everything else, and if they would come out and help to whip him and to take his plunder, it should all be divided with those in the fort. They promised that when Jackson came they would then come out and help to whip him. It was about an hour by the sun in the morning when we got near the fort. We were piloted by friendly Indians and divided as we had done on a former occasion, so as to go to the right and left of the fort, and, consequently, of the warriors who were camped near it. Our lines marched on as before, till they met in front, and then closed in the rear, forming again into a hollow square. We then sent on old Major Russel with his spy company, to bring on the battle; Captain Evans' company went also. When they got near the fort, the top of it was lined with the friendly Indians, crying out as loud as they could roar, "How-dy-do, brother, how-dy-do?" They kept this up till Major Russel had passed by the fort, and was moving on towards the warriors. They were all painted as red as scarlet, and were just as naked as they were born. They had concealed themselves under the bank of a branch that ran partly around the fort, in the manner of a half moon. Russell was going right into their circle, for he couldn't see them, while the Indians on the top of the fort were trying every plan to show him his danger. But he couldn't understand them. At last, two of them jumped from it, and ran and took his horse by the bridle, and pointing to where they were, told him there were thousands of them lying under the bank. This brought them to a halt, and about this moment the Indians fired on them, and came rushing forth like a cloud of Egyptian locusts, and screaming like all the young devils had been turned loose, with the old devil of all at their head. Russell's company quit their horses and took into the fort, and their horses ran up to our line, which was then in full view. The warriors then came yelling on, meeting us, and continued till they were within shot of us, when we fired and killed a considerable number of them. They then broke like a gang of steers, and ran across to the other line, where they were again fired on; and so we kept them running from one line to the other, constantly under a heavy fire, till we had killed upwards of four hundred of them. They fought with guns, and also with their bows and arrows; but at length they made their escape through a part of our line which was made up of drafted militia, which broke ranks and they passed. We lost fifteen of our men, as brave fellows as ever lived or died. We buried them all in one grave, and started back to our fort; but before we got there, two more of our men died of wounds they had received, making our total loss seventeen good fellows in that battle.*

We now remained at the fort a few days, but no provision came yet, and we were all likely to perish. The weather also began to get very cold; and our clothes were nearly worn out, and horses getting very feeble and poor. Our officers proposed to General Jackson to let us return home and get fresh horses and fresh clothing, so as to be better prepared for another campaign, for our sixty days had long been out, and that was the time we entered for.

But the general took "the responsibility" on himself, and refused. We were, however, determined to go, as I am to put back the deposites, *if I can*. With this, the general issued his orders against it, as he has against the bank. But we began to fix for a start, as provisions were too scarce, just as Clay, and Webster, and myself, are preparing to fix bank matters, on account of the scarcity of money. The general went and placed his cannon on a bridge we had to cross, and ordered out his regulars and drafted men to keep us from crossing; just as he has planted his Globe and K. C. to alarm the bank men, while his regulars and militia in Congress are to act as artillery men. But when the militia started to guard the bridge, they would holler back to us to bring their knapsacks along when we come, for they wanted to go as bad as we did, just as many a good fellow now wants his political knapsack brought along, that, if when we come to vote, he sees he has a *fair shake to go*, he may join in and help us to take back the deposites.

We got ready and moved on till we came near the

* This is the famous battle of Taladega, fought under Jackson's immediate command, Dec. 7, 1813.

bridge where the general's men were all strung along on both sides, just like the office-holders are now, to keep us from getting along to the help of the country and the people. But we all had our flints ready picked, and our guns ready primed, that if we were fired on we might fight our way through, or all die together, just as we are now determined to save the country from ready ruin, or to sink down with it. When we came still nearer the bridge we heard the guards cocking their guns, and we did the same, just as we have had it in Congress, while the "government" regulars and the people's volunteers have all been setting their political triggers. But, after all, we marched boldly on, and not a gun was fired, nor a life lost, just as I hope it will be again, that we shall not be afraid of the general's Globe, nor his K. C., nor his regulars, nor their trigger snapping, but just march boldly over the executive bridge, and take the deposites back where the law placed them and where they ought to be. When we had passed, no further attempt was made to stop us; but the general said we were "the damned'st volunteers he had ever seen in his life; that we would volunteer and go out and fight, and then at our pleasure would *volunteer* and go home again in spite of the devil." But we went on, and near Huntsville we met a reinforcement who were going on to join the army. It consisted of a regiment of volunteers, and was under the command of some one whose name I can't remember. They were sixty day volunteers.

We got home pretty safely, and in a short time we had procured fresh horses and a supply of clothing better suited for the season; and then we returned to Fort Deposite, where our officers held a sort of a *"national convention"* on the subject of a message they had received from General Jackson,—demanding that on our return we should serve out *six months*. We had already served three months instead of two, which was the time we had volunteered for. On the next morning the officers reported to us the conclusions they had come to; and told us, if any of us felt bound to go on and serve out the six months, we could do so; but that they intended to go back home. I knowed if I went back home I wouldn't rest, for I felt it my duty to be out; and when out I was, somehow or other, always delighted to be in the very thickest of the danger. A few of us, therefore, determined to push on and join the army. The number I do not recollect, but it was very small.

When we got out there, I joined Major Russell's company of spies. Before we reached the place, General Jackson had started. We went on likewise, and overtook him at a place where we established a fort, called Fort Williams, and leaving men to guard it, we went ahead; intending to go to a place called the Horseshoe bend on the Talapoosa river. When we came near that place, we began to find Indian sign plenty, and we struck up camp for the night. About two hours before day we heard our guard firing, and we were all up in little or no time. We mended up our camp fires, and then fell back in the dark, expecting to see the Indians pouring in; and intending, when they should do so, to shoot them by the light of our own fires. But it happened they did not rush in as we had expected, but commenced a fire on us as we were. We were encamped in a hollow square, and we not only returned the fire, but continued to shoot as well as we could in the dark, till day broke, when the Indians disappeared.

The only guide we had in shooting was to notice the flash of their guns, and then shoot as directly at the place as we could guess.

In this scrape we had four men killed and several wounded, but whether we killed any of the Indians or not we never could tell, for it is their custom always to carry off their dead, if they can possibly do so. We buried ours, and then made a large log heap over them and set it on fire, so that the place of their deposite might not be known to the savages, who we knew would seek for them that they might scalp them. We made some horse litters for our wounded, and took up a retreat. We moved on till we came to a large creek which we had to cross; and about half our men had crossed, when the Indians commenced firing on our left wing, and they kept it up very warmly. We had left Major Russell and his brother at the camp we had moved from that morning, to see what discovery they could make as to the movements of the Indians; and about this time, while a warm fire was kept up on our left, as I have just stated, the major came up in our rear, and was closely pursued by a large number of Indians, who immediately commenced a fire on our artillery men. They hid themselves behind a large log, and could kill one of our men almost every shot, they being in open ground and exposed. The worst of all was, two of our colonels just at this trying moment left their men, and by a *forced march,* crossed the creek out of the reach of the fire. Their names, at this late day, would do the world no good, and my object is history alone, and not the slightest interference with character. An opportunity was now afforded for Governor Carroll to distinguish himself, and on this occasion he did so, by greater bravery than I ever saw any other man display. In truth, I believe, as firmly as I do that General Jackson is President, that if it hadn't been for Carroll, we should all have been genteely licked that time, for we were in a devil of a fix; part of our men on one side of the creek, and part on the other, and the Indians all the time pouring it on us, as hot as fresh mustard to a sore shin. I will not say exactly that the old general was whipped; but I will say, that if we escaped it at all, it was like old Henry Snider going to heaven, "mit a dam tite squeeze." I think he would confess himself, that he was nearer whipp'd this time than he was at any other, for I know that all the world couldn't make him acknowledge that he was *pointedly* whipped. I know I was mighty glad when it was over, and the savages quit us, for I begun to think there was one behind every tree in the woods.*

Soon after this, an army was to be raised to go to Pensacola, and I determined to go again with them, for I wanted a small taste of British fighting, and I supposed they would be there.

Here again the entreaties of my wife were thrown in the way of my going, but all in vain; for I always had a way of just going ahead at whatever I had a mind to. One of my neighbours, hearing I had determined to go, came to me, and offered me a hundred dollars to go in his place as a substitute, as he had been drafted. I told him I was better raised than to hire myself out to be shot at; but that I would go, and he should go too, and in that way the government would have the services of us both. But we didn't call General Jackson "the government" in those

---

* This was the battle of Enstichopco, fought January 23d. 1814. Jackson in command.

days, though we used to go to fight under him in the war.

I fixed up, and joined old Major Russell again; but we couldn't start with the main army, but followed on in a little time, after them. In a day or two, we had a hundred and thirty men in our company; and we went over and crossed the Muscle Shoals at the same place where I had crossed when first out, and when we burned the Black Warrior's town. We passed through the Choctaw and Chickasaw nations, on to Fort Stephens, and from thence to what is called the Cut-off, at the junction of the Tom-Bigby with the Alabama river. This place is near old Fort Mimms, where the Indians committed the great butchery at the commencement of the war.

We were here about two days behind the main army, who had left their horses at the Cut-off, and taken it on foot; and they did this because there was no chance for forage between there and Pensacola. We did the same, leaving men enough to take care of our horses, and cut on foot for that place. It was about eighty miles off; but in good heart we shouldered our guns, blankets, and provisions, and trudged merrily on. About twelve o'clock the second day, we reached the encampment of the main army, which was situated on a hill, overlooking the city of Pensacola. My commander Major Russell, was a great favorite with General Jackson, and our arrival was hailed with great applause, though we were a little after the feast; for they had taken the town and fort before we got there. That evening we went down into the town, and could see the British fleet lying in sight of the place. We got some liquor, and took a "horn" or so, and went back to the camp. We remained there that night, and in the morning we marched back towards the Cut-off. We pursued this direction till we reached old Fort Mimms, where we remained two or three days. It was here that Major Russell was promoted from his command, which was only that of a captain of spies, to the command of a major in the line. He had been known long before at home as old Major Russell, and so we continued to call him in the army. A Major Childs, from East Tennessee, also commanded a battalion, and he, and the one Russell was appointed to command, composed a regiment, which, by agreement with General Jackson, was to quit his army and go to the south, to kill up the Indians on the Scamby river.

General Jackson and the main army set out the next morning for New Orleans, and a Colonel Blue took command of the regiment which I have before described. We remained, however, a few days after the general's departure, and then started also on our route.

As it gave rise to so much war and bloodshed, it may not be improper here to give a little description of Fort Mimms, and the manner in which the Indian war commenced. The fort was built right in the middle of a large old field, and in it the people had been forted so long and so quietly, that they didn't apprehend any danger at all, and had, therefore, become quite careless. A small negro boy, whose business it was to bring up the calves at milking time, had been out for that purpose, and on coming back, he said he saw a great many Indians. At this the inhabitants took the alarm, and closed their gates and placed out their guards, which they continued for a few days. But finding that no attack was made, they concluded the little negro had lied; and again threw their gates open and set all their hands out to work their fields. The same boy was out again on the same errand, when, returning

in great haste and alarm, he informed them that he had
seen the Indians as thick as trees in the woods. He was
not believed, but was tucked up to receive a flogging for
the supposed lie; and was actually getting badly licked at
the very moment when the Indians came in a troop,
loaded with rails, with which they stopp'd all the port-
holes of the fort on one side except the bastion; and then
they fell in to cutting down the picketing. Those inside
the fort had only the bastion to shoot from, as all the other
holes were spiked up; and they shot several of the Indians, while engaged in cutting. But as fast as one would
call, another would seize up the axe and chop away, until
they succeeded in cutting down enough of the picketing
to admit them to enter. They then began to rush through,
and continued until they were all in. They immediately
commenced scalping, without regard to age or sex; having
forced the inhabitants up to one side of the fort, where
they carried on the work of death as a butcher would in
a slaughter pen.

The scene was particularly described to me by a young
man who was in the fort when it happened, and subse-
quently went on with us to Pensacola. He said he saw his
father, and mother, his four sisters, and the same number
of brothers, all butchered in the most shocking manner,
and that he made his escape by running over the heads
of the crowd, who were against the fort wall, to the top of
the fort, and then jumping off, and taking to the woods.
He was closely pursued by several Indians, until he came
to a small bayou, across which there was a log. He knew
the log was hollow on the under side, so he slipp'd under
the log and hid himself. He said he heard the Indians
walk over him several times back and forward. He re-

mained, nevertheless, still till night, when he came out and finished his escape. The name of this young man has entirely escaped my recollection, though his tale greatly excited my feelings. But to return to my subject. The regiment marched from where General Jackson had left us to Fort Montgomery, which was distant from Fort Mimms about a mile and a half, and there we remained for some days.

Here we supplied ourselves pretty well with beef, by killing wild cattle which had formerly belonged to the people who perished in the fort, but had gone wild after their massacre.

When we marched from Fort Montgomery, we went some distance back towards Pensacola; then we turned to the left, and passed through a poor piny country, till we reached the Scamby river, near which we encamped. We had about one thousand men, and as a part of that number, one hundred and eighty-six Chickesaw and Choctaw Indians with us. That evening a boat landed from Pensacola, bringing many articles that were both good and necessary; such as sugar and coffee, and liquors of all kinds. The same evening, the Indians we had along proposed to cross the river, and the officers thinking it might be well for them to do so, consented; and Major Russell went with them, taking sixteen white men, of which number I was one. We camped on the opposite bank that night, and early in the morning we set out. We had not gone far before we came to a place where the whole country was covered with water, and looked like a sea. We didn't stop for this, though, but just put in like so many spaniels, and waded on, sometimes up to our arm-pits, until we reached the pine hills, which made our distance through the water about a mile and a half. Here we struck up a fire to warm ourselves, for it was cold, and we were chilled through by being so long in the water. We again moved on, keeping our spies out; two to our left near the bank of the river, two straight before us, and five others on our right. We had gone in this way about six miles up the river, when our spies on the left came to us leaping the brush like so many old bucks, and informed us that they had discovered a camp of Creek Indians, and that we must kill them. Here we paused for a few minutes, and the prophets pow-wowed over their men awhile and then got out their paint, and painted them, all according to their custom when going into battle. They then brought their paint to old Major Russell, and said to him, that as he was an officer, he must be painted too. He agreed, and they painted him just as they had done themselves.

We let the Indians understand that we white men would first fire on the camp, and then fall back so as to give the Indians a chance to rush in and scalp them. The Chickesaws marched on our left hand, and the Choctaws on our right, and we moved on till we got in hearing of the camp, where the Indians were employed in beating up what they called chainy briar root. On this they mostly subsisted. On a nearer approach, we found they were on an island, and that we could not get to them. While we were chatting about this matter, we heard some guns fired, and in a very short time after, a keen whoop, which satisfied us that wherever it was, there was war on a small scale. With that, we all broke like quarter horses, for the firing; and when we got there, we found it was our two front spies, who related to us the following

story:—As they were moving on, they had met with two
Creeks who were out hunting their horses; as they approached each other, there was a large cluster of green
bay bushes exactly between them, so that they were
within a few feet of meeting before either was discovered.
Our spies walked up to them, and, speaking in the Shaw-
nee tongue, informed them that General Jackson was at
Pensacola, and they were making their escape, and wanted
to know where they could get something to eat. The
Creeks told them that nine miles up the Conaker, the
river they were then on, there was a large camp of
Creeks, and they had cattle and plenty to eat; and further,
that their own camp was on an island about a mile off,
and just below the mouth of the Conaker. They held
their conversation, and struck up a fire and smoked together, and shook hands and parted. One of the Creeks
had a gun, the other had none; and as soon as they had
parted, our Choctaws turned round and shot down the
one that had the gun, and the other attempted to run
off. They snapped several times at him, but the gun still
missing fire, they took after him, and overtaking him, one
of them struck him over the head with his gun, and followed up his blows till he killed him.

The gun was broken in the combat, and they then
fired off the gun of the Creek they had killed, and raised
the war-whoop. When we reached them, they had cut off
the heads of both the Indians; and each of those Indians
with us would walk up to one of the heads, and taking
his war-club would strike on it. This was done by every
one of them; and when they had got done, I took one of
their clubs and walked up as they had done, and struck
it on the head also. At this, they all gathered round me,

and patting me on the shouder, would call me "Warrior, warrior."

They scalped the heads, and then we moved on a short distance to where we found a trace leading in towards the river. We took this trace and pursued it, till we came to where a Spaniard had been killed and scalped, together with a woman who we supposed to be his wife, and also four children. I began to feel mighty ticklish along about this time, for I knowed if there was no danger then, there had been, and I felt exactly like there still was. We, however, went on till we struck the river, and then continued down it till we came opposite to the Indian camp, where we found they were still beating their roots.

It was now late in the evening, and they were in a thick cane-brake. We had some few friendly Creeks with us, who said they could decoy them. So we all hid behind trees and logs while the attempt was made. The Indians would not agree that we should fire, but picked out some of their best gunners and placed them near the river. Our Creeks went down to the river's side, and hailed the camp in the Creek language. We heard the answer, and an Indian man started down towards the river, but didn't come in sight. He went back and again commenced beating his roots and sent a squaw. She came down and talked to our Creeks until dark came on. They told her they wanted her to bring them a canoe. To which she replied that their canoe was on our side; that two of their men had gone out to hunt their horses, and hadn't yet returned. They were the same two we had killed. The canoe was found, and forty of our picked Indian warriors were crossed over to take the camp. There was at last only one man in it, and he escaped; and they took two squaws and ten children, but killed none of them, of course.

We had run nearly out of provisions, and Major Russell had determined to go up the Conaker to the camp we had heard of from the Indians we had killed. I was one that he selected to go down the river that night for provisions, with the canoe, to where we had left our regiment. I took with me a man by the name of John Guess and one of the friendly Creeks, and cut out. It was very dark, and the river was so full, that it overflowed the banks and the adjacent low bottoms. This rendered it very difficult to keep the channel, and particularly as the river was very crooked. At about ten o'clock at night we reached the camp, and were to return by morning to Major Russell, with provisions for his trip up the river; but on informing Colonel Blue of this arrangement, he vetoed it as quick as General Jackson did the bank bill, and said, if Major Russell didn't come back the next day, it would be bad times for him. I found we were not to go up the Conaker to the Indian camp, and a man of my company offered to go up in my place to inform Major Russell. I let him go; and they reached the Major, as I was told, about sunrise in the morning, who immediately returned with those who were with him, to the regiment, and joined us where we crossed the river, as hereafter stated.

The next morning we all fixed up, and marched down the Scamby to a place called Miller's Landing, where we swam our horses across, and sent on two companies down on the side of the bay, opposite to Pensacola, where the Indians had fled when the main army first marched to that place. One was the company of Captain William

Russell, a son of the old Major, and the other was commanded by a Captain Trimble. They went on, and had
a little skirmish with the Indians. They killed some, and
took all the balance prisoners, though I don't remember
the numbers.

CHAPTER SEVEN

I Return Home

When we made a move from the point where we met the companies, we set out for Chatahachy, the place for which we had started when we left Fort Montgomery. At the start, we had taken only twenty days' rations of flour, and eight days' rations of beef, and it was now thirty-four days before we reached that place. We were, therefore, in extreme suffering for want of something to eat, and exhausted with our exposure and the fatigues of our journey. I remember well, that I had not myself tasted bread but twice in nineteen days. I had brought a pretty good supply of coffee from the boat that had reached us from Pensacola, on the Scamby, and on that we chiefly subsisted. At length, one night our spies came in, and informed us they had found Holm's village on the Chatahachy river; and we made an immediate push for that place. We traveled all night expecting to get something to

eat when we got there. We arrived about sunrise, and
near the place prepared for battle. We were all so furious,
that even the certainty of a pretty hard fight could not
have restrained us. We made a furious charge on the
town; but to our great mortification and surprise, there
was not a human being in it. The Indians had all run off
and left it. We burned the town, however, but, melancholy to tell, we found no provision whatever. We then
turned about, and went back to the camp we had left the
night before, as nearly starved as any set of poor fellows
ever were in the world.

We staid there only a little while, when we divided our
regiment; and Major Childs, with his men, went back the
way we had come for a considerable distance, and then
turned to Baton-Rouge, where they joined General Jackson and the main army on their return from Orleans.
Major Russell and his men struck for Fort Decatur, on the
Talapoosa river. Some of our friendly Indians, who knew
the country, went on ahead of us, as we had no trail except
the one they made to follow. With them we sent some of
our ablest horses and men, to get us some provisions, to
prevent us from absolutely starving to death. As the army
marched, I hunted every day, and would kill every hawk,
bird, and squirrel that I could find. Others did the same;
and it was a rule with us, that when we stop'd at night,
the hunters would throw all they had killed in a pile, and
then we would make a general division among all the
men. One evening I came in, having killed nothing that
day. I had a very sick man in my mess, and I wanted something for him to eat, even if I starved myself. So I went to
the fire of a Captain Cowen, who commanded my company after the promotion of Major Russell, and informed

him that I was on the hunt of something for a sick man to eat. I know'd the captain was as bad off as the rest of us, but I found him broiling a turkey's gizzard. He said he had divided the turkey out among the tick, that Major Smiley had killed it, and that nothing else had been killed that day. I immediately went to Smiley's fire, where I found him broiling another gizzard. I told him that it was the first turkey I had ever seen have two gizzards. But so it was, I got nothing for my sick man. And now, seeing that every fellow must shift for himself, I determined that in the morning I would come up missing; so I took my mess, and cut out to go ahead of the army. We know'd that nothing more could happen to us if we went than if we staid, for it looked like it was to be starvation any way; we therefore determined to go on the old saying, root hog or die. We passed two camps, at which our men, that had gone on before us, had killed Indians. At one they had killed nine, and at the other three. About daylight we came to a small river, which I thought was the Scamby; but we continued on for three days, killing little or nothing to eat; till, at last, we all began to get nearly ready to give up the ghost, and lie down and die; for we had no prospect of provision, and we knew we couldn't go much further without it.

We came to a large prairie, that was about six miles across it, and in this I saw a trail which I knowed was made by bear, deer, and turkeys. We went on through it till we came to a large creek, and the low grounds were all set over with wild rye, looking as green as a wheat field. We here made a halt, unsaddled our horses, and turned them loose to graze.

One of my companions, a Mr. Vanzant, and myself,

then went up the low grounds to hunt. We had gone some distance, finding nothing; when, at last, I found a squirrel, which I shot, but he got into a hole in the tree. The game was small, but necessity is not very particular; so I thought I must have him, and I climbed that tree thirty feet high, without a limb, and pulled him out of his hole. I shouldn't relate such small matters, only to show what lengths a hungry man will go to, to get something to eat. I soon killed two other squirrels, and fired at a large hawk. At this a large gang of turkeys rose from the cane brake, and flew across the creek to where my friend was, who had just before crossed it. He soon fired on a large gobler, and I heard it fall. By this time, my gun was loaded again, and I saw one sitting on my side of the creek, which had flew over when he fired; so I blazed away, and down I brought him. I gathered him up, and a fine turkey he was. I now began to think we had struck a breeze of luck, and almost forgot our past sufferings, in the prospect of once more having something to eat. I raised the shout, and my comrade came to me, and we went on to our camp with the game we had killed. While we were gone, two of our mess had been out, and each of them had found a bee tree. We turned into cooking some of our game, but we had neither salt nor bread. Just at this moment, on looking down the creek, we saw our men, who had gone on before us for provisions, coming to us. They came up, and measured out to each man a cupfull of flour. With this, we thickened our soup, when our turkey was cooked, and our friends took dinner with us, and then went on.

We now took our tomahawks, and went out and cut our bee trees, out of which we got a fine chance of honey; though we had been starving so long that we feared to eat much at a time, till, like the Irish by hanging, we got used to it again. We rested that night without moving our camp; and the next morning myself and Vanzant again turned out to hunt. We had not gone far, before I wounded a fine buck very badly; and while pursuing him, I was walking on a large tree that had fallen down, when from the top of it a large bear broke out and ran off. I had no dogs, and I was sorry enough for it; for of all the hunting I ever did, I have always delighted most in bear hunting. Soon after this, I killed a large buck; and we had just gotten him to camp, when our poor starved army came up. They told us, that to lessen their sufferings as much as possible, Captain William Russell had had his horse led up to be shot for them to eat, just at the moment that they saw our men returning, who had carried on the flour.

We were now about fourteen miles from Fort Decatur, and we gave away all our meat and honey, and went on with the rest of the army. When we got there, they could give us only one ration of meat, but not a mouthful of bread. I immediately got a canoe, and taking my gun, crossed over the river, and went to the Big Warriors' town. I had a large hat, and I offered an Indian a silver dollar for my hat full of corn. He told me that his corn was all *"shuestea,"* which in English means, it was all gone. But he showed me where an Indian lived, who, he said, had corn. I went to him and made the same offer. He could talk a little broken English, and said to me, "You got any powder? You got bullet?" I told him I had. He then said, "Me swap my corn for powder and bullet." I took out about ten bullets, and showed him; and he proposed to give me a hat full of corn for them. I took him up mighty quick. I then offered to give him ten charges of powder for another hat full of corn. To this he agreed very willingly. So I took off my hunting shirt, and tied up my corn; and though it had cost me very little of my powder and lead, yet I wouldn't have taken fifty silver dollars for it. I returned to the camp, and the next morning we started for the Hickory Ground, which was thirty miles off. It was here that General Jackson met the Indians, and made peace with the body of the nation.

We got nothing to eat at this place, and we had yet to go forty-nine miles, over a rough and wilderness country, to Fort Williams. Parched corn, and but little even of that, was our daily subsistence. When we reached Fort Williams, we got one ration of pork, and one of flour, which was our only hope until we could reach Fort Strother.

The horses were now giving out, and I remember to have seen thirteen good horses left in one day, the saddles and bridles being thrown away. It was thirty-nine miles to Fort Strother, and we had to pass directly by Fort Talladega, where we first had the big Indian battle with the eleven hundred painted warriors. We went through the old battle ground, and it looked like a great gourd patch; the skulls of the Indians who were killed, still lay scattered all about, and many of their frames were still perfect, as the bones had not separated. But about five miles before we got to this battle ground, I struck a trail, which I followed until it led me to one of their towns. Here I swapp'd some more of my powder and bullets for a little corn.

I pursued on, by myself, till some time after night, when I came up to the rest of the army. That night my company and myself did pretty well, as I divided out my corn among them. The next morning we met the East Tennessee troops, who were on the road to Mobile, and my youngest brother was with them. They had plenty of corn and provisions, and they gave me what I wanted for myself and my horse. I remained with them that night, though my company went across the Coosa river to the fort, where they also had the good fortune to find plenty of provisions. Next morning, I took leave of my brother and all my old neighbours, for there were a good many of them with him, and crossed over to my men at the fort. Here I had enough to go on, and after remaining a few days, cut out for home. Nothing more, worthy of the reader's attention, transpired till I was safely landed at home once more with my wife and children. I found them all well and doing well; and though I was only a rough sort of backwoodsman, they seemed mighty glad to see me, however little the quality folks might suppose it. For I do reckon we love as hard in the backwood country, as any people in the whole creation.

But I had been home only a few days, when we received orders to start again, and go on to the Black Warrior and Cahawba rivers, to see if there were no Indians there. I know'd well enough there was none, and I wasn't willing to trust my craw any more where there was neither any fighting to do, nor anything to go on; and so I agreed to give a young man, who wanted to go, the balance of my wages if he would serve out my time, which was about a month. He did so, and when they returned, sure enough they hadn't seen an Indian, any more than if they had been all the time chopping wood in my clearing. This closed my career as a warrior, and I am glad of it, for I like life now a heap better than I did then; and I am glad all over that I lived to see these times, which I should not have done if I had kept fooling along in war, and got used up at it. When I say I am glad, I just mean I am glad that I am alive, for there is a confounded heap of things I an't glad of at all. I an't glad, for example, that the "government" moved the deposites, and if my military glory should take such a turn as to make me president after the general's time, I'll move them back; yes, I, the "government" will "take the responsibility," and move them back again. If I don't, I wish I may be shot.

But I am glad that I am now through war matters, and I reckon the reader is too, for they have no fun in them at all; and less, if he had had to pass through them first, and then write them afterwards. But for the dullness of their narrative, I must try to make amends by relating some of the curious things that happened to me in private life, and when *forced* to become a public man, as I shall have to be again, if ever I consent to take the presidential chair.

CHAPTER EIGHT

I Marry Again

I continued at home now, working my farm for two years, as the war finally closed soon after I quit the service. The battle at New Orleans had already been fought, and treaties were made with the Indians, which put a stop to their hostilities.

But in this time, I met with the hardest trial which ever falls to the lot of man. Death, that cruel leveler of all distinctions—to whom the prayers and tears of husbands, and of even helpless infancy, are addressed in vain, —entered my humble cottage, and tore from my children an affectionate good mother, and from me a tender and loving wife.

It is a scene long gone by, and one which it would be supposed I had almost forgotten; yet when I turn my memory back on it, it seems as but the work of yesterday. It was the doing of the Almighty, whose ways are always right, though we sometimes think they fall heavily on us; and as painful as is even yet the remembrance of her sufferings, and the loss sustained by my little children and myself, yet I have no wish to lift up the voice of complaint. I was left with three children; the two eldest were sons, the youngest a daughter, and, at that time, a mere infant. It appeared to me, at that moment, that my situation was the worst in the world. I couldn't bear the thought of scattering my children, and so I got my youngest brother, who was also married, and his family to live with me. They took as good care of my children as they well could, but yet it wasn't all like the care of a mother. And though their company was to me in every respect like that of a brother and sister, yet it fell far short of being like that of a wife. So I came to the conclusion it wouldn't do, but that I must have another wife.

There lived in the neighborhood, a widow lady whose husband had been killed in the war. She had two children, a son and daughter, and both quite small, like my own. I began to think, that as we were both in the same situation, it might be that we could do something for each other; and therefore began to hint a little around the matter, as we were once in a while together. She was a good industrious woman, and owned a snug little farm, and lived quite comfortable. I soon began to pay my respects to her in real good earnest; but I was as sly about it as a fox when he is going to rob a hen-roost. I found that my company wasn't at all disagreeable to her: and I thought I could treat her children with so much friendship as to make her a good stepmother to mine, and in this I wasn't mistaken, as we soon bargained, and got married, and then went ahead. In a great deal of peace we raised our first crop of children, and they are all married and doing well. But we had a second crop together; and I shall notice them as I go along, as my wife and myself both had a hand in them, and they therefore belong to the history of my second marriage.

The next fall after this marriage, three of my neighbors and myself determined to explore a new country. Their names were Robinson, Frazier, and Rich. We set out for the Creek country, crossing the Tennessee river; and after having made a day's travel, we stopp'd at the house of one of my old acquaintances, who had settled there after the war. Resting here a day, Frazier turned out to hunt, being a great hunter; but he got badly bit by a very poisonous snake, and so we left him and went on. We passed through a large rich valley, called Jones's Valley, where several other families had settled, and continued our course till we came near to the place where Tuscaloosa now stands. Here we camped, as there were no inhabitants, and hobbled out our horses for the night. About two hours before day, we heard the bells on our horses going back the way we had come, as they had started to leave us. As soon as it was daylight, I started in pursuit of them on foot, and carrying my rifle, which was a very heavy one. I went ahead the whole day, wading creeks and swamps, and climbing mountains; but I couldn't overtake our horses, though I could hear of them at every house they passed. I at last found I couldn't catch up with them, and so I gave up the hunt, and turned back to the last house I had passed, and staid there till morning. From the best calculation we could make, I had walked over fifty miles that day; and the next morning I was so sore, and fatigued, that I felt like I couldn't walk any more. But I was anxious to get back to where I had left my company, and so I started and went on, but mighty slowly, till after the middle of the day. I now began to feel mighty sick, and had a dreadful headache. My rifle was so heavy, and I felt so weak, that I lay down by the side of the trace, in a perfect wilderness too, to see if I wouldn't get better. In a short time some Indians came along. They had some ripe melons, and wanted me to eat some, but I was so sick I couldn't. They then signed to me, that I would die, and be buried; a thing I was confoundly afraid of myself. But I asked them how near it was to any house? By their signs, again, they made me understand it was a mile and a half. I got up to go; but when I rose, I reeled about like a cow with the blind staggers, or a fellow who had taken too many "horns." One of the Indians proposed to go with me, and carry my gun. I gave him half a dollar, and accepted his offer. We got to the house, by which time I was pretty far gone, but was kindly received, and got on to a bed. The woman did all she could for me with her warm teas, but I still continued bad enough, with a high fever, and generally out of my senses. The next day two of my neighbors were passing the road, and heard of my situation, and came to where I was. They were going nearly the route I had intended to go, to look at the country; and so they took me first on one of their horses, and then on the other, till they got me back to where I had left my company. I expected I would get better, and be able to go on with them, but, instead of this, I got worse and worse; and when we got there, I wasn't able to sit up at all. I thought now the jig was mighty nigh up with me, but I determined to keep a stiff upper lip. They carried me to a house, and each of my comrades bought him a horse, and they all set out together, leaving me behind. I knew but little that was going on for about two weeks; but the family treated me with every possible kindness in their power, and I shall always feel thankful to them. The man's name was Jesse Jones. At the end of two weeks I began to mend without the help of a doctor, or of any doctor's means. In this time, however, as they told me, I was speechless for five days, and they had no thought that I would ever speak again,—in Congress or anywhere else. And so the woman, who had a bottle of Bateman's drops, thought if they killed me, I would only die any how, and so she would try it with me. She gave me the whole bottle, which throwed me into a sweat that continued on me all night; when at last I seemed to wake up, and spoke, and asked her for a drink of water. This almost alarmed her, for she was looking every minute for me to die. She gave me the water, and, from that time, I began slowly to mend, and so kept on till I was able at last to walk about a little. I might easily have been mistaken for one of the Kitchen Cabinet,* I looked so much like a ghost. I have been particular in giving a history of this sickness, not because I believe it will interest any body much now, nor, indeed, do I *certainly* know that it ever will. But if I should be forced to take the "white house," then it will be a good history; and every one will look on it as important. And I can't, for my life, help laughing now, to think, that when all my folks get around me, wanting good fat offices, how so many of them will say, "What a good thing it was that

---

* The "Kitchen Cabinet" refers to the coterie of advisers to President Andrew Jackson who met with him unofficially in the kitchen of the White House for the discussion of public affairs. They were not members of the official cabinet.

that kind woman had a bottle of drops that saved PRESI-
DENT CROCKETT's life,—the second greatest and best"!!!!!
Good, says I, my noble fellow! You take the post office;
or the navy; or the war office; or, may be, the treasury.
But if I give him the treasury, there's no devil if I don't
make him agree first to fetch back them deposites. And if
it's even the post office, I'll make him promise to keep his
money 'counts without any figuring, as that throws the
whole concern heels over head in debt, in little or no time.

But when I got so I could travel a little, I got a
wagoner who was passing along to haul me to where he
lived, which was about twenty miles from my house. I
still mended as we went along, and when we got to his
stopping place, I hired one of his horses, and went on
home. I was so pale, and so much reduced, that my face
looked like it had been half soled with brown paper.

When I got there, it was to the utter astonishment of
my wife; for she supposed I was dead. My neighbors who
had started with me had returned and took my horse
home, which they had found with theirs; and they
reported that they had seen men who had helped to bury
me; and who saw me draw my last breath. I know'd this
was a whopper of a lie, as soon as I heard it. My wife
had hired a man, and sent him out to see what had
become of my money and other things; but I had missed
the man as I went in, and he didn't return until some
time after I got home, as he went all the way to where
I lay sick, before he heard that I was still in the land of
the living and a-kicking.

The place on which I lived was sickly, and I was determined to leave it. I therefore set out the next fall to look
at the country which had been purchased of the Chicke-

saw tribe of Indians. I went on to a place called Shoal Creek, about eighty miles from where I lived, and here again I got sick. I took the ague and fever, which I supposed was brought on by my camping out. I remained here for some time, as I was unable to go farther; and in that time I became so well pleased with the country about there, that I resolved to settle in it. It was just only a little distance in the purchase, and no order had been established there; but I thought I could get along without order as well as anybody else. And so I moved and settled myself down on the head of Shoal Creek. We remained here some two or three years, without any law at all; and so many bad characters began to flock in upon us, that we found it necessary to set up a sort of temporary government of our own. I don't mean that we made any president, and called him the "government," but we met and made what we called a corporation; and I reckon we called *it* wrong, for it wasn't a bank, and hadn't any deposites; and now they call the bank a corporation. But be this as it may, we lived in the backwoods, and didn't profess to know much, and no doubt used many wrong words. But we met, and appointed magistrates and constables to keep order. We didn't fix any laws for them, though; for we supposed they would know law well enough, whoever they might be; and so we left it to themselves to fix the laws.

I was appointed one of the magistrates; and when a man owed a debt, and wouldn't pay it, I and my constable ordered our warrant, and then he would take the man, and bring him before me for trial. I would give judgment against him, and then an order for an execution would easily scare the debt out of him. If any one was charged with marking his neighbor's hogs, or with stealing anything,—which happened pretty often in those days,—I would have him taken, and if there were tolerable grounds for the charge, I would have him well whipp'd and cleared. We kept this up till our Legislature added us to the white settlements in Giles county, and appointed magistrates by law, to organize matters in the parts where I lived. They appointed nearly every man a magistrate who had belonged to our corporation. I was then, of course, made a squire, according to law; though now the honor rested more heavily on me than before. For, at first, whenever I told my constable, says I—"Catch that fellow and bring him up for trial,"—away he went, and the fellow must come, dead or alive; for we considered this a good warrant, though it was only in verbal writing. But after I was appointed by the assembly, they told me my warrants must be in real writing, and signed; and that I must keep a book, and write my proceedings in it. This was a hard business on me, for I could just barely write my own name; but to do this, and write the warrants too, was at least a huckleberry over my persimmon. I had a pretty well informed constable, however, and he aided me very much in this business. Indeed, I had so much confidence in him, that I told him, when we should happen to be out anywhere, and see that a warrant was necessary, and would have a good effect, he needn't take the trouble to come all the way to me to get one, but he could just fill out one; and then on the trial I could correct the whole business if he had committed any error. In this way I got on pretty well, till by care and attention I improved my handwriting in such a manner as to be able to prepare my warrants, and keep my record book without much difficulty. My judgments were never appealed

from, and if they had been, they would have stuck like
wax, as I gave my decisions on the principles of common
justice and honesty between man and man, and relied on
natural born sense, and not on law learning to guide
me; for I had never read a page in a law book in all my
life.

CHAPTER NINE

On the Stump

About the time we were getting under good headway in our new government, a Captain Matthews came to me and told me he was a candidate for the office of colonel of a regiment, and that I must run for first major in the same regiment. I objected to this, telling him that I thought I had done my share of fighting, and that I wanted nothing to do with military appointments.

He still insisted, until at last I agreed, and of course had every reason to calculate on his support in my election. He was an early settler in that country, and made rather more corn than the rest of us; and knowing it would afford him a good opportunity to electioneer a little, he made a great corn husking, and a great frolic, and gave a general treat, asking everybody over the whole country. Myself and my family were, of course, invited. When I got there, I found a very large collection of people, and some friend of mine soon informed me that the captain's son was going to offer against me for the office of major, which he had seemed so anxious for me to get. I cared nothing about the office, but it put my dander up high enough to see, that after he had pressed me so hard to offer, he was countenancing, if not encouraging, a secret plan to beat me.

I took the old gentleman out, and asked him about it. He told me it was true his son was going to run as a candidate, and that he hated worse to run against me than any man in the county. I told him his son need give himself no uneasiness about that; that I shouldn't run against him for major, but against his daddy for colonel. He took me by the hand, and we went into the company. He then made a speech and informed the people that I was his opponent. I mounted up for a speech too. I told the people the cause of my opposing him, remarking that as I had the whole family to run against any way, I was determined to levy on the head of the mess. When the time for election came, his son was opposed by another man for major; and he and his daddy were both badly beaten. I just now began to take a rise, as in a little time I was asked to offer for the Legislature in the counties of Lawrence and Heckman.

I offered my name in the month of February, and started about the first of March with a drove of horses to the lower part of the State of North Carolina. This was in the year of 1821, and I was gone upwards of three months. I returned, and set out electioneering, which was a bran-fire new business to me. It now became necessary that I should tell the people something about the government, and an eternal sight of other things that I knowed nothing more about than I did about Latin, and law, and such things as that. I have said before that in those days none of us called General Jackson the government, nor did he seem in as fair a way to become so as I do now; but I knowed so little about it, that if any one had told me he was "the government," I should have believed it, for I had never read even a newspaper in my life, or anything else, on the subject. But over all my difficulties, it seems to me I was born for luck, though it would be hard for any one to guess what sort. I will, however, explain that hereafter.

I went first into Heckman county, to see what I could do among the people as a candidate. Here they told me that they wanted to move their town nearer to the centre of the county, and I must come out in favor of it. There's no devil if I knowed what this meant, or how the town was to be moved; and so I kept dark, going on the identical same plan that I now find is called *"noncommittal."* About this time there was a great squirrel hunt on Duck river, which was among my people. They were to hunt two days; then to meet and count the scalps, and have a big barbecue, and what might be called a tip-top country frolic. The dinner, and a general treat, was all to be paid for by the party having taken the fewest scalps. I joined one side, taking the place of one of the hunters, and got a gun ready for the hunt. I killed a great many squirrels, and when we counted scalps, my party was victorious.

The company had every thing to eat and drink that could be furnished in so new a country, and much fun and good humor prevailed. But before the regular frolic commenced, I mean the dancing, I was called on to make a speech as a candidate; which was a business I was as ignorant of as an outlandish negro.

A public document I had never seen, nor did I know there were such things; and how to begin I couldn't tell. I made many apologies, and tried to get off, for I know'd I had a man to run against who could speak prime, and I know'd, too, that I wasn't able to shuffle and cut with him. He was there, and knowing my ignorance as well as I did myself, he also urged me to make a speech. The truth is, he thought my being a candidate was a mere matter of sport; and didn't think for a moment, that he was in any danger from an ignorant backwoods bear hunter. But I found I couldn't get off, and so I determined just to go ahead, and leave it to chance what I should say. I got up and told the people I reckoned they know'd what I had come for, but if not, I could tell them. I had come for their votes, and if they didn't watch mighty close I'd get them too. But the worst of all was, that I could not tell them anything about government. I tried to speak about something, and I cared very little what, until I choked up as bad as if my mouth had been jamm'd and cramm'd chock full of dry mush. There the people stood, listening all the while, with their eyes, mouths, and ears all open, to catch every word I would speak.

At last I told them I was like a fellow I had heard of not long before. He was beating on the head of an empty barrel near the road-side, when a traveler, who was passing along, asked him what he was doing that for? The fellow replied that there was some cider in that barrel a few days before, and he was trying to see if there was any then, but if there was he couldn't get at it. I told them that there had been a little bit of a speech in me a while ago, but I believed I couldn't get it out. They all roared out in a mighty laugh, and I told some other anecdotes, equally amusing to them, and believing I had them in a first-rate way, I quit and got down, thanking the people for their attention. But I took care to remark that I was as dry as a powder-horn, and that I thought it was time for us all to wet our whistles a little: and so I put off to the liquor stand, and was followed by the greater part of the crowd.

I felt certain this was necessary, for I knowed my competitor could talk government matters to them as easy as he pleased. He had, however, mighty few left to hear him, as I continued with the crowd, now and then taking a horn, and telling good-humored stories, till he was done speaking. I found I was good for the votes at the hunt, and when we broke up I went on to the town of Vernon, which was the same they wanted me to move. Here they pressed me again on the subject, and I found I could get either party by agreeing with them. But I told them I didn't know whether it would be right or not, and so couldn't promise either way.

Their court commenced on the next Monday, as the barbecue was on a Saturday, and the candidates for Governor and for Congress, as well as my competitor and myself, all attended.

The thought of having to make a speech made my knees feel mighty weak, and set my heart to fluttering almost as bad as my first love scrape with the Quaker's niece. But as good luck would have it, these big candidates spoke nearly all day, and when they quit, the people were worn out with fatigue, which afforded me a good apology for not discussing the government. But I listened mighty close to them, and was learning pretty fast about political matters. When they were all done, I got up and told some laughable story, and quit. I found I was safe in those parts, and so I went home, and did not go back again till after the election was over. But to cut this matter short, I was elected, doubling my competitor, and nine votes over.

A short time after this, I was in Pulaski, where I met with Colonel Polk, now a member of Congress from Tennessee.* He was at that time a member elected to the Legislature, as well as myself; and in a large company he said to me, "Well, colonel, I suppose we shall have a radical change of the judiciary at the next session of the Legislature." "Very likely, sir," says I; and I put out quicker, for I was afraid some one would ask me what the judiciary was; and if I knowed I wish I may be shot. I don't indeed believe I had ever before heard that there was any such thing in all nature; but still I was not willing that the people there should know how ignorant I was about it.

When the time for meeting of the Legislature arrived, I went on, and before I had been there long, I could have told what the judiciary was, and what the government was too; and many other things that I had known nothing about before.

About this time I met with a very severe misfortune, which I may be pardoned for naming, as it made a great change in my circumstances, and kept me back very much in the world. I had built an extensive grist mill, and powder mill, all connected together, and also a large distillery. They had cost me upwards of three thousand dollars; more than I was worth in the world. The first

* James Knox Polk was later elected President of the United States and served from 1845 to 1849.

news that I heard after I got to the Legislature, was, that
my mills were—not blown up sky high, as you would
guess, by my powder establishment—but swept away all
to smash by a large fresh, that came soon after I left home.
I had, of course, to stop my distillery, as my grinding was
broken up; and, indeed, I may say, that the misfortune
just made a complete mash of me. I had some likely
negroes, and a good stock of almost everything about me,
and, best of all, I had an honest wife. She didn't advise me,
as is too fashionable, to smuggle up this, and that, and
t'other, to go on at home; but she told me, says she, "Just
pay up, as long as you have a bit's worth in the world; and
then everybody will be satisfied, and we will scuffle for
more." This was just such talk as I wanted to hear, for a
man's wife can hold him devilish uneasy, if she begins to
scold and fret, and perplex him, at a time when he has a
full load for a railroad car on his mind already.

And so, you see, I determined not to break full handed,
but thought it better to keep a good conscience with an
empty purse, than to get a bad opinion of myself, with a
full one. I therefore gave up all I had, and took a bran-
fire new start.

CHAPTER TEN

I Go A-Hunting

Having returned from the Legislature, I determined to make another move, and so I took my eldest son with me, and a young man by the name of Abram Henry, and cut out for the Obion. I selected a spot when I got there, where I determined to settle; and the nearest house to it was seven miles, the next nearest was fifteen, and so on to twenty. It was a complete wilderness, and full of Indians who were hunting. Game was plenty of almost every kind, which suited me exactly, as I was always fond of hunting. The house which was nearest me, and which, as I have already stated, was seven miles off, and on the different side of the Obion river, belonged to a man by the name of Owens; and I started to go there. I had taken one horse along, to pack our provision, and when I got to the water I hobbled him out to graze, until I got back; as there was no boat to cross the river in, and it was so high that it had overflowed all the bottoms and low country near it.

We now took water like so many beavers, notwithstanding it was mighty cold, and waded on. The water would sometimes be up to our necks, and at others not so deep; but I went, of course, before, and carried a pole, with which I would feel along before me, to see how deep it was, and to guard against falling into a slough, as there was many in our way. When I would come to one, I would take out my tomahawk and cut a small tree across it, and then go ahead again. Frequently my little son would have to swim, even where myself and the young man could wade; but we worked on till at last we got to the channel of the river, which made it about half a mile we had waded from where we took water. I saw a large tree that had fallen into the river from the other side, but it did not reach across. One stood on the same bank where we were, that I thought I could fall, so as to reach the other; and so at it we went with my tomahawk, cutting away till we got it down; and, as good luck would have it, it fell right, and made us a way that we could pass.

When we got over this, it was still a sea of water as far as our eyes could reach. We took into it again, and went ahead, for about a mile, hardly ever seeing a single spot of land, and sometimes very deep. At last we came in sight of land, which was a very pleasing thing; and when we got out, we went but a little way, before we came in sight of the house, which was more pleasing than ever; for we were wet all over, and mighty cold. I felt mighty sorry when I would look at my little boy, and see him shaking like he had the worst sort of an ague, for there was no time for fever then. As we got near to the house, we saw Mr. Owens and several men that were with him, just starting away. They saw us, and stopp'd, but looked much astonished until we got up to them, and I made myself known. The men who were with him were the owners of a boat which was the first that ever went that far up the Obion river; and some hands he had hired to carry it about a hundred miles still further up, by water, though it was only about thirty by land, as the river is very crooked.

They all turned back to the house with me, where I found Mrs. Owens, a fine, friendly old woman; and her kindness to my little boy did me ten times as much good as anything she could have done for me, if she had tried her best. The old gentleman set out his bottle to us, and I concluded that if a horn wasn't good then, there was no use for its invention. So I swigg'd off about a half a pint, and the young man was by no means bashful in such a case; he took a strong pull at it too. I then gave my boy some, and in a little time we felt pretty well. We dried ourselves by the fire, and were asked to go on board the boat that evening. I agreed to do so, but left my son with the old lady, and myself and the young man went to the boat with Mr. Owens and the others. The boat was loaded with whiskey, flour, sugar, coffee, salt, castings, and other articles suitable for the country; and they were to receive five hundred dollars to land the load at McLe-more's Bluff, beside the profit they could make on their load. This was merely to show that boats could get up to that point. We staid all night with them, and had a high night of it, as I took steam enough to drive out all the cold that was in me, and about three times as much more.

In the morning, we concluded to go on with the boat to where a great *harricane* had crossed the river, and blowed all the timber down into it. When we got there, we found the river was falling fast, and concluded we couldn't get through the timber without more rise; so we dropp'd down opposite Mr. Owens' again where they determined to wait for more water.

The next day it rained rip-roariously, and the river rose pretty considerable, but not enough yet. And so I got the boatsmen all to go out with me to where I was going to settle, and we slapped up a cabin in little or no time. I got from the boat four barrels of meal, and one of salt, and about ten gallons of whiskey.

To pay for these, I agreed to go with the boat up the river to their landing place. I got also a large middling of bacon, and killed a fine deer, and left them for my young man and my little boy, who were to stay at my cabin till I got back, which I expected would be in six or seven days. We cut out and moved up to the hurricane, where we stopp'd for the night. In the morning, I started about daylight intending to kill a deer, as I had no thought they would get the boat through the timber that day. I had gone but a little way before I killed a fine buck, and started to go back to the boat; but on the way I came on the tracks of a large gang of elks, and so I took after them. I had followed them only a little distance when I saw them, and directly after I saw two large bucks. I shot one down, and the other wouldn't leave him; so I loaded my gun and shot him down too. I hung them up, and went ahead again after my elks. I pursued on till after the middle of the day before I saw them again; but they took the hint before I got in shooting distance, and run off. I still pursued on till late in the evening, when I found I was about four miles from where I had left the boat, and as hungry as a wolf, for I hadn't eaten a bite that day.

I started down the edge of the river low grounds giving out the pursuit of my elks, and hadn't gone hardly any distance at all, before I saw two more bucks, very large fellows too. I took a blizzard at one of them and up he tumbled. The other ran off a few jumps and stopp'd; and stood there till I loaded again, and fired at him. I knock'd his trotters from under him, and then I hung them both up. I pushed on again, and about sunset I saw three other bucks. I down'd with one of them and the other two ran off. I hung this one up also, having now killed six that day. I then pushed on till I got to the harricane, and at the lower edge of it, about where I expected the boat was. Here I hollered as hard as I could roar, but could get no answer. I fired off my gun, and the men on the boat fired one too; but quite contrary to my expectation, they had got through the timber, and were about two miles above me. It was now dark, and I had to crawl through the fallen timber the best way I could; and if the reader don't know it was bad enough, I am sure I do. For the vines and briers had grown all through it, and so thick that a good fat coon couldn't much more than get along. I got through at last, and went on near to where I had killed my last deer, and once more fired off my gun, which was again answered from the boat which was still a little above me. I moved on as fast as I could, but soon came to water, and not knowing how deep it was I halted, and hollered till they came to me with a skiff. I now got to the boat, without further difficulty; but the briers had worked on me at such a rate that I felt like I wanted sewing up all over. I took a pretty stiff horn,* which soon made me feel much better; but I was so tired that I could hardly work my jaws to eat.

In the morning, myself and a young man started and brought in the first buck I had killed, and after breakfast we went and brought in the last one. The boat then started, but we again went and got the two I had killed just as I turned down the river in the evening; and we then pushed on and overtook the boat, leaving the other two hanging in the woods, as we had now as much as we wanted.

We got up the river very well, but quite slowly, and we landed on the eleventh day at the place the load was delivered at. They here gave me their skiff, and myself and a young man by the name of Flavius Harris, who had determined to go and live with me, cut out down the river for my cabin, which we reached safely enough.

We turned in, and cleared a field and planted our corn; but it was so late in the spring we had no time to make rails, and therefore we put no fence around our field. There was no stock, however, nor anything else to disturb our corn except the wild *varments,* and the old serpent himself, with a fence to help him, couldn't keep them out. I made corn enough to do me, and during that spring I killed ten bears, and a great abundance of deer. But in all this time, we saw the face of no white person in that country, except Mr. Owens' family and a very few passengers, who went out there looking at the country. Indians, though, were still plenty enough. Having laid by my crap,† I went home, which was a distance

* Drinking cups or beakers having been originally made of the horns of cattle, the word "horn" came to be used for "a drink."

† The word meant was obviously "crop."

of about a hundred and fifty miles, and when I got there
I was met by an order to attend a call-session of our
Legislature. I attended at, and served out my time, and
then returned and took my family and what little plunder
I had, and moved to where I had built my cabin, and made
my crap.

I gathered my corn, and then set out for my Fall's
hunt. This was in the last of October, 1822. I found bear
very plenty, and, indeed, all sorts of game and wild varments, except buffalo. There was none of them. I hunted
on till Christmas, having supplied my family very well
all along with wild meat, at which time my powder gave
out; and I had none either to fire Christmas guns, which is
very common in that country, or to hunt with. I had a
brother-in-law who had now moved out and settled about
six miles west of me, on the opposite side of Rutherford's
fork of the Obion river, and he had brought me a keg of
powder, but I had never gotten it home. There had just
been another of Noah's freshes, and the low grounds were
flooded all over with water. I know'd the stream was at
least a mile wide which I would have to cross, as the
water was from hill to hill, and yet I determined to go
on over in some way or other, so as to get my powder. I
told this to my wife, and she immediately opposed it with
all her might. I still insisted, telling her we had no powder
for Christmas, and, worse than all, we were out of meat.
She said, we had as well starve as for me to freeze to death
or to get drowned, and one or the other was certain if I
attempted to go.

But I didn't believe the half of this; and so I took
my woolen wrappers, and a pair of moccasins, and put
them on, and tied up some dry clothes, and a pair of

shoes and stockings, and started. But I didn't before know how much anybody could suffer and not die. This, and some of my other experiments in water, learned me something about it, and I therefore relate them.

The snow was about four inches deep when I started; and when I got to the water, which was only about a quarter of a mile off, it looked like an ocean. I put in, and waded on till I come to the channel, where I crossed that on a high log. I then took water again, having my gun and all my hunting tools along, and waded till I came to a deep slough, that was wider than the river itself. I had crossed it often on a log; but behold, when I got there, no log was to be seen. I knowed of an island in the slough, and a sapling stood on it close to the side of that log, which was now entirely under water. I knowed further, that the water was about eight or ten feet deep under the log, and I judged it to be about three feet deep over it. After studying a little what I should do, I determined to cut a forked sapling, which stood near me, so as to lodge it against the one that stood on the island, in which I succeeded very well. I then cut me a pole, and then crawled along on my sapling till I got to the one it was lodged against, which was about six feet above the water. I then felt about with my pole till I found the log, which was just about as deep under the water as I had judged. I then crawled back and got my gun, which I had left at the stump of the sapling I had cut, and again made my way to the place of lodgment, and then climbed down the other sapling so as to get on the log. I then felt my way along with my feet, in the water, about waist deep, but it was a mighty ticklish business. However, I got over, and by this time I had very little feeling in my feet and legs, as I had been all the time in the water, except what time I was crossing the high log over the river, and climbing my lodged sapling.

I went but a short distance before I came to another slough, over which there was a log, but it was floating on the water. I thought I could walk it, and so I mounted on it; but when I had got about the middle of the deep water, somehow or somehow else, it turned over, and in I went up to my head. I waded out of this deep water, and went ahead till I came to the highland, where I stopp'd to pull off my wet clothes, and put on the others, which I had held up with my gun, above the water, when I fell in. I got them on, but my flesh had no feeling in it, I was so cold. I tied up the wet ones, and hung them up in a bush. I now thought I would run, so as to warm myself a little, but I couldn't raise a trot for some time; indeed, I couldn't step more than half the length of my foot. After a while I got better, and went on five miles to the house of my brother-in-law, having not even smelt fire from the time I started. I got there late in the evening, and he was much astonished at seeing me at such a time. I staid all night, and the next morning was most piercing cold, and so they persuaded me not to go home that day. I agreed, and turned out and killed him two deer; but the weather still got worse and colder, instead of better. I staid that night, and in the morning they still insisted I couldn't get home. I knowed the water would be frozen over, but not hard enough to bear me, and so I agreed to stay that day. I went out hunting again, and pursued a big *he-bear* all day, but didn't kill him. The next morning was bitter cold, but I knowed my family was without meat, and I determined to get home to them, or die a-trying.

I took my keg of powder, and all my hunting tools, and cut out. When I got to the water, it was a sheet of ice as far as I could see. I put on to it, but hadn't got far before it broke through with me; and so I took out my tomahawk, and broke my way along before me for a considerable distance. At last I got to where the ice would bear me for a short distance, and I mounted on it, and went ahead; but it soon broke in again, and I had to wade on till I came to my floating log. I found it so tight this time, that I know'd it couldn't give me another fall, as it was frozen in with the ice. I crossed over it without much difficulty, and worked along till I got to my lodged sapling, and my log under the water. The swiftness of the current prevented the water from freezing over it, and so I had to wade, just as I did when I crossed it before. When I got to my sapling, I left my gun, and climbed out with my powder keg first, and then went back and got my gun. By this time I was nearly frozen to death, but I saw all along before me, where the ice had been fresh broke, and I thought it must be a bear straggling about in the water. I, therefore, fresh primed my gun, and, cold as I was, I was determined to make war on him, if we met. But I followed the trail till it led me home, and I then found it had been made by my young man that lived with me, who had been sent by my distressed wife to see, if he could, what had become of me, for they all believed that I was dead. When I got home, I wasn't quite dead, but mighty nigh it; but had my powder, and that was what I went for.

CHAPTER ELEVEN

I Meet Up with a Big Bear

That night there fell a heavy rain, and it turned to a sleet. In the morning all hands turned out hunting. My young man, and a brother-in-law who had lately settled close by me, went down the river to hunt for turkeys; but I was for larger game. I told them I had dreamed the night before of having had a hard fight with a big black nigger, and I know'd it was a sign that I was to have a battle with a bear; for in a bear country, I never know'd such a dream to fail. So I started to go up above the hurricane, determined to have a bear. I had two pretty good dogs, and an old hound, all of which I took along. I had gone about six miles up the river, and it was then about four miles across to the main Obion; so I determined to strike across to that, as I had found nothing yet to kill. I got on the river, and turned down it; but the sleet was still getting worse and worse. The bushes were all bent down and locked together with ice, so that it was almost impossible to get along. In a little time my dogs started a large gang of old turkey gobblers, and I killed two of them of the biggest sort. I shouldered them up, and moved on, until I got through the hurricane, when I was so tired that I laid my gobblers down to rest, as they were confounded heavy, and I was mighty tired. While I was resting, my old hound went to a log, and smelt it awhile, and then raised his eyes towards the sky, and cried out. Away he went, and my other dogs with him, and I shouldered up my turkeys again, and followed on as hard as I could drive. They were soon out of sight, and in a very little time I heard them begin to bark. When I got to them they were barking up a tree, but there was no game there. I concluded it had been a turkey, and that it had flew away.

When they saw me coming, away they went again; and, after a little time, began to bark as before. When I got near them, I found they were barking up the wrong tree again, as there was no game there. They served me in this way three or four times, until I was so infernal mad, that I determined, if I could get near enough, to shoot the old hound at least. With this intention, I pushed on the harder, till I came to the edge of an open prairie, and looking on before my dogs, I saw in and about the biggest bear that ever was seen in America. He looked, at the distance he was from me, like a large black bull. My dogs were afraid to attack him, and that was the reason they had stopp'd so often, that I might overtake them. They were now almost up with him, and I took my gobblers from my back and hung them up in a sapling, and broke like a quarter horse after my bear, for the sight of him had put new springs in me. I soon got near to them, but they were just getting into a roaring thicket, and so I couldn't run through it, but had to pick my way along, and had close work even at that.

In a little time I saw the bear climbing up a large black oak tree, and I crawled on until I got within about eighty yards of him. He was setting with his breast to me: and so I put fresh priming in my gun, and fired at him. At this he raised one of his paws and snorted loudly. I loaded again as quick as I could, and fired as near the same place in his breast as possible. At the crack of my gun here he came tumbling down; and the moment he touched the ground, I heard one of my best dogs cry out. I took my tomahawk in one hand, and my big butcher-knife in the other, and run up within four or five paces of him, at which he let my dog go, and fixed his eyes on me. I got back in all sorts of a hurry, for I knowed if he got hold of me, he would hug me altogether too close for comfort. I went to my gun and hastily loaded her again, and shot him the third time, which killed him good.

I now began to think about getting him home, but I didn't know how far it was. So I left him and started; and in order to find him again, I would blaze a sapling every little distance, which would show me the way back. I continued this until I got within about a mile of home, for there I knowed very well where I was, and that I could easily find my way back to my blazes. When I got home, I took my brother-in-law, and my young man, and four horses, and went back. We got there just before dark, and struck up a fire, and commenced butchering my bear. It was some time in the night before we finished it; and I can assert, on my honor, that I believed he would have weighed six hundred pounds. It was the second largest I ever saw. I killed one, a few years after, that weighed six hundred and seventeen pounds. I now felt fully compensated for my sufferings in going after my powder; and well satisfied that a dog might sometimes be doing a good business, even when he seemed to be *barking up the wrong tree.* We got our meat home, and I had the pleasure to know that we now had plenty, and that of the best; and I continued through the winter to supply my family abundantly with bearmeat and venison from the woods.*

* The bear appears to have been the Colonel's favorite game. Indeed, with the exception of the deer and the wild turkey, it seems there was no other large game to be found in that part of Tennessee where he was settled. Buffaloes were only to be found farther to the west, and panthers were very rare. [Footnote in 1880 edition.]

CHAPTER TWELVE

I Run for Congress

I had on hand a great many skins, and so, in the month of February, I packed a horse with them, and taking my eldest son along with me, cut out for a little town called Jackson, situated about forty miles off. We got there well enough, and I sold my skins, and bought me some coffee, and sugar, powder, lead, and salt. I packed them all up in readiness for a start, which I intended to make early the next morning. Morning came, but I concluded, before I started, I would go and take a horn with some of my old fellow-soldiers that I had met with at Jackson.

I did so; and while we were engaged in this, I met with three candidates for the Legislature. A Doctor Butler, who was, by marriage, a nephew to General Jackson, a Major Lynn, and a Mr. McEver, all first-rate men. We all took a horn together, and some person present said to me, "Crockett, you must offer for the Legislature." I told

him I lived at least forty miles from any white settlement; and had no thought of becoming a candidate at
that time. So we all parted, and I and my little boy went on
home.

It was about a week or two after this, that a man came
to my house, and told me I was a candidate. I told
him not so. But he took out a newspaper from his pocket,
and showed me where I was announced. I said to my wife
that this was all a burlesque on me, but I was determined
to make it cost the man who had put it there at least the
value of the printing, and of the fun he wanted at my
expense. So I hired a young man to work in my place on
my farm, and turned out myself electioneering. I hadn't
been out long, before I found the people began to talk
very much about the bear hunter, the man from the cane;
and the three gentlemen, who I have already named, soon
found it necessary to enter into an agreement to have a
sort of caucus at their March court, to determine which
of them was the strongest, and the other two was to withdraw and support him. As the court came on, each one of
them spread himself, to secure the nomination; but it fell
on Dr. Butler, and the rest backed out. The doctor was a
clever fellow, and I have often said he was the most
talented man I ever run against for any office. His being
related to General Jackson also helped him on very
much; but I was in for it, and I was determined to push
ahead and go through, or stick. Their meeting was held
in Madison county, which was the strongest in the representative district, which was composed of eleven counties,
and they seemed bent on having the member from there.

At this time Colonel Alexander was a candidate for
Congress, and attending one of his public meetings one

day, I walked to where he was treating the people, and he gave me an introduction to several of his acquaintances, and informed them that I was out electioneering. In a little time my competitor, Doctor Butler, came along; he passed by without noticing me, and I supposed, he did not recognize me. But I hailed him, as I was for all sorts of fun; and when he turned to me, I said to him, "Well, doctor, I suppose they have weighed you out to me; but I should like to know why they fixed your election for *March* instead of *August?* This is," said I, "a branfire new way of doing business, if a caucus is to make a representative for the people!" He now discovered who I was, and cried out, "D—n it, Crockett, is that you?" "Be sure it is," said I, "but I don't want it understood that I have come electioneering. I have just crept out of the cane, to see what discoveries I could make among the white folks." I told him that when I set out electioneering, I would go prepared to put every man on as good a footing when I left him as I found him on. I would therefore have me a large buckskin hunting-shirt made, with a couple of pockets holding about a peck each; and that in one I would carry a great big twist of tobacco, and in the other my bottle of liquor; for I knowed when I met a man and offered him a dram, he would throw out his quid of tobacco to take one, and after he had taken his horn, I would out with my twist, and give him another chew. And in this way he would not be worse off than when I found him; and I would be sure to leave him in a first-rate good humor. He said I could beat him electioneering all hollow. I told him I would give him better evidence of that before August, notwithstanding he had many advantages over me, and particularly in the way of money;

but I told him I would go on the products of the country; that I had industrious children, and the best of coondogs; and they would hunt every night till midnight to support my election; and when the coon fur wasn't good, I would myself go a wolfing, and shoot down a wolf, and skin his head, and his scalp would be good to me for three dollars, in our State Treasury money; and in this way I would get along on the big string. He stood like he was both amused and astonished, and the whole crowd was in a roar of laughter. From this place I returned home, leaving the people in a first-rate way, and I was sure I would do a good business among them. At any rate, I was determined to stand up to my lick-log, salt or no salt.

In a short time there came out two other candidates, a Mr. Shaw and a Mr. Brown. We all ran the race through; and when the election was over, it turned out that I beat them all by a majority of two hundred and forty-seven votes, and was again returned as a member of the Legislature from a new region of the country, without losing a session. This reminded me of the old saw—"A fool for luck, and a poor man for children."

I now served two years in that body from my new district, which was the years 1823 and 1824. At the session of 1823, I had a small trial of my independence, and whether I would forsake principle for party, or for the purpose of following after big men.

The term of Col. John Williams had expired, who was a senator in Congress from the State of Tennessee. He was a candidate for another election, and was opposed by Pleasant M. Miller, Esq., who it was believed, would not be able to beat the Colonel. Some two or three others were spoken of, but it was at last concluded that the only man

who could beat him was General Jackson. So, a few days
before the election was to come on, he was sent for to
come and run for the senate. He was then in nomination
for the presidency; but sure enough he came, and did run
as the opponent of Colonel Williams, and beat him too,
but not by my vote. The vote was, for Jackson, *thirty-five;*
for Williams, *twenty-five.* I thought the Colonel had
honestly discharged his duty, and even the mighty name
of Jackson couldn't make me vote against him.

But voting against the old chief was found a mighty
up-hill business to all of them except myself. I never
would, nor never did, acknowledge I had voted wrong;
and I am more certain now that I was right than ever.

I told the people it was the best vote I ever gave; that
I had supported the public interest, and cleared my conscience in giving it, instead of gratifying the private
ambition of a man.

I let the people know as early as then, that I wouldn't
take a collar around my neck.

During these two sessions of the Legislature, nothing
else turned up which I think it worth while to mention;
and, indeed, I am fearful that I am too particular about
many small matters; but if so, my apology is, that I
want the world to understand my true history, and how
I worked along to rise from the cane-brake to my present
station in life.

Col. Alexander was the representative in Congress of
the district I lived in, and his vote on the tariff law of
1824 gave a mighty heap of dissatisfaction to his people.*

---

* The tariff of 1824 raised the rates on woolen goods, glass, iron,
lead and hemp. The act was opposed by the Southern cotton planters
who imported most of these goods and thus had to pay a higher price
for them.

They therefore began to talk pretty strong of running me for Congress against him. At last I was called on by a good many to be a candidate. I told the people that I couldn't stand that; it was a step above my knowledge, and I know'd nothing about Congress matters.

However, I was obliged to agree to run, and myself and two other gentlemen came out. But Providence was a little against two of us this hunt, for it was the year that cotton brought twenty-five dollars a hundred; and so Colonel Alexander would get up and tell the people, it was all the good effect of this tariff law; that it had raised the price of their cotton, and that it would raise the price of every thing else they made to sell. I might as well have sung *psalms* over a dead horse, as to try to make the people believe otherwise; for they know'd their cotton had raised, sure enough, and if the colonel hadn't done it, they didn't know what had. So he rather made a mash of me this time, as he beat me exactly *two* votes, as they counted the polls, though I have always believed that many other things had been as fairly done as that same count.

He went on, and served out his term, and at the end of it cotton was down to *six* or *eight* dollars a hundred again; and I concluded I would try him once more, and see how it would go with cotton at the common price, and so I became a candidate.

CHAPTER THIRTEEN

More Bear Hunting

But the reader, I expect, would have no objection to know a little about my employment during the two years while my competitor was in Congress. In this space I had some pretty tough times, and will relate some few things that happened to me. So here goes, as the boy said when he run by himself.

In the fall of 1825, I concluded I would build two large boats, and load them with pipe staves for market. So I went down to the lake, which was about twenty-five miles from where I lived, and hired some hands to assist me, and went to work; some at boat building, and others to getting staves. I worked on with my hands till the bears got fat, and then I turned out to hunting, to lay in a supply of meat. I soon killed and salted down as many as was necessary for my family; but about this time, one of my old neighbors who had settled down on the lake about twenty-

five miles from me, came to my house and told me he
wanted me to go down and kill some bears about in his
parts. He said they were extremely fat, and very plenty.
I knowed that when they were fat they were easily taken,
for a fat bear can't run fast or long. But I asked a bear no
favors, no way, further than civility, for I now had eight
large dogs, and as fierce as painters, so that a bear stood no
chance at all to get away from them. So I went home with
him and then went on down towards the Mississippi and
commenced hunting.

We were out two weeks, and in that time killed fifteen
bears. Having now supplied my friend with plenty of
meat, I engaged occasionally again with my hands in our
boat building, and getting staves. But I at length couldn't
stand it any longer without another hunt. So I concluded
to take my little son and cross over the lake, and take a
hunt there. We got over, and that evening turned out and
killed three bears in little or no time. The next morning
we drove up four forks, and made a sort of scaffold, on
which we salted up our meat, so as to have it out of the
reach of the wolves, for as soon as we would leave our
camp, they would take possession. We had just eat our
breakfast, when a company of hunters came to our camp
who had fourteen dogs, but all so poor, that when they
would bark they would almost have to lean up against a
tree and take a rest. I told them their dogs couldn't run in
smell of a bear, and they had better stay at my camp and
feed them on the bones I had cut out of my meat. I left
them there and cut out; but I hadn't gone far, when my
dogs took a first rate start after a very large fat old he-bear,
which run right plump towards my camp. I pursued on,
but my other hunters had heard my dogs coming, and

met them and killed the bear before I got up with him.
I gave him to them, and cut out again for a creek called
Big Clover, which wasn't very far off. Just as I got there,
and was entering a cane brake, my dogs all broke and went
ahead, and in a little time they raised a fuss in the cane,
and seemed to be going every way. I listened a while, and
found my dogs was in two companies, and that both was
in a snorting fight. I sent my little son to one and I broke
for t'other. I got to mine first, and found my dogs had a
two-year-old bear down a-wooling away on him, so I just
took out my big butcher, and went up and slapp'd it into
him, and killed him without shooting. There was five of
the dogs in my company. In a short time I heard my little
son fire at his bear; when I went to him he had killed it
too. He had two dogs in his team. Just at this moment we
heard my other dog barking a short distance off, and all
the rest immediately broke to him. We pushed on too, and
when we got there, we found that he had still a larger bear
than either of them we had killed, treed by himself. We
killed that one also, which made three we had killed in
less than half an hour. We turned in and butchered them,
and then started to hunt for water and a good place to
camp. But we had no sooner started, than our dogs took
a start after another one, and away they went like a
thundergust and was out of hearing in a minute. We followed the way they had gone for some time, but at length
we gave up the hope of finding them, and turned back.
As we were going back, I came to where a poor fellow was
grubbing, and he looked like the very picture of hard
times. I asked him what he was doing away there in the
woods by himself? He said he was grubbing for a man who
intended to settle there; and the reason why he did it

was, that he had no meat for his family, and he was working for a little.

I was mighty sorry for the poor fellow, for it was not only a hard but a very slow way to get meat for a hungry family; so I told him if he would go with me, I would give him more meat than he could get by grubbing in a month. I intended to supply him with meat, and also to get him to assist my little boy in packing and salting up my bears. He had never seen a bear killed in his life. I told him I had six killed then, and my dogs were hard after another. He went off to his little cabin, which was a short distance in the brush, and his wife was very anxious he should go with me. So we started and went to where I had left my three bears, and made a camp. We then gathered my meat, and salted and scaffold it, as I had done the other. Night now came on, but no word from my dogs yet. I afterwards found they had treed the bear about five miles off, near to a man's house, and had barked at it the whole enduring night. Poor fellows! many a time they looked for me, and wondered why I didn't come, for they know'd there was no mistake in me, and I know'd they were as good as ever fluttered. In the morning, as soon as it was light enough to see, the man took his gun and went to them, and shot the bear and killed it. My dogs, however, wouldn't have anything to say to this stranger; so they left him, and came early in the morning back to me.

We got breakfast and cut out again, and we killed four large and very fat bears that day. We hunted out the week, and in that time we killed seventeen, all of them first rate. When we closed our hunt, I gave the man over a thousand weight of fine, fat bear-meat, which pleased him mightily, and made him feel as rich as a Jew. I saw him the next fall, and he told me he had plenty of meat to do him the whole year from his week's hunt. My son and me now went home. This was the week between Christmas and New Year, that we made this hunt.

When I got home, one of my neighbors was out of meat, and wanted me to go back, and let him go with me, to take another hunt. I couldn't refuse; but I told him I was afraid the bear had taken to house by that time, for after they get very fat in the fall and early part of the winter, they go into their holes, in large hollow trees, or into hollow logs, or their cane-houses, or the harricanes; and lie there till spring, like frozen snakes. And one thing about this will seem mighty strange to many people. From about the first of January to about the last of April, these varments lie in their holes altogether. In all that time they have no food to eat; and yet when they come out, they are not an ounce lighter than when they went to house. I don't know the cause of this, and still I know it is a fact; and I leave it for others who have more learning than myself to account for it. They have not a particle of food with them, but they just lie and suck the bottom of their paw all the time. I have killed many of them in their trees, which enables me to speak positively on this subject. However, my neighbor, whose name was McDaniel, and my little son and me, went on down to the lake to my second camp, where I had killed my seventeen bears the week before, and turned out to hunting. But we hunted hard all day without getting a single start. We had carried but little provisions with us, and the next morning was entirely out of meat. I sent my son about three miles off, to the house of an old friend, to get some. The old gentleman was much pleased to hear I was hunting in those parts, for the year before the bears had killed a great many of his hogs. He was that day killing his bacon hogs, and so he gave my son some meat, and sent word to me that I must come in to his house that evening, that he would have plenty of feed for my dogs, and some accommodations for ourselves; but before my son got back, we had gone out hunting, and in a large cane brake my dogs found a big bear in a cane-house, which he had fixed for his winter-quarters, as they sometimes do.

When my lead dog found him, and raised the yell, all the rest broke to him, but none of them entered his house until we got up. I encouraged my dogs, and they knowed me so well, that I could have made them seize the old serpent himself, with all his horns and heads, and cloven foot and ugliness into the bargain, if he would only have come to light, so that they could have seen him. They bulged in, and in an instant the bear followed them out, and I told my friend to shoot him, as he was mighty wrathy to kill a bear. He did so, and killed him prime. We carried him to our camp, by which time my son had returned; and after we got our dinners we packed up, and cut for the house of my old friend, whose name was Davidson.

We got there, and staid with him that night; and the next morning, having salted up our meat, we left it with him, and started to take a hunt between the Obion lake and the Red foot lake; as there had been a dreadful harricane, which passed between them, and I was sure there must be a heap of bears in the fallen timber. We had gone about five miles without seeing any sign at all; but at length we got on some high cany ridges, and, as we rode along, I saw a hole in a large black oak, and on examining more closely, I discovered that a bear had clomb the tree. I could see his tracks going up, but none coming down, and so I was sure he was in there. A person who is acquainted with bear-hunting, can tell easy enough when the varment is in the hollow; for as they go up they don't slip a bit, but as they come down they make long scratches with their nails.

My friend was a little ahead of me, but I called him back, and told him there was a bear in that tree, and I must have him out. So we lit from our horses, and I found a small tree which I thought I could fall so as to lodge against my bear tree, and we fell to work chopping it with our tomahawks. I intended, when we lodged the tree against the other, to let my little son go up, and look into the hole, for he could climb like a squirrel. We had chopp'd on a little time and stopp'd to rest, when I heard my dogs barking mighty severe at some distance from us, and I told my friend I knowed they had a bear; for it is the nature of a dog, when he finds you are hunting bears, to hunt for nothing else; he becomes fond of the meat, and considers other game as "not worth a notice," as old Johnson said of the devil.

We concluded to leave our tree a bit, and went to my dogs, and when we got there, sure enough they had an eternal great big fat bear up a tree, just ready for shooting. My friend again petitioned me for liberty to shoot this one also. I had a little rather not, as the bear was so big, but I couldn't refuse; and so he blazed away, and down came the old fellow like some great log had fell. I now missed one of my dogs, the same that I before spoke of as having treed the bear by himself sometime before, when I had started the three in the cane brake. I told my friend that my missing dog had a bear somewhere, just as sure as fate; so I left them to butcher the one we had just killed, and I went up on a piece of high ground to listen for my dog. I heard him barking with all his might some distance off, and I pushed ahead for him. My other dogs hearing him broke to him, and when I got there, sure enough again he had another bear ready treed; if he hadn't, I wish I may be shot. I fired on him, and brought him down; and then went back, and help'd finish butchering the one at which I had left my friend. We then packed both to our tree where we had left my boy. By this time, the little fellow had cut the tree down that we intended to lodge, but it fell the wrong way; he had then feather'd in on the big tree, to cut that, and had found that it was nothing but a shell on the outside, and all doted in the middle, as too many of our big men are in these days, having only an outside appearance. My friend and my son cut away on it, and I went off about a hundred yards with my dogs to keep them from running under the tree when it should fall. On looking back at the hole, I saw the bear's head out of it, looking down at them as they were cutting. I hollered to them to look up, and they did so; and McDaniel catched up his gun, but by this time the bear was out, and coming down the tree. He fired at it, and as soon as it touched the ground the dogs were all round it, and they had a roll-and-tumble fight to the foot of the hill, where they stopp'd him. I ran up, and putting my gun against the bear, fired and killed him. We had now three, and so we made our scaffold and salted them up.

CHAPTER FOURTEEN

Perilous Adventures on the Hunt

In the morning I left my son at the camp, and we started on towards the harricane; and when we had went about a mile, we started a very large bear, but we got along mighty slow on account of the cracks in the earth occasioned by the earthquakes. We, however, made out to keep in hearing of the dogs for about three miles, and then we come to the harricane. Here we had to quit our horses, as old Nick himself couldn't have got through it without sneaking it along in the form that he put on, to make a fool of our old grandmother Eve. By this time several of my dogs had got tired and come back; but we went ahead on foot for some little time in the harricane, when we met a bear coming straight to us, and not more than twenty or thirty yards off. I started my tired dogs after him, and McDaniel pursued them, and I went on to where my other dogs were. I had seen the track of the bear they were after, and I knowed he was a screamer. I followed on to about the middle of the harricane, but my dogs pursued him so close, that they made him climb an old stump about twenty feet high. I got in shooting distance of him and fired, but I was all over in such a flutter from fatigue and running, that I couldn't hold steady; but, however, I broke his shoulder, and he fell. I run up and loaded my gun as quick as possible, and shot him again and killed him. When I went to take out my knife to butcher him, I found I had lost it in coming through the harricane. The vines and briers was so thick that I would sometimes have to get down and crawl like a varment to get through at all; and a vine had, as I supposed, caught in the handle and pulled it out. While I was standing and studying what to do, my friend came to me. He had followed my trail through the harricane, and had found my knife, which was mighty good news to me; as a hunter hates the worst in the world to lose a good dog, or any part of his hunting tools. I now left McDaniel to butcher the bear, and I went after our horses, and brought them as near as the nature of the case would allow. I then took our bags, and went back to where he was; and when we had skinned the bear, we fleeced off the fat and carried it to our horses at several loads. We then packed it up on our horses, and had a heavy pack of it on each one. We now started and went on till about sunset, when I concluded we must be near our camp; so I hollered and my son answered me, and we moved on in the direction to the camp. We had gone but a little way when I heard my dogs make a warm start again; and I jumped down from my horse and gave him up to my friend, and told him I would follow them. He went on to the camp, and I went ahead after my dogs with

all my might for a considerable distance, till at last night
came on. The woods were very rough and hilly, and all
covered over with cane.

I now was compelled to move on more slowly; and
was frequently falling over logs, and into the cracks made
by the earthquakes, so that I was very much afraid I
would break my gun. However, I went on about three
miles, when I came to a good big creek, which I waded.
It was very cold, and the creek was about knee-deep;
but I felt no great inconvenience from it just then, as I
was all over wet with sweat from running, and I felt hot
enough. After I got over this creek and out of the cane,
which was very thick on all our creeks, I listened for my
dogs. I found they had either treed or brought the bear
to a stop, as they continued barking in the same place.
I pushed on as near in the direction of the noise as I
could, till I found the hill was too steep for me to climb,
and so I backed and went down the creek some distance,
till I came to a hollow, and then took up that, till I came
to a place where I could climb up the hill. It was mighty
dark, and was difficult to see my way, or anything else.
When I got up the hill, I found I had passed the dogs;
and so I turned and went to them. I found, when I got
there, they had treed the bear in a large forked poplar,
and it was setting in the fork.

I could see the lump, but not plain enough to shoot
with any certainty, as there was no moonlight; and so I
set into hunting for some dry brush to make me a light;
but I could find none, though I could find that the ground
was torn mightily to pieces by the cracks.

At last I thought I could shoot by guess, and kill him; so
I pointed as near the lump as I could, and fired away. But
the bear didn't come, he only clumb up higher, and got

out on a limb, which helped me to see him better. I now
loaded up again and fired, but this time he didn't move
at all. I commenced loading for a third fire, but the first
thing I knowed, the bear was down among my dogs, and
they were fighting all around me. I had my big butcher
in my belt, and I had a pair of dressed buckskin breeches
on. So I took out my knife, and stood, determined, if he
should get hold of me, to defend myself in the best
way I could. I stood there for some time, and could now
and then see a white dog I had, but the rest of them, and
the bear, which were dark colored, I couldn't see at all,
it was so miserable dark. They still fought around me, and
sometimes within three feet of me; but, at last, the bear
got down into one of the cracks that the earthquakes had
made in the ground, about four feet deep, and I could
tell the biting end of him by the hollering of my dogs. So
I took my gun and pushed the muzzle of it about, till I
thought I had it against the main part of his body, and
fired; but it happened to be only the fleshy part of his
foreleg. With this he jumped out of the crack, and he
and the dogs had another hard fight around me, as before.
At last, however, they forced him back into the crack
again, as he was when I had shot.

I had laid down my gun in the dark, and I now began
to hunt for it; and, while hunting, I got hold of a pole,
and I concluded I would punch him awhile with that. I
did so, and when I would punch him, the dogs would
jump in on him, when he would bite them badly, and
they would jump out again. I concluded, as he would
take punching so patiently, it might be that he would
lie still enough for me to get down in the crack, and
feel slowly along till I could find the right place to give
him a dig with my butcher. So I got down, and my

dogs got in before him and kept his head towards them, till I got along easily up to him; and placing my hand on his rump, felt for his shoulder, just behind which I intended to stick him. I made a lunge with my long knife, and fortunately stuck him right through the heart, at which he just sank down, and I crawled out in a hurry. In a little time my dogs all come out too, and seemed satisfied, which was the way they always had of telling me that they had finished him.

I suffered very much that night with cold, as my leather breeches, and everything else I had on, was wet and frozen. But I managed to get my bear out of this crack after several hard trials, and so I butchered him and laid down to try to sleep. But my fire was very bad, and I couldn't find anything that would burn well to make it any better; and so I concluded I should freeze, if I didn't warm myself in some way by exercise. So I got up and hollered awhile, and then I would just jump up and down with all my might, and throw myself into all sorts of motions. But all this wouldn't do; for my blood was now getting cold, and the chills coming all over me. I was so tired, too, that I could hardly walk; but I thought I would do the best I could to save my life, and then, if I died, nobody would be to blame. So I went to a tree about two feet through, and not a limb on it for thirty feet, and I would climb up to the limbs, and then lock my arms together around it, and slide down to the bottom again. This would make the insides of my legs and arms feel mighty warm and good. I continued this till daylight in the morning, and how often I clumb up my tree and slid down I don't know, but I reckon at least a hundred times.

In the morning I got my bear hung up so as to be safe, and then set out to hunt for my camp. I found it after awhile, and McDaniel and my son were very much rejoiced to see me get back, for they were about to give me up for lost. We got our breakfasts, and then secured our meat by building a high scaffold, and covering it over. We had no fear of its spoiling, for the weather was so cold that it couldn't.

We now started after my other bear, which had caused me so much trouble and suffering; and before we got him, we got a start after another, and took him also. We went on to the creek I had crossed the night before, and camped, and then went to where my bear was that I had killed in the crack. When we examined the place, McDaniel said he wouldn't have gone into it, as I did, for all the bears in the woods.

We then took the meat down to our camp and salted it, and also the last one we had killed; intending in the morning, to make a hunt in the harricane again.

We prepared for resting that night, and I can assure the reader I was in need of it. We had laid down by our fire, and about ten o'clock there came a most terrible earthquake, which shook the earth so, that we were rocked about like we had been in a cradle. We were very much alarmed; for though we were accustomed to feel earthquakes, we were now right in the region which had been torn to pieces by them in 1812, and we thought it might take a notion and swallow us up, like the big fish did Jonah.

In the morning we packed up and moved to the harricane, where we made another camp, and turned out that evening and killed a very large bear, which made eight we had now killed in this hunt.

The next morning we entered the harricane again, and in a little or no time my dogs were in full cry. We pursued them, and soon came to a thick cane-brake, in which they had stopp'd their bear. We got up close to him, as the cane was so thick that we couldn't see more than a few feet. Here I made my friend hold the cane a little open with his gun till I shot the bear, which was a mighty large one. I killed him dead in his tracks. We got him out and butchered him, and in a little time started another and killed him, which now made ten we had killed; and we knowed we couldn't pack any more home, as we had only five horses along; therefore we returned to the camp and salted up all our meat, to be ready for a start homeward next morning.

The morning came, and we packed our horses with the meat, and had as much as they could possibly carry, and sure enough cut out for home. It was about thirty miles, and we reached home the second day. I had now accommodated my neighor with meat enough to do him, and had killed in all, up to that time, fifty-eight bears, during the fall and winter.

As soon as the time come for them to quit their houses and come out again in the spring, I took a notion to hunt a little more, and in about one month I killed forty-seven more, which made one hundred and five bears which I had killed in less than one year from that time.*

* These bear hunts of the Colonel entirely surpass anything on record. Mr. Gordon Cumming's record of his fights with lions, elephants, giraffes, hippopotamuses, and African buffaloes, is full of excitement and interest; but in real peril and adventure, they by no means surpass Colonel Crockett's bear fights. [Footnote in 1880 edition]

CHAPTER FIFTEEN

I Go Down the Mississippi

Having now closed my hunting for that winter, I returned to my hands, who were engaged about my boats and staves, and made ready for a trip down the river. I had two boats and about thirty thousand staves, and so I loaded with them, and set out for New Orleans. I got out of the Obion river, in which I had loaded my boats, very well; but when I got into the Mississippi, I found all my hands were bad scared, and in fact I believe I was scared a little the worst of any; for I had never been down the river, and I soon discovered that my pilot was as ignorant of the business as myself. I hadn't gone far before I determined to lash the two boats together; we did so, but it made them so heavy and obstinate, that it was next akin to impossible to do anything at all with them, or to guide them right in the river.

That evening we fell in company with some Ohio

boats; and about night we tried to land, but we could not. The Ohio men hollered to us to go on and run all night. We took their advice, though we had a good deal rather not; but we couldn't do any other way. In a short distance we got into what is called the *"Devil's Elbow;"* and if any place in the wide creation has its own proper name, I thought it was this. Here we had about the hardest work that I ever was engaged in, in my life, to keep out of danger; and even then we were in it all the while. We twice attempted to land at Wood-yards, which we could see but couldn't reach.

The people would run out with lights, and try to instruct us how to get to shore; but all in vain. Our boats were so heavy that we couldn't take them much any way, except the way they wanted to go, and just the way the current would carry them. At last we quit trying to land, and concluded just to go ahead as well as we could, for we found we couldn't do any better. Some time in the night I was down in the cabin of one of the boats, sitting by the fire, thinking on what a hobble we had got into; and how much better bear-hunting was on hard land, than floating along on the water, when a fellow had to go ahead whether he was exactly willing or not.

The hatchway into the cabin came slap down, right through the top of the boat; and it was the only way out except a small hole in the side, which we had used for putting our arms through to dip up water before we lashed the boats together.

We were now floating sideways, and the boat I was in was the hindmost as we went. All at once I heard the hands begin to run over the top of the boat in great confusion, and pull with all their might; and the first thing I know'd after this we went broadside full tilt against the head of an island where a large raft of drift timber had lodged. The nature of such a place would be, as everybody knows, to suck the boats down, and turn them right under this raft; and the uppermost boat would, of course, be suck'd down and go under first. As soon as we struck, I bulged for my hatchway, as the boat was turning under sure enough. But when I got to it, the water was pouring through in a current as large as the hole would let it, and as strong as the weight of the river would force it. I found I couldn't get out here, for the boat was now turned down in such a way, that it was steeper than a house-top. I now thought of the hole in the side, and made my way in a hurry for that. With difficulty I got to it, and when I got there, I found it was too small for me to get out by my own power, and I began to think that I was in a worse box than ever. But I put my arms through and hollered as loud as I could roar, as the boat I was in hadn't yet quite filled with water up to my head, and the hands who were next to the raft, seeing my arms out, and hearing me holler, seized them, and began to pull. I told them I was sinking, and to pull my arms off, or force me through, for now I know'd well enough it was neck or nothing, come out or sink.

By a violent effort they jerked me through; but I was in a pretty pickle when I got through. I had been sitting without any clothing over my shirt; this was torn off, and I was literally skin'd like a rabbit. I was, however, well pleased to get out in any way, even without shirt or hide; as before I could straighten myself on the boat next to the raft, the one they pull'd me out of went entirely under, and I have never seen it any more to this day. We all escaped on to the raft, where we were compelled to sit all night about a mile from land on either side. Four of my company were bareheaded, and three barefooted; and of that number I was one. I reckon I looked like a pretty cracklin ever to get to Congress!!!

We had now lost all our loading; and every particle of our clothing, except what little we had on; but over all this, while I was setting there, in the night, floating about on the drift, I felt happier and better off than I had ever had in my life before, for I had just made such a marvellous escape, that I had forgot almost every thing else in that; and so I felt prime.

In the morning about sunrise, we saw a boat coming down, and we hailed her. They sent a large skiff, and took us all on board, and carried us down as far as Memphis. Here I met with a friend, that I never can forget as long as I am able to go ahead at anything; it was a Major Winchester, a merchant of that place: he let us all have hats, and shoes, and some little money to go upon, and so we all parted.

A young man and myself concluded to go on down to Natchez, to see if we could hear anything of our boats; for we supposed they would float out from the raft, and keep on down the river. We got on a boat at Memphis, that was going down, and so cut out. Our largest boat, we were informed, had been seen about fifty miles below where we stove, and an attempt had been made to land her, but without success, as she was as hard headed as ever.

This was the last of my boats, and of my boating; for it went so badly with me, along at the first, that I had not much mind to try it any more. I now returned home again, and as the next August was the Congressional election, I began to turn my attention a little to that matter, as it was beginning to be talked of a good deal among the people.

CHAPTER SIXTEEN

I Get Elected to Congress

I have, heretofore, informed the reader that I had determined to run this race to see what effect *the price of cotton* would have again on it. I now had Colonel Alexander to run against once more, and also General William Arnold.

I had difficulties enough to fight against this time, as every one will suppose; for I had no money, and a very bad prospect, so far as I know'd, of getting any to help me along. I had, however, a good friend, who sent for me to come and see him. I went, and he was good enough to offer me some money to help me out. I borrowed as much as I thought I needed at the start, and went ahead. My friend also had a good deal of business about over the district at the different courts; and if he now and then slipp'd in a good word for me, it is nobody's business. We frequently met at different places, and, as he thought I needed, he would occasionally hand me a little more cash; so I was able to buy a little of "the *creature*," to put my friends in a good humor, as well as the other gentlemen, for they all treat in that country; not to get elected, of course—for that would be against the law; but just, as I before said, to make themselves and their friends feel their keeping a little.

Nobody ever did know how I got money to get along on, till after the election was over, and I had beat my competitors twenty-seven hundred and forty-eight votes. Even the price of cotton couldn't save my friend Aleck this time. My rich friend, who had been so good to me in the way of money, now sent for me, and loaned me a hundred dollars, and told me to go ahead; that that amount would bear my expenses to Congress, and I must then shift for myself. I came on to Washington, and draw'd two hundred and fifty dollars, and purchased with it a check on the bank at Nashville, and enclosed it to my friend; and I may say, in truth, I sent this money with a mighty good will, for I reckon nobody in this world loves a friend better than me, or remembers a kindness longer.

I have now given the close of the election, but I have skipp'd entirely over the canvass, of which I will say a very few things in this place, as I know very well how to tell the truth, but not much about placing them in book order, so as to please critics.

Col. Alexander was a very clever fellow, and principal surveyor at that time; so much for one of the men I had to run against. My other competitor was a major-general in the militia, and an attorney-general at the law, and quite a smart, clever man also; and so it will be seen I had war work as well as law trick to stand up under.

Taking both together, they make a pretty considerable of a load for any one man to carry. But for war claims. I consider myself behind no man except "the government," and mighty little, if any, behind him; but this the people will have to determine hereafter, as I reckon it won't do to quit the work of "reform and retrenchment" yet for a spell.

But my two competitors seemed some little afraid of the influence of each other, but not to think me in their way at all. They, therefore, were generally working against each other, while I was going ahead for myself, and mixing among the people in the best way I could. I was as cunning as a little red fox, and wouldn't risk my tail in a "committal trap."

I found the sign was good, almost every where I went. On one occasion, while we were in the eastern counties of the district, it happened that we all had to make a speech, and it fell on me to make the first one. I did so after my manner, and it turned pretty much on the old saying, "A short horse is soon curried," as I spoke not very long. Colonel Alexander followed me, and then General Arnold come on.

The general took much pains to reply to Alexander, but didn't so much as let on that there was any such candidate as myself at all. He had been speaking for a considerable time, when a large flock of guinea-fowls came very near to where he was, and set up the most unmerciful chattering that ever was heard, for they are a noisy little brute any way. They so confused the general, that he made a stop, and requested that they might be driven away. I let him finish his speech, and then walking up to him, said aloud, "Well, colonel, you are the first man I ever saw that understood the language of fowls." I told him that he had not had the politeness to name me in his speech, and that when my little friends, the guinea-fowls, had come up and began to holler, "Crockett, Crockett, Crockett," he had been ungenerous enough to stop, and drive *them* all away. This raised a universal shout among the people for me, and the general seemed mighty bad plagued. But he got more plagued than this at the polls in August, as I have stated before.

This election was in 1827, and I can say, on my conscience, that I was without disguise, the friend and supporter of General Jackson, upon his principles as he had laid them down, and as *"I understood them,"* before his election as President. During my two first sessions in Congress, Mr. Adams was president, and I worked along with what was called the Jackson party pretty well. I was re-elected to Congress in 1829, by an overwhelming majority; and soon after the commencement of this second term, I saw, or thought I did, that it was expected of me that I would bow to the name of Andrew Jackson, and follow him in all his motions, and windings, and turnings, even at the expense of my conscience and judgment. Such a thing was new to me, and a total stranger to my principles. I know'd well enough, though, that if I didn't "hurra" for his name, the hue and cry was to be raised against me, and I was to be sacrificed, if possible. His famous, or rather I should say in*famous*, Indian bill*

---

* Jackson supported Georgia, Mississippi and Alabama when these states violated Federal treaties with the Cherokee, Creek, Choctaw and Chickesaw Indians, and annexed their territory. In his message to Congress, Jackson upheld the states in their harsh treatment of the Indians, and advocated removing the tribes west of the Mississippi.

Davy Crockett's championship of the rights of the Indians is reported briefly in the following statement in the *Register of Debates, United States Congress*, for January 31, 1831 (Vol. VII, p. 543) : "Mr. Crockett was brought forward, and I opposed it from the purest motives in the world. Several of my colleagues got around me, and told me how well they loved me, and that I was ruining myself. They said this was a favorite measure of the president, and I ought to go for it. I told them I believed it was a wicked, unjust measure, and that I should go against it, let the cost to myself be what it might; that I was willing to go with General Jackson in everything that I believed was honest and right;* but, further than this, I wouldn't go for him, or any other man in the whole creation; that I would sooner be honestly and politically d—nd, than hypocritically immortalized. I had been elected by a majority of three thousand five hundred and eighty-five votes, and I believed they were honest men, and wouldn't want me to vote for any unjust notion, to please Jackson or any one else; at any rate, I was of age, and determined to trust them. I voted against this Indian bill, and my conscience yet tells me that I gave a good honest vote, and one that I believe will not make me ashamed in the day of judgment. I served out my term, and though many amusing things happened, I am not disposed to swell my narrative by inserting them.

When it closed, and I returned home, I found the storm had raised against me sure enough; and it was echoed from side to side, and from end to end of my

presented the petition of three Cherokee Indians, who are entitled to reserves of six hundred and forty acres of land each, and moved its reference to the Committee of Claims."

* Davy Crockett did support Jackson on issues he thought were right even when he opposed him bitterly on other questions. At the same time that he opposed Jackson's position on the United States Bank, he supported his land bill. The *Congressional Globe* reported him as praising Jackson for advocating giving "every citizen a portion of the public lands who would settle upon it. No act of the President's life pleased him so much as the avowal of this sentiment." (Vol. II, 1833-35, p. 241.)

district, that I had turned against Jackson. This was considered the unpardonable sin. I was hunted down like a wild varment, and in this hunt every little newspaper in the district, and every little pin-hook lawyer was engaged. Indeed, they were ready to print anything and everything that the ingenuity of man could invent against me. Each editor was furnished with the journals of Congress from head-quarters; and hunted out every vote I had missed in four sessions, whether from sickness or not, no matter: and each one was charged against me at *eight* dollars. In all I had missed about *seventy* votes, which they made amount to five hundred and sixty dollars; and they contended that I had swindled the government out of this sum, as I received my pay, as other members do. I was now again a candidate in 1830, while all the attempts were making against me; and every one of these little papers kept up a constant war on me, fighting with every scurrilous report they could catch.

Over all I should have been elected, if it hadn't been that but a few weeks before the election, the little four-pence-ha'-penny limbs of the law fell on a plan to defeat me, which had the desired effect. They agreed to spread out over the district, and make appointments for me to speak almost everywhere to clear up the Jackson question. They would give me no notice of these appointments, and the people would meet in great crowds to hear what excuse Crockett had to make for quitting Jackson.

But instead of Crockett's being there, this small-fry of lawyers would be there, with their saddle-bags full of the little newspapers and their journals of Congress, and would get up and speak, and read their scurrilous attacks

on me, and would then tell the people that I was afraid
to attend; and in this way would turn many against me.
All this intrigue was kept a profound secret from me,
till it was too late to counteract it; and when the election
came, I had a majority in seventeen counties, putting all
their votes together, but the eighteenth beat me; and
so I was left out of Congress during those two years. The
people of my district were induced, by these tricks, to take
a stay on me for that time; but they have since found out
that they were imposed on, and on re-considering my case,
have reversed that decision, which, as the Dutchman said,
"is as fair a ding as eber was."

When I last declared myself a candidate, I knew that
the district would be divided by the Legislature before
the election would come on; and I moreover knew, that
from the geographical situation of the country, the
county of Madison, which was very strong, and which
was the county that had given the majority that had
beat me in the former race, should be left off from my
district.

But when the Legislature met, as I had been informed,
and I have no doubt of the fact, Mr. Fitzgerald, my competitor, went up and informed his friends in that body,
that if Madison county was left off, he wouldn't run; for
"that Crockett could beat Jackson himself in those parts,
in any way they could fix it."

The liberal Legislature you know, of course, gave him
that county; and it is too clear to admit of dispute, that
it was done to make a mash of me. In order to make my
district in this way, they had to form the southern district
of a string of counties around three sides of mine, or very

nearly so.* Had my old district been properly divided, it would have made two nice ones in convenient nice form. But as it is, they are certainly the most unreasonably laid off of any in the State, or perhaps in the nation, or even in the tetotal creation.

However, when the election came on, the people of the district and of Madison county among the rest, seemed disposed to prove to Mr. Fitzgerald and the Jackson Legislature, that they were not to be transferred like hogs, and horses, and cattle in the market; and they determined that I shouldn't be broke down, though I had to carry Jackson, and the enemies of the bank, and the legislative works all at once. I had Mr. Fitzgerald, it is true, for my open competitor, but he was helped along by all his little lawyers again, headed by old Black Hawk, as he is sometimes called, (alias) Adam Huntsman, with all his talents for writing *"Chronicles,"* and such like foolish stuff.

But one good thing was, and I must record it, the papers in the district were now beginning to say "fair play a little," and they would publish on both sides the question. The contest was a warm one, and the battle well fought; but I gained the day, and the Jackson horse was left a little behind. When the polls were compared, it turned out I had beat Fitz just two hundred and two votes, having made a mash of all their intrigues.

* This practice is known as "gerrymander." It is named after Elbridge Gerry who was responsible for many redistrictings of this type when he was Governor of Massachusetts (1810-1811).

CHAPTER SEVENTEEN

I Set Out for the East

During the session of this Congress, I thought I would take a travel through the Northern States. I had braved the lonely forests of the West, I had shouldered the warrior's rifle in the far South; but the North and East I had never seen. I seemed to like members of Congress who came from these parts, and wished to know what kind of constituents they had. These considerations, in addition to my physician's advice to travel a little for my health, induced me to leave Washington on the 25th day of April, 1834, and steer for the North.

I arrived the same evening at Barnum's Hotel, in Baltimore. Uncle Davy, as he is often called, was right glad to see me, perhaps, because we were namesakes; or may-be he always likes to see folks patronize his house. He has a pleasant face, any how, and his acts don't belie it. No one need look for better quarters; if they do, it will be because they don't know when they are satisfied.

Shortly after I arrived, I was called upon and asked to eat supper with a number of gentlemen. I went and passed the evening pleasantly with my friend Wilkes and others.

Early next morning, I started for Philadelphia, a place where I had never been. I sort of felt lonesome as I went down to the steamboat. The idea of going among a new people, where there are tens of thousands who would pass me by without knowing or caring who I was, who are all taken up with their own pleasures or their own business, made me feel small; and, indeed, if any one who reads this book has a grand idea of his own importance, let him go to a big city, and he will find that he is not higher valued than a coon-skin.

The steamboat was the Carroll of Carrollton, a fine craft, with the rum old commodore Chaytor for head man. A good fellow he is—all sorts of a man—bowing and scraping to the ladies, nodding to the gentlemen, cursing the crew, and his right eye broad-cast upon the "opposition line," all at the same time. "Let go!" said the old one, and off we walked in prime style.

We immediately came past Fort McHenry, justly celebrated for its gallant defence under Armistead, Stewart, Nicholson, Newcomb, and others, during the last war; and shortly after we passed North Point, where the British landed to make, what they never dared, an attack on Baltimore.

Our passage down the Chesapeake bay was very pleasant; and in a very short run we came to the place where we were to get on board of the railroad cars.

This was a clean new sight to me; about a dozen big stages hung on to one machine, and to start up hill. After a good deal of fuss, we all got seated and moved slowly off, the engine wheezing as if she had the tizzick. By-and-by she began to take short breaths, and away we went with a blue streak after us. The whole distance is seventeen miles, and it was run in fifty-five minutes.

While I was whizzing along, I burst out a laughing. One of the passengers asked me what it was at. "Why," says I, "it's no wonder the fellow's horses run off." A Carolina wagoner had just crossed the rail-road, from Charleston to Augusta, when the engine hove in sight with the cars attached. It was growing dark, and the sparks were flying in all directions. His horses ran off, broke his wagon, and smashed his combustibles into items. He run to a house for help, and when they asked him what scared his horses, he said he did not jist know, but it must be hell in harness.

At Delaware City, I again embarked on board of a splendid steamboat, which ran to Philadelphia.

When dinner was ready, I set down with the rest of the passengers; among them was the Rev. O. B. Brown of the Post Office Department, who sat near me. During dinner, the parson called for a bottle of wine, and called on me for a toast. Not knowing whether he intended to compliment me, or abash me among so many strangers, or have some fun at my expense, I concluded to go ahead, and give him and his likes a blizzard. So our glasses being filled, the word went round, "a toast from Colonel Crockett." I gave it as follows: "Here's wishing the bones of tyrant kings may answer in hell, in place of gridirons, to roast the souls of Tories on." At this the parson appeared as if he was stump't. I said, "Never heed; it was meant for where it belonged." He did not repeat his invitation, and I eat my dinner quietly.

After dinner I went up on the deck, and saw the captain hoisting three flags. Says I, "What does that mean?" He replied, that he was under promise to the citizens of Philadelphia, if I was on board, to hoist his flags, as a friend of mine had said he expected I would be along soon.

We went on till we came in sight of the city; and as we advanced towards the wharf, I saw the whole face of the earth covered with people, all anxiously looking on towards the boat. The captain and myself were standing on the bow-deck; he pointed his finger at me, and people slung their hats, and huzzaed for Colonel Crockett. It struck me with astonishment, to hear a strange people huzzaing for me, and made me feel sort of queer. It took me so uncommon unexpected, as I had no idea of attracting attention. But I had to meet it, and so I stepped on to the wharf, where the folks came crowding around me, saying, "Give me the hand of an honest man." I did not know what all this meant: but some gentleman took hold of me, and pressing through the crowd, put me into an elegant barouche, drawn by four fine horses; they then told me to bow to the people: I did so, and with much difficulty we moved off. The streets were crowded to a great distance, and the windows full of people, looking out I supposed, to see the wild man. I thought I had rather be in the wilderness with my gun and dogs, than to be attracting all that fuss. I had never seen the like before, and did not know exactly what to say or do. After some time we reached the United States Hotel in Chesnut Street.

The crowd had followed me, filling up the street, and pressing into the house to shake hands. I was conducted up stairs, and walked out on a platform, drew off my hat, and bowed round to the people. They cried out from all quarters, "A speech, a speech, Colonel Crockett."

After the noise had quit, so I could be heard, I said to them the following words:

"GENTLEMEN OF PHILADELPHIA:—My visit to your city is rather accidental. I had no expectation of attracting any uncommon attention. I am traveling for my health, without the least wish of exciting the people in such times of high political feeling. I do not wish to encourage it. I am unable at this time to find language suitable to return my gratitude to the citizens of Philadelphia. However, I am almost induced to believe it flattery—perhaps a burlesque. This is new to me, yet I see nothing but friendship in your faces; and if your curiosity is to hear the backwoodsman, I will assure you I am illy prepared to address this most enlightened people. However, gentlemen, if this is a curiosity to you, if you will meet me to-morrow, at one o'clock, I will endeavor to address you in my plain manner." So I made my obeisance to them, and retired into the house.

After night, when I could walk out unknown, I went up street or down, I don't know which, but took good care not to turn any corners, for fear I might get lost. I soon found that the streets were laid off square. This I thought was queer enough for a Quaker city, for they don't generally come up square to nothing; even their coats have a kind of slope, at least so they have cut Mister Penn's coat in the capitol. This may be wrong, too, for I was told that when the man who made him, first knocked off "the kivers" of the house where he worked at him, he had cut out Mister Penn with a regular built continental cocked hat on; and it was so much laughed at, to see such a hat on a Quaker, that as soon as Congress rose, he cut off his head, and worked on a new one, with a rale sloped broad brim. Which is the honest George Fox hat, I leave for Philadelphia lawyers and persons to decide.

When I went to my room, and got to bed, I could not sleep, thinking over all that passed, and my promise also to speak the next day; but at last I composed myself with the reflection that I had got through many a scrape before, so I thought I'd trust again to good luck.

Next morning I had the honor of being called on by some old friends whom I knew at Washington—Judge Baldwin, Judge Hemphill, John Sergeant, and others, and I took it right kind in them to do so.

Early after breakfast I was taken to the Water-works, where I saw several of the gentlemen managers. This is a grand sight, and no wonder the Philadelphians ask every one that comes, "Have you seen the Water-works?" Just think of a few wheels throwing up more water than five hundred thousand people can use: yes, and waste, too; for such scrubbing of steps, and even the very pavements under your feet, I never saw. Indeed, I looked close to see if the house-maids had not web-feet, they walked so well in water; and as for a fire, it has no chance at all; they just screw on a long hollow leather with a brass nose on it, dash up stairs, and seem to draw on Noah's flood.

The next place I visited was the Mint. Here I saw them coining gold and silver in abundance, and they were the rale "e pluribus unum;" not this electioneering trash, that they sent out to cheat the poor people, telling them they would all be paid in gold and silver, when the poor deceived creatures had nothing coming to them. A chip with a spit on the back of it, is as good currency as an eagle, provided you can't get the image of the bird. It's all nonsense. The President, both cabinets and Congress to boot, can't enact poor men into rich. Hard knocks, and plenty of them, can only build up a fellow's self.

I asked if the workmen never stole any of the coin. They said not: they got used to it. Well, I thought that was what my parson would call heterodox doctrine, that the longer a man was in temptation, the more he would not sin. But I let it pass, for I had heard that they had got "new lights" in this city, and, of course, new and genuine doctrines—so that the Bible-doxy stood no chance. I could not help, barring the doctrine, giving these honest men great credit; especially when I recollected an old sancti-moniouslyfied fellow, who made his negroes whistle while they were picking cherries, for fear they should eat some.

From the Mint I was taken to the Asylum for insane persons, went through different apartments, saw men and women, some quite distracted, others not so bad. This was a very unpleasant sight. I am not able, nor do I wish I was able, to describe it. I felt monstrous solemn, and could not help thanking God I was not one of them; and I felt grateful in their stead to that city for caring for those who could not take care of themselves, and feeding them that heeded not the hand and heart that provided for them.

On returning to the hotel, the hour had nearly arrived when I was to visit the Exchange. I asked Colonel Dorrance, the landlord, to go with me. He is a very clever man, and made me feel quite at home in his house. Whoever goes there once, will go back again. So he agreed, and off we started.

I had made set speeches in Congress, and especially on my Tennessee land bill, when all my colleagues were against me; I had made stump speeches at home, in the face of all the little office yelpers who were opposed to me; but, indeed, when I got within sight of the Exchange, and saw the streets crowded, I most wished to take back my promise; but I was brought up by hearing a youngster say, as I passed by, "Go ahead, Davy Crockett." I said to myself, "I have faced the enemy; these are friends. I have fronted the savage red man of the forest; these are civilized. I'll keep cool, and let them have it."

I was conducted to the house of a Mr. Neil; where I met several gentlemen, and took some refreshment, not passing by a little Dutch courage. Of the latter there was plenty; and I observed the man of the house, when he asked me to drink, he didn't stand by to see what I took, but turned away, and told me to help myself. That's what I call genteel.

Arrived at the Exchange, I crowded through, went up to the second floor, and walked out on the porch, drew off my hat, and made my bow; speaking was out of the question, the huzzas for Crockett were so loud and so long.

The time had come when my promise must be kept. There must have been more than five thousand people, and they were still gathering from all parts. I spoke for about half an hour.

Three times three cheers closed the concern, and I came down to the door, where it appeared as if all the world had a desire to shake hands with me. I stood on the door-

step, and, as Major Jack Downing said, shook hands as
hard as I could spring for near an hour. After this I returned to the hotel, and remained until night, when I
was asked to visit the theatre in Walnut street. The landlord, Dorrance, and others, were to go with me, to see
Jim Crow. While we were talking about it, one of them
said he could go all over the world "To crow juicy." Some
laughed very hearty, and others did not. I was among the
latter, for I considered it a dry joke, although there was
something *juicy* in it. Some of them said it was Latin;
and that proved to me the reason why I did not laugh—
I was tired of the "old Roman." But these Philadelphians
are eternally cutting up jokes on words; so I puts a con-
undrum to them; and says I, "Can you tell me why the
sacking of Jerusalem was like a cider-mill?" Well, they
all were stumped, and gave it up. "Because it made the
Jews fly." Seeing them so much pleased with this, says I,
"Why is a cow like a razor-grinder?" No one could answer.
"Well," says I, "I thought you could find that out, for I
don't know myself."

We started for the theatre, and found a very full house,
and Jim a-playing for the dear life. Jim makes as good a
nigger as if he was clean black, except the bandy legs.

Everybody seemed pleased, particularly when I laughed;
they appeared to act as if I knew exactly when to laugh,
and then they all followed.

What a pity it is that these theatres are not contrived
that everybody could go; but the fact is, backwoodsman
as I am, I have heard some things in them that was a
leetle too tough for good women and modest men; and
that's a great pity, because there are thousands of scenes
of real life that might be exhibited, both for amusement

and edification, without offending. Folks pretend to say that high people don't mind these things. Well, it may be that they are better acquainted with vice than we plain folks; but I am yet to live and see a woman polished out of the natural feelings, or too high not to do things that ain't quite reputable in those of low degree.

Their fiddling was pretty good, considering every fellow played his own piece; and I would have known more about it, if they had played a tune, but it was all twee-wee-tadlum-tadlum-tum-tum, tadle-leedle-tadle-leedle-lee. The "Twenty-second of February," or the "Cuckoo's Nest," would have been a treat.

I do not think, however, from all I saw, that the people enjoyed themselves better than we do at a country frolic, where we dance till daylight, and pay off the score by giving one in our turn. It would do you good to see our boys and girls dancing. None of your stradling, mincing, sadying; but a regular sifter, cut-the-buckle, chicken-flutter set-to. It is good wholesome exercise; and when one of our boys puts his arm round his partner, it is a good hug, and no harm in it.

Next morning I was waited on by some gentlemen, who presented me with a seal for my watch-chain, which cost forty dollars. I told them I always accepted a present, as a testimony of friendship. The engraving on the stone represents the great match race, two horses in full speed, and over them the words "Go ahead." It is the finest seal I ever saw; and when I returned to Washington, the members almost used it up, making copies to send all over the country.

I was hardly done making my bow to these gentlemen, before Mr. James M. Sanderson informed me that the

young whigs* of Philadelphia had a desire to present me
with a fine rifle, and had chosen him to have her made
agreeable to my wishes. I told him that was an article that
I knew somewhat about, and gave him the size, weight, &c.

You can't imagine how I was crowded to get through
every thing. Colonel Pulaski called to take me in his
carriage to the Naval Hospital, where they stow away the
old sailors on dry land, and a splendid building it is; all
made of marble. I did not like the situation: but I suppose it was the best they could get, with so much ground
to it.

From there we went to the Navy Yard, and examined
the largest ship ever made in the United States. She was
what they called "in the stocks."

I then surveyed the artillery, and the balance of the
shipping, not forgetting to pay my respects to the officers
of the yard, and then returned home with the colonel,
where I was kindly treated, both in eating and drinking:
and so ended another day.

The next morning the land admiral, Colonel Reeside,
asked me to call on him and take a ride. I did so; and he
carried me out to the rail-road and Schuylkill bridge. I
found that the rail-road was finished near a hundred miles
into the interior of the State, and is only one out of many;
and yet they make no fuss about it.

We drove in past the Girard school—that old man
that gave so many millions to Philadelphia, and cut out
his kin with a crumb. Well, thinks I, blood is thicker than
water, and the remembrance of friends better than a big
name. I'd have made them all rich, and give away the

* The Whig Party was an anti-Jackson coalition organized in 1834.

balance. But, maybe, French people don't think like me.*

This being my last night in Philadelphia, Dorrance gave me what they call a "pick knick" supper; which means as much as me and all my company could eat and drink, and nothing to pay.

I had forgot to say that I had spent part of the evening before this with Colonel Saint.

* Stephen Girard, Philadelphia businessman, banker and philan-
thropist, was born in Bordeaux, France. In his will he left $140,000 to
relatives and several million dollars in cash and real estate to different
philanthropic causes in which he was interested. Some of his heirs
tried to set the will aside, but the Supreme Court upheld its validity.

CHAPTER EIGHTEEN

"Wild Man of the West" in New York

Next morning, Wednesday the 29th, I was invited by Captain Jenkins, of the steamboat New Philadelphia, to go on with him to New York, I accepted his offer and started. I saw nothing very particular along the Delaware river, except the place where all the hard stone coal comes to, from the interior of Pennsylvania; where, I am told, they have mountains of it. After some time, we got upon a rail-road where they say we run twenty-five miles to the hour. I can only judge of the speed by putting my head out to spit, which I did and overtook it so quick that it hit me smack in the face. We soon arrived at Amboy, and took the water again; and soon came in sight of the great city of New York, and a bulger of a place it is. The number of the ships beat me all hollow, and looked for all the world like a big clearing in the West, with the dead trees all standing.

When we swung round to the wharf, it was covered with people, who inquired if I was on board; and when the captain told them I was, they slung their hats and gave three cheers.

Immediately a committee came on board, representing the young whigs, and informed me they were appointed to wait upon me, and invite me to the American Hotel. I accepted their offer, and went with them to the hotel, where I was friendly received; conducted to a large parlor, where I was introduced to a great many gentlemen.

I was invited to visit the new and elegant fire-engine, and took some refreshment with the managers, and returned in time to visit the Park theatre, and see Miss Fanny Kemble play in grand style. The house was better filled, and the fixings looked nicer than the one in Philadelphia; but any of them is good enough, if they have such pretty play-actors as Miss Kemble. In fact, she is like a handsome piece of changeable silk; first one color, then another, but always the clean thing.

I returned home, as I am told all great folks do, after the lady actor was done; and, sitting with my friends, the cry of "fire, fire," struck my ear. I bounced from my chair, and ran for my hat. "Sit down, colonel," said one of the gentlemen, "it's not near us." "A'n't you going to help put it out?" "No," said he, laughing, "we have fire companies here, and we leave it to them." Well, to me this seemed queer enough, for at home I would have jumped on the first horse at hand, and rode full flight bare-backed, to help put out a fire.

I forgot that I was in a city where you may live, as they tell me, years, and not know who lives next door to you: still, I felt curious to see how they managed; and Colonel Jackson went with me. As it was late, the engines were only assembling when we got there; but when they began to spirt, they put out a four story house that was all in a blaze, in less than no time. I asked the colonel where they got so much water from. He said it was raised by the Manhattan Bank, out of a charter got by Aaron Burr.

Next morning I was invited by Colonel Mapes to walk down to some of the newspaper offices. I proposed to go to the Courier and Enquirer and Star offices: we did so. I like Webb,* for he comes out plump with what he has to say. Mr. Noah has another way of using a fellow up: he holds him uneasy; laughs at him, and makes other folks do so; teazes him; roasts him, until he don't know what ails him, nor what hurt him, but he can't help limping.

We went into Pearl street; and I could not help wondering if they had as many boxes and bags and things inside of the houses as they had out. Elegant place for a lame man to walk, for every one is like him—first up, then down; then one side, then another, like a pet in a squirrel box. Shortly we came to the Exchange—the place where the merchants assemble every day at one o'clock, to hear all they can, and tell as little as possible; and where two lines from a knowing correspondent, prudently used, may make a fortune.

I had not been long here before I was surrounded, and called on for a speech. I made many apologies, but none seem'd to hit right; and was so hard pressed, that I had

* Colonel James Watson Webb was editor of the New York *Courier and Enquirer* and one of the founders of the Whig Party.

no corner to get into: so, taking my stand upon the steps above them, I spoke awhile.

I returned to the hotel, where I found a great many gentlemen waiting to see the wild man from the far West. After spending some time with them, I was taken to Peale's museum. I shall not attempt to describe the curiosities here; it is above my bend. I could not help, however, thinking what pleasure or curiosity folks could take in sticking up whole rows of little bugs, and such like varmints. I saw a boy there that had been born without any hands or arms; and he took a pair of scissors in his toes, and cut his name in full, and gave it to me. This I called a miracle.

From thence I went to the City Hall, and was introduced to the mayor of the city and several of the aldermen. The mayor is a plain, common-sense-looking man. I was told he had been a tanner: that pleased me; for I thought both him and me had clumb up a long way from where we had started: and it is truly said, "Honor and fame from no condition rise." It's the grit of a fellow that makes the man.

On my return, I received an invitation from Colonel Draper to dine with him, informing me also, that the rale Major Jack Downing was expected to be there. When the hour arrived, I started to walk there, as it was but a short distance. On my way I saw a white man who was in a great rage, cursing a white man-servant. I stopped, and said to him, "Hellow, mister! if you was to talk that way to a white man in my country, he'd give you first rate hell." He looked at me and said nothing, but walked off. Sure enough, when I got to Colonel Draper's I was introduced to the major. We sat down to a splendid dinner, and amused ourselves with some good jokes. But as this was a private party, I don't think it gentlemanly to tell what was said at this time, and especially as this was not the only communication I had with the major. One observation, however, was made by him, and I gave him an answer which could not offend anybody. "Colonel," says he, "what d'ye sort o' think about gineral matters and things in purticlur?" Knowing him to be a Yankee, I tried to answer him in his own way. So says I, "Major, the Ginneral's matters are all wrong; but some purticklar things are very well: such, for instance, as the honor I have in dining with you at Colonel Draper's." "Good," says the major, "and we'll talk about them there matters some other time." "Agreed," says I, "major, always at your sarvice."

I found a large company waiting for me when I got back to the hotel, and invitation to sup with the young Whigs. Well, now, thinks I, they had better keep some of these things to eat for somebody else, for I'm sure I'm as full as a young cub. But right or wrong, I must go in. There I met the honorable Augustus S. Clayton, of Georgia, and was right glad to see him, for I knew I could get him to take some of the speaking off of me. He speaks prime, and is always ready, and never goes off half-cock.

Upwards of one hundred sat down to supper. They were going to toast me, but I told some of them near me to toast Judge Clayton first; that there should be more rejoicing over one that was lost and found again, than over ninety and nine such as me, that had never strayed away. They did so; and he made a speech that fairly made the tumblers hop. He rowed the Tories up and over Salt River.

Then they toasted me as "the undeviating supporter of the constitution and laws." I made a short speech, and concluded with the story of the "Red Cow," which was, that as long as General Jackson went straight, I followed him; but when he began to go this way, and that way, and every way, I wouldn't go after him; like the boy whose master ordered him to plough across the field to the red cow. Well, he began to plough and she began to walk; and he ploughed all forenoon after her. So when the master came, he swore at him for going so crooked. "Why, sir," said the boy, "you told me to plough to the red cow, and I kept after her, but she always kept moving."

Next morning being the first day of May, I went to some of the newspaper offices, read the news, and returned to take a ride with Colonel S. D. Jackson, in an elegant barouche. We drove up to the city, and took a view of the improvements and beautiful houses in the new part. By the time we returned down Broadway, it seemed to me that the city was flying before some awful calamity. "Why," said I, "Colonel, what under heaven is the matter? Everybody appears to be pitching out their furniture, and packing it off." He laughed, and said this was the general "moving day." Such a sight nobody ever saw unless it was in this same city. It seemed a kind of frolic, as if they were changing houses just for fun. Every street was crowded with carts, drays, and people. So the world goes. It would take a good deal to get me out of my log-house; but here, I understand, many persons "move" every year.

Having alighted, and taken some refreshment, I asked Colonel Webb to go with me to the "Five Points," a noted place near the centre of the city. This is the place where Van Buren's warriors came from during the election, when the wild Irish, with their clubs and bludgeons, knocked down every one they could find that would not huzza for Jackson. However, I had a great curiosity to see them; and on we went, the major and me, and in the midst of that great city we came to a place where five streets all come together; and from this it takes the name of the "Five Points." The buildings are little, old, frame houses, and looked like some little country village. The houses all had cellars; and as that day was fashionable to move, they were moving too. The streets looked like a *clearing,* in my part of the world, as they were emptying and burning the straw out of their beds. It appeared as if the cellars were jam full of people; and such fiddling and dancing nobody ever before saw in this world. I thought they were the true "heaven-borns." Black and white, white and black, all hugemsnug together, happy as lords and ladies, sitting sometimes round in a ring, with a jug of liquor between them: and I do think I saw more drunken folks, men and women, that day than I ever saw before. This is part of what is called by the Regency the "glorious sixth ward"—the regular Van Buren ground-floor. I thought I would rather risk myself in an Indian fight than venture among these creatures after night. I said to the colonel, "God deliver me from such constituents, or from a party supported by such. In my country, when you meet an Irishman, you find a first rate gentleman; but these are worse than savages; they are too mean to swab hell's kitchen." He took me to the place where the election was held. It appeared to me that all the place round was made ground, and that there was more room in the houses under ground than above: and I suppose there must have been a flood of rain during the election, which forced those rats out of their holes. There is more people stowed away together here than any place I ever saw. I heard a story, and it is asserted to be true, that about here, some years ago, a committee visited all the houses, to see how they were coming on. One house, that was four stories high, and four rooms on a floor, had sixteen families in it, and four in the garret, which was divided into four parts by a streak of charcoal. An old lady, that was spinning up there, was asked how they made out. She said, pretty well; and that they would be quiet enough if it was not for the old woman in the opposite corner, and she took boarders, and they often made a noise. I believe it is true. What a miserable place a city is for poor people: they are half starved, poorly clothed, and perished for fire. I sometimes wonder they do not clear out to a new country, where every skin hangs by its own tail: but I suppose they think an hour's indulgence in vice is sweet enough for the bitter of the rest.

Coming home, I took notice that the rear of the City Hall was of brown stone, while the front and sides were of white marble. I asked the Colonel why that was so. He said the Poor House stood behind when they built the Hall. That is like many a great man: if he gets a fine breast to his jacket, he will make the back of fustian—and like thousands of great people, who think that any thing will do for poor folks to look at, or eat, or wear. Another thing seemed queer to me, and that was a bell hanging outside of the steeple of the Hall. It was so big that they could not get it in, and rather than lose the money, they hung it outside; never reflecting that even a backwoodsman must laugh at such a Dutch blunder.

On the same walk I was introduced to the honorable Albert Gallatin. He had an old straw hat in his hand, and like every body else, was "mooving," and said he was sorry not to have more time to be acquainted with me. He pointed to the house he was leaving, and said it and several others were to be torn down to build a big tavern. It was a very fine house, fit for any man to live in; but in a few hours I saw men on the top of it, and before the next evening the daylight was through it. This tavern is to be near the park, and is building by John Jacob Astor. It is to cost seven hundred thousand dollars, and covers a whole square. Mr. Astor, I am told, begun business in New York as a dealer in furs, and is now worth millions. Lord help the beavers and otters! they must have most got used to being skinned by this time. And what a meeting of friends and kin there must have been in his warehouse. "Farewell," said the otter to the beaver, "I never expect to see you again, my dear old friend." "Never mind, my dear fellow," said the beaver, "don't be too much distressed, we'll soon meet at the hatter's shop."

This day a new flag was to be hoisted, down on the Battery, and I was invited to attend. The artillery, under command of General Morton, paraded; and he invited many of his friends to be present: among the rest, the mayor, Gideon Lee, was there, and addressed the people. Among other things he told them that that flag-staff was placed where the old one stood when the British evacuated New York; that they left the flag flying, and greased the pole, so that it could not be clim up; but at last a sailor got up and tore it down, and hoisted the American flag in its place; and when he came down, the people filled his hat with money.

General Morton is a revolutioner, and an officer in the society of old soldiers, called the "Cincinnati Society," and wears its badge on his breast. He gave an entertainment to his friends on this occasion; for you must know that nobody thinks any thing well done in this place, without eating and drinking over it.

This battery a'n't a place, as its name looks like, for keeping and shooting off cannon. It might have been so, long ago; but it is a beautiful meadow of a place, all measured off, with nice walks of gravel between the grass plats, full of big shade-trees, and filled with people and a great many children, that come there to get the fresh air that comes off the water of the bay. This is a beautiful place; and you can see Long Island, and Staten Island, and many others from it. Here is likewise Castle Garden, and the bridge that Van Buren wanted to drown the president off of, when him and Major Jack most fell in. The fact is, the plan was well enough, but General Jackson did not know of it. It was concluded, you see, that the president should make all his big secretaries and Colonel Reeside go before, and him come after; and then slam should go the bridge, with the old fellow on it. But he went foremost, and when it fell, they didn't catch any but Governor Cass, secretary of war; and he only lost his hat and wig, which they say the porpusses carried off and gave to the sea serpent, so that he might be on their side in the next oyster war.

After all this, I went that same day to see my young friend Walden, and enjoyed myself with some friends till evening.

When I got back to the hotel, I found the bill for the Bowery theatre; and it stated I was to be there. Now I knew I had never given the manager any authority to use my name, and I determined not to go. After some time, I was sent for, and refused; and then the head manager came himself. I told him I did not come for a show; I did not come for the citizens of New York to look at, I come to look at them. However, my friends said it would be a great disappointment, and might harm the managers; and so I went, and was friendly received. I remained a short time, and returned. So ended the first day of May, 1834; and I should like to see any body who saw more sights in once waking up. In fact, when I got to bed and begun to think them over, I found it would take me to daylight; so I just broke off, and went to sleep.

Next morning, Colonel Mapes told me he was requested to invite me to come over to Jersey City, to see some shooting with a rifle. In the mean time, I had been very kindly invited by Captain Comstock to go that day, at half-past three o'clock, with him to Boston. I concluded to go, as I might never have another opportunity, and it took only eighteen hours to go there.

I went with the colonel to see little Thawburn's seed store; and a great place it is, for he has got all kinds of things there; and for fear his bird-seed should not be fresh, he keeps a few hundred birds to eat it up in short order; and to prove that his flower-seed is prime, he keeps thousands of little pots growing, and mostly gits five times as much for the proof as he does for the seed. He is a little, old, weezened-up man, talks broad Scotch, and is as active as a terrier dog.

I now started to Jersey City, where I found a great

many gentlemen shooting rifles, at the distance of one hundred yards with a rest. One gentleman gave me his gun, and asked me to shoot. I raised up, off-hand, and cut within about two inches of the centre. I told him my distance was forty yards, off-hand. He loaded his gun, and we walked down to within forty yards, when I fired, and was deep in the paper. I shot a second time, and did the same. Colonel Mapes then put up a quarter of a dollar in the middle of the black spot, and asked me to shoot at it. I told him he had better mark the size of it and put his money in his pocket. He said, "Fire away." I did so, and made slight-of-hand work with his quarter. It was now time to return, and prepare for my trip to Boston.

CHAPTER NINETEEN

I Am Welcomed in Boston

At three o'clock I left the hotel, and went over to where the steamboat lay. When I went on board, the captain showed me into a splendid state-room, which I was to occupy for the voyage. So, when I had made toilet (as great folks say), that is, combed my hair, and taken a glass of brandy and water, I went on deck. There I saw almost as many people as were when I landed; and they kept gathering until the whole ground was covered; and when we started, they cheered me for some time; and all I could do was to stand and bow to them. This brought me into new trouble; for the passengers found I was on board, and came round me, so that I missed seeing the city until we got past it.

Soon, however, we came to the place called Hell's Gate; so called, I suppose, because the water boils, and foams, and bounces, about as if it was in a pot. I don't think,

however, that this is a good name for it, because we are
told in the good book, that hell's gate is a mighty slick
place, and easy to get into. Here I first saw a large square-
sailed British merchant ship, under full sail. She was
coming in through the channel, and I was glad to see
that, for when we were voting for an appropriation for a
fort to defend this place, I heard it said that no foreign
ship ever attempted coming in that way. But these are the
kind of arguments used most generally by those who
oppose internal improvements, harbors, &c., &c.; they
fancy things, and speak them for truth.

We went on very pleasantly till night; and the captain
told me if I would rise at daylight, we would be out of
sight of land. So I went to bed, and rose as soon as I
could see. I walked out on deck, and sure enough, there
was no land to be seen. We were coming near Fort
Juda, a place where, the captain informed me, people on
board was often very sea-sick. So I set myself down for a
case, but was disappointed; it was quite calm, and a clear
fine morning, and when the sun rose, it came up like a
ball of fire out of the water, and looked, for all the world,
as if it had been made for the first time. We went around
Point Juda, and kept in sight of land on our left hand.
There was very little timber to be seen; the whole country
appeared to be laid off in fields, divided by stone fences.
These were a great curiosity to me, and I could not help
thinking that their cattle must be well schooled here; for
one of my cows would pitch over a dozen such fences,
without flirting her tail.

We went by the great fort at the Naraganset bay, and
landed at Newport for a short time. From thence we took
our way again to Providence. There I met a large number

of the citizens. They cheered me on my arrival, and wanted me to stay and partake of a dinner with them. I declined, and took my seat in the fast stage. The driver was ordered to go ahead, and sure enough he did. It was forty miles to Boston, and we run it down in four hours.

What mighty hard land it is on this road, and seems as if the whole face of the earth had been covered over with stones, as thick as Kentuck land titles; but they have got them strung up into fences, as many as they can, by picking of them off; but they won't stay picked, for every time they plough, a new crop comes up.

It was somewhere away long here that the Pilgrims landed at Plymouth, and begun to people this part of the world; and a hard time they must have had of it in this barren country; and it seems odd that they should come all the way across the sea, and not look out for good land. However, I suppose it was all right, or God would have given them better pilots. If they had had fine land, they would not have ventured so much on the ocean, and would have had less necessity to work hard, and bring up their children to industry, and give them such cute teaching as makes them know how to make ducks and drakes of us out yonder, when they come among us.

You would be as much struck as I was with the handsome houses and nice farms; but when I came to find all out, I didn't wonder so much. This was Captain A, and that B's house; and they made money on sea, and spent it on land; that's the truth; for Adam himself could not have made it out of the land. So I found out that the most of them owned a little plantation on shore, and the run of the sea to work on besides.

One of the passengers, who came from beyond Boston,

while we were talking over these things, asked me if I knew Captain Silsbee. I told him no. "I guess you do," says he, "he's our senator in Congress; but to home, we old folks call him captain." I told him, certainly I did, but never knew him by that title. "Well, we know that none on 'em boxed a compass longer nor better, and he made a power of money, and during the last war planked up more gold and silver to lend the government than Benton ever counted."

But I must quit philosophy, and tell you where I stopped in Boston—and that was just where any one that has plenty of cash, and plenty of good-will for pleasure, would like—in a clean street, with a tavern on one side, and the theatre on the other, and both called Tremont. Mr. Boyden did not know me, nor me him; but when I told him my name, where they put it on the bar-book, he treated me like an old friend, and continued to do so all the time I was there. He gave me a good room and nice bed; and did not, like many landlords, let a stranger take care of himself, but attended to me the kindest in the world. I had seen a great many fine taverns; but take this out and out, and Tremont House is a smart chance ahead. It is lately built, and has every new arrangement; and for a house with a couple of hundred people about it, is the quietest I ever was in. His head man of the gap, in the bar, has eyes all round him; and Will Scarlet, as he is called by a friend of mine, has the sound of every bell in the house by heart. When I arrived, I knew no one, but in a short time I made many acquaintances, and, indeed, was very kindly treated by every person I met. There is a great deal of friendly feeling with the eastern people; and folks need not go out of Boston to find rale hospitality.

Next morning I was invited by Mr. Harding to visit his gallery of paintings, where he had a great many specimens of the fine arts; and finally he asked me to sit for him until he could get my likeness, which I did, during my stay, and he has it now, hung up among the rest of the fine arts. From there I went to Faneuil Hall, where General Davis showed me all the accoutrements of war for several companies of infantry and riflemen, that was deposited in it. These are in snug rooms on each side of the second story; and in the middle is the parade-room, where, summer and winter, the companies meet to drill. This is doing things in true style, that is all for use, and no show about it. So, instead of hearing a great fuss with volunteers, and drilling, and all that, wheeling and marching, handle cartridge, eyes right—you see a squad of fine soldiers coming out of this same place, and squared up as if they were the rale breed.

General Davis informed me this was the house that was called the "cradle of liberty." I reckon old king George thought they were thundering fine children that was rocked in it, and a good many of them; and that no wonder his red-coats were licked, when the children came out with soldier clothes on, and muskets in their hands. God grant that the liberty-tree bough on which this cradle rocks may never break.

From here I went to the market, which is a small circumstance ahead of anything I ever saw, and just where it should be. Now, in Philadelphia, it looks like a long feeding-trough, stuck up in the middle of the city. And how d'ye think it was done? Why, they put a man of head in, as mayor, who laid all his plans, counted the cost, cyphered out the profits, and so forth, and then made one pitch right "ahead:" and before the ninnies and scarey folks had half done telling their long stories about the dreadful expense, Mayor Quincy's hammers were keeping time on the big granite stones, and the beautiful pillars were rising up as if he had just ordered them. In this market-house everything looks like so many different shops or stores, and you are quite indoors, instead of sellers and buyers both being exposed to wet, heat, and cold. The market appeared to be abundantly supplied, but, as I thought, rather dear.

After returning home, I was invited over to Roxborough, where they make the Indian-rubber clothing, shoes, &c. This is done by dissolving the rubber, and putting it on silk and other cloth, which entirely turns the rain, and still is pliable, and not heavy. The proprietor made me a present of a hunting coat, which I have tried, and would risk my powder under it for forty days and nights. It was a great curiosity to see the young ladies cutting out the clothes, and sticking them together without sewing them. I went also through the shoe factory, where they make shoes in the same way without stitching them. I could not help thinking of the Philadelphia girls —thought they ought to have them, to keep their feet dry.

We often wonder how things are made so cheap among the Yankees. Come here, and you will see women doing men's work, and happy and cheerful as the day is long: and why not? Is it not much better for themselves and families, instead of sitting up all day busy about nothing? It ain't hard work, neither, and looked as queer to me as it would to one of my countrywomen to see a man milking the cows, as they do here.

After I had seen all that was to be seen here, I was taken to Colonel Perkins' carpet factory. There I saw the widest web I ever saw, and they were glossing and stamping it in handsome style. I was quite friendly received by the colonel. He is said to be a very rich man; is quite old, but firm and healthy in appearance; and uses his riches in the best possible way—by keeping a great many people busy. And he is not one of those foolish people, neither, that strive all their days to see how rich they can die: for he gives with his hands open. I saw one house in Boston which he gave to keep the blind in, and was told it was worth fifty thousand dollars. What a comfort the old gentleman must have when he looks at his great possessions, and is calculating, not how much he can hoard up, but how much he can give away. God never made such men to be envied, or I could begrudge him a few of his blessings from the poor and destitute.

At the invitation of the owners of the Indian-rubber factory, I met a number of the citizens of Roxborough, and passed a short time with them very pleasantly.

When I returned to the Tremont, I received an invitation from the young Whigs, to sup with them at eight o'clock. I accepted their invitation, and then went over to the Navy Yard, at Charlestown. I saw many fine ships, and among them was the splendid old Constitution. She was lying in dry dock, and had been new timbered in grand style. The likeness of Andrew Jackson was placed on her for a figure-head. I was asked if it was a good likeness. I said I had never seen him misrepresented; but that they had fixed him just where he had fixed himself, that was, before the Constitution.

We then went up to the old battle-ground on Bunker's hill, where they were erecting a monument to those who fell in that day-break battle of our rising glory. I felt as if I wanted to call them up, and ask them to tell me how to help to protect the liberty they bought for us with their blood; but as I could not do so, I resolved on that holy ground, as I had done elsewhere, to go for my country, always and everywhere.

When I came back from Bunker's hill, I received about a half a dozen invitations from distinguished citizens of Boston, to dine or sup with them, so that it was impossible to attend to all of them unless I had the digestion of a cassowary. I must here state that the citizens generally of Boston are uncommon kind and civil; and if they understand the art of making money they know how to spend it. I was entertained like a prince, and could have lived there, I suspect, on the same terms for much longer. They appear to me to live generally in New England more snugly, and have more kind feelings to one another, and live in more peace and harmony than any people I ever was among. And another good thing—they don't forget one another when they are among strangers; old New England binds them hard together; and this gives them, as it ought to do, strength and confidence, and influence; and with us in the South Yankee cunning is assuming the true name—Yankee knowledge of business, and perseverance in whatever they undertake.

During the afternoon many gentlemen came to see me, and we spent our time pleasantly until the time came for me to attend upon the young Whigs. A coach and four fine horses was sent for me. This I considered as too much honor; but as I take all things as they come, and everything for the best, I stepped into it, and off they whirled with the backwoods hunter. Which way they drove I did not know, nor did I care. I knew they would not eat supper till I got there; and that they would not serve me as Lafayette was served at a certain place where he was expected to land and dine. The steamboat went wrong and he did not arrive; so they eat their dinners and took out the frolic. About sundown, the boat came up, the orator of the day was called for; he was as blind as a pup; but the moment the old general touched the ground, he put at him with abundance of welcomes and compliments about his heroism, until he got up in the pathetics, when he said, "Glorious Lafayette, the blood you have shed, and the treasures you expended in defence of the liberties of this country, call for our gratitude. I want words to convey my ideas; in fact, (striking his hand on his belly instead of his heart) I'm too full to proceed." The old gentleman seized his hand, gave it a hearty shake, and so the oration ended.

We came to the appointed place, where I was taken in and introduced to about one hundred young gentlemen, true chips of the old block, ready to be rocked in the old cradle, whether for fight or frolic, war or electioneering. They gave me a hearty welcome, and made me feel all as one of themselves. So down we sat to an elegant supper, with the best of wine, and the champagne foaming up as if you were supping fog out of speaking-trumpets.

After the cloth was removed and several toasts drank, they toasted me very warmly. I rose and addressed them.

Early next morning I got up, and my health being much

improved, I felt just like I was in peace with myself and all the world. After breakfast, I took a long walk through the city, and passed through the Mall. This is a beautiful green of something like forty acres, I should judge, and looks refreshing in the midst of a city. From the top of the State-house I had a fine view of the city, and was quite amused to see the representation of a large codfish hung up in the House of Assembly, or General Court, as they call it—to remind them either that they depended a good deal on it for food, or made money by the fisheries. This is quite natural to me, for at home I have on one end of my house the antlers of a noble buck, and the heavy paws of a bear.

I did not like the statue of General Washington in the State-house. They have a Roman gown* on him, and he was an American; this ain't right. They did the thing better at Richmond, in Virginia, where they have him in the old blue and buff. He belonged to this country— heart, soul, and body, and I don't want any other to have any part of him—not even his clothes.

I return the officers in the State-house my thanks for their civility. I can't remember all their names, and there- fore I won't name any of them.

When I returned to Tremont house, a gentleman in- vited me to walk with him to the old State-house. When I reached that I saw a great crowd. General Davis con- ducted me into the house, and we went up stairs, where there was a platform. I drew off my hat, and bowed to the people; they immediately cheered me, and called for a speech which I had to make.

* This is a mistake. Chantrey's statue of Washington represents him in the costume of the Revolution with a military cloak.

Here now comes a poser. I was invited to dine out; but if I can mind the gentleman's name I wish I may be shot. He lived near Tremont; and I hope, if he has curiosity enough to read this here book, that he will write me a letter, so that in my second edition, I may give his name as large as life, and I beg him to recollect that it ain't every one that signs a letter that makes himself known. Let him write it plain—none of your hieroglyphics—or I won't put him in.

Some would say that they were mortified that they forgot this gentleman's name. I ain't; I'm sorry—but the truth is, I saw so many folks, and so many new things, that it's no wander I should not mind everything. He was a clever fellow, and I know he will forgive me.

When I went home, there I met a young man that was stone blind. "Well," says you, "that's no new thing." Stop, if you please: that puts me in mind of an old parson and a scolding woman that belonged to his church. She told him, in one of her tantrums, that she could preach as well as he could, and he might select the text. "Well," said the old man, "I'll give you one, and you can study over it —'It is better to dwell on the house-top than in a wide house with a brawling woman.'" "You good-for-nothing, impudent, old—what shall I say? do you go for to call me a brawling woman?" "Dear mistress," said the good old man, "you'll have to study a while longer, for you come to the application of the text before you discuss the doctrine."

Now it was not that I met a blind boy in Tremont house that was any curiosity, but it was his errand. He inquired of the barkeeper for me, as I was standing by him, and said he was sent by the teacher of the blind, to

invite me to visit the institution, and that he would show
me the way.

I was told by the gentlemen present that he could go
all over Boston. A gentleman accompanied me, and we
went on till we came to a fine house where the institution
was kept. We went, and were introduced to the teacher.
He asked me if I wished to hear some of them read. I said
I did, and he ordered a little girl, perhaps ten or twelve
years old, to get her book, asked her to find a certain
chapter in the Old Testament, and read it. She took up
the book and felt with her fingers until she found it. He
then told her to read, and she did so, with a clear, distinct
voice. This was truly astonishing; but on examining their
books I found that the letters were stamped on the under
side of the paper, so as to raise them above the surface of
the upper side; and such was the keenness of their touch
that, by passing the end of the finger over the word, it
served them for sight, and they pronounced the word.
There was a little boy learning to cipher in the same way.
The teacher put several questions to him aloud; and
putting his fingers together and working with them for a
short time, he answered all the questions correctly.

That kind of education astonished me more than anything I ever saw. There were a great many of them. Some
were learning to play on the piano-forte; and many of
them were busy making pretty little baskets, such as are
carried by the ladies.

They asked me if I would like to hear them sing; and
telling them it would please me very much, a number of
them came up, and some had musical instruments: one
had a large thing which I never saw before, nor did I ask
the name; one had a clarionet, and one had a flute. They

played and sung together beautifully, and, indeed, I never saw happier people in my life. I remained some time with them going over the establishment. This is the house that I mentioned before was given by Colonel Perkins to the blind. There is not such a grand house owned by any person in Washington. What a satisfaction it must be to this old gentleman and others who have helped these unfortunates, to see them surrounded with so many comforts!*

* Colonel Thomas Handaside Perkins was one of the "merchant princes" of Boston. The property which he gave to the Asylum for the Blind, was valued at fifty thousand dollars; and it was given on condition that the citizens of Boston should raise by subscription fifty thousand dollars in thirty days, to be given to the Asylum, which condition was promptly complied with.

CHAPTER TWENTY

I Tour New England

When I returned, there were some gentlemen that invited me to go to Cambridge, where the big college or
university is, where they keep ready-made titles or nick-
names to give people. I would not go, for I did not know
but they might stick an LL. D. on me before they let me
go; and I had no idea of changing "Member of the House
of Representatives of the United States," for what stands
for "lazy lounging dunce," which I am sure my constituents would have translated my new title to be, knowing
that I had never taken any degree, and did not own to any
except a small degree of good sense not to pass for what I
was not—I would not go it. There had been one doctor
made from Tennessee already, and I had no wish to put
on the cap and bells. I recollect the story of a would-be-
great man who put on his sign after his name, in large
capitals, D. Q. M. G., which stood for Deputy Quarter

Master General; but, which one of his neighbors, to the great diversion of all the rest, and to his mortification, translated into "damn'd quick made gentleman." No, indeed, not me—anything you please but Granny Crockett; I leave that for others, I'll throw that in to make chuck full the measure of their country's glory.

I told them I did not go to this branding school; I did not want to be tarred with the same stick; one dignitary was enough from Tennessee; that as far as my learning went, I would stand over it, and spell a strive or two with any of them, from *a-b-ab* to *crucifix*, which was where I left off at school.

This day I dined out again; but I'm most tired talking of dinners, especially after I have eaten them. I went to the theatre that night. The acting was pretty considerable, considering that one actress, who, it was very plain, was either a married woman or "had ought to be," as they say there, was playing in the character of a young lady; and one fellow tried to sing that was not half up to a Mississippi boat horn.

We got a little dry or so, and wanted a horn, but this was a temperance house, and there was nothing to treat a friend to that was worth shaking a stick at, so says I, "When there was a famine in the land of Canaan, there was plenty of corn in Egypt; let us go over to the Tremont, Boyden keeps stuff that runs friends together, and makes them forget which is which." Over we went, and soon forgot all about the theatre.

I had promised next morning to go to Lowell with Mr. Lawrence, Mr. Harding, and others; but when I woke up it was pouring down rain, so that kept me in the house all day.

I was not idle, for I had a heap of talk with the folks in the house. One gentleman asked me to come and see him; but he gave me so many directions about getting to where he lived that I asked him to write it down, and told him if ever he came to my part of the country, I hoped he would call and see me. "Well," said he, "how will I find where you live?" "Why, sir, run down the Mississippi till you come to the Obion river, run a small streak up that, jump ashore anywhere and inquire for me."

Says I to one of them, "Do you believe in the sea-sarpint?" "If I don't, there's no snakes. I believe it to be as much true as there is lie in our deacon when he says his red face ain't made by drinking 'New England.' " "Do you consider him dangerous, or is he peaceable?" "Well, now, to keep the truth, I never saw him; but Capting Hodijah Folger said as how he considered the critter as a sort o' so, and a sort o' not." "Had he a long tail?" "Tail, did you say? You'd a died to hear Didge tell about that verming. Didge said he was like skying a copper—head or tail—but you had to guess which. Ses Didge to me, 'Don't you mind,' ses he, 'that are angel what stood with one leg on the sea, and t'other on the dry land?' 'I guess I do.' 'Well,' ses he to me, 'that are sarpint's skin was long enough to a queued his hair.' "

I was asked to sup with a Mr. Richards, whom I had seen at Washington. He had a house full of ladies and gentlemen, collected to see me: so I was on my manners, and I hope they were all as much gratified as I was. We had a fine supper, plenty of conversation, and some fun. I don't think the northern ladies talk as much publicly as they do in the south and west. In private conversation they are ready enough.

When I got back, I saw my old cock again. "Well," says I, "what do you think of nullification up here?" "Why, they say, some of them, that it was got and bred by the tariff. Squire Williams, my neighbor, said he didn't think so: it was a kind of come-by-chance, that was too wicked to know its own kin; and he thought it was a very ugly thing." "Well," says I to him, "squire, setting a case as how the Congress of Jacksonmen should pass a law taxing of all the looms and spindles, and letting cottons and woolens come in from foreign parts, free of duty —what should we do?" "Why, ask 'em to repeal it." "Suppose they would not do it; and when we were growing poorer and poorer, the tax-gatherer should come to sell you out, stock and fluke." "Why, I'd dispute his authority desperately; and if that would not do, I'd fight him, by the blue blazes." "And so would I: but ain't that nullifying, or something mighty like it?" "Why," ses he, "the toe that's tramped on feels most; and a man that don't swear, had better try a stumpy field with a young yoke of cattle." "Well," ses I, "them there people down there fought desperate in the old war. They whipped Captain Cornwallis, and scared Sir Harry Clinton out and out; and I reckon then no more nor now they don't like nobody to wrong them out of their rights. But I'm glad it's all over: and I tell you what I think; you don't work hard enough in the south, and take good care of your grounds, and cattle, and so on; at least, I hearn Josiah Norton say so, when he come home from down to south, where he had been pedling a spell. Si ses to me, ses he, 'Please goodness! but that's a poor country down yander; it makes the tears come into the kildear's eyes when they fly over the old fields. Dod drot me, if you can ever get a drink of cider!! They ain't got no apples but little runts of things, about as big us your thumb, and so sour, that when a pig sticks his tooth into 'em, he lays back his jaw, and hollers, you might hear him a mile: but it's 'eat, pig, or die'—for it's all he's got. And then again they're great for huntin of foxes; and if you were to see their hounds! lean, lank, labber-sided pups, that are so poor they have to prop up agin a post-and-rail fence, 'fore they can raise a bark at my tin-cart. It's the poorest place was ever made.' " "So," said I, "stranger, you had better come down and judge for yourself, both as to principles and habits: you would be as much pleased, I am sure, as I have been in coming north."

Next morning I rose early, and started for Lowell in a fine carriage, with three gentlemen who had agreed to accompany me. I had heard so much of this place that I longed to see it; not because I had heard of the "mile of gals;" no, I left that for the gallantry of the president, who is admitted, on that score, to be abler than myself: but I wanted to see the power of the machinery, wielded by the keenest calculations of human skill; I wanted to see how it was that these northerners could buy our cotton, and carry it home, manufacture it, bring it back, and sell it for half nothing; and, in the mean time, be well to live, and make money besides.

We stopped at the large stone house at the head of the falls of the Merrimac river, and having taken a little refreshment, went down among the factories. The dinner bells were ringing, and the folks pouring out of the houses like bees out of a gum. I looked at them as they passed, all well dressed, lively, and genteel in their appearance;

indeed, the girls looked as if they were coming from a quilting frolic.* We took a turn round, and after dining on a fine salmon, again returned, and entered the factories.

The out-door appearance was fully sustained by the whole of the persons employed in the different rooms. I went in among the young girls, and talked with many of them. Not one expressed herself as tired of her employment, or oppressed with work: all talked well, and looked healthy. Some of them were very handsome; and I could not help observing that they kept the prettiest inside, and put the homely ones on the outside rows.

I could not help reflecting on the difference of condition between these females, thus employed, and those of other populous countries, where the female character is degraded to abject slavery. Here were thousands, useful to others, and enjoying all the blessings of freedom, with the prospect before them of future comfort and respectability: and however we, who only hear of them, may call their houses workshops and prisons, I assure my neighbors there is every enjoyment of life realized by these persons, and there can be but few who are not happy. It cannot be otherwise: respectability depends upon being neighbor-like: here everybody works, and therefore no one is degraded by it; on the contrary, these who don't work are not estimated.

There are more than five thousand females employed in Lowell; and when you come to see the amount of labor performed by them, in superintending the different machinery, you will be astonished.

* For an interesting comment on Crockett's visit to the Lowell mills, see Arthur M. Schlesinger, Jr., *The Age of Jackson*, Boston, 1945, p. 278.

Twelve years ago, the place where Lowell now rises in all its pride was a sheep-pasture. It took its name from Francis C. Lowell, the protector of its manufactories, and was incorporated in 1826—then a mere village. The fall, obtained by a canal from the Merrimac river, is thirty-two feet, affording two levels for mills, of thirteen and seventeen feet; and the whole waters of the river can be used.

There are about fourteen thousand inhabitants. It contains nine meeting-houses; appropriates seven thousand five hundred dollars for free schools; provides instruction for twelve hundred scholars, daily; and about three thousand annually partake of its benefits. It communicates with Boston by the Middlesex canal (the first ever made in the United States); and in a short time the railroad to Boston will be completed, affording every facility of intercourse to the seaboard.

This place has grown by, and must depend on, its manufactures. Its location renders it important, not only to the owners, but to the nation. Its consumption not only employs the thousands of its own population, but many thousands far away from them. It is calculated not only to give individual happiness and prosperity, but to add to our national wealth and independence; and instead of depending on foreign countries, to have our own material worked up in our own country.

Some of the girls attended three looms; and they make from one dollar seventy-five cents to three dollars per week, after paying their board. These looms weave fifty-five yards per day; so that one person makes one hundred and sixty-five yards per day. Everything moves on like clock-work, in all the variety of employments; and the whole manufacture appears to be of the very best.

The owner of one of the mills, Mr. Lawrence, presented me with a suit of broadcloth, made out of wool bought from Mark Cockral, of Mississippi, who sold them about four thousand pounds, and it was as good cloth as the best I ever bought for best imported.

The calico made here is beautiful, and of every variety of figure and color. To attempt to give a description of the manner in which it is stamped and colored is far beyond my abilities. One thing I must state, that after the web is wove, and before they go further, it is actually passed over *a red-hot cylinder,* to scorch off the furze. The number of different operations is truly astonishing; and if one of my country-women had the whole of the persons in her train that helped to make her gown, she should be like a captain on a field muster: and yet, when you come to look at the cost, it would take a trunk full of them to find these same people in living for one day.

I never witnessed such a combination of industry, and perhaps never will again. I saw the whole process, from the time they put in the raw material, until it came out completely finished. In fact, it almost came up to the old story of a fellow walking into a patent machine with a bundle of wool under his am, and coming out at the other end with a new coat on.

Nothing can be more agreeable than the attention that is paid by every one connected with these establishments. Nothing appears to be kept secret—every process is shown and with great cheerfulness. I regret that more of our southern and western men do not go there, as it would help much to do away with their prejudices against these manufactories.

I met the young gentlemen of Lowell, by their particular request, at supper. About one hundred sat down. Everything was in grand order, and went off well. They toasted *me,* and I enlightened *them* by a speech as good as I could make; and, indeed, I considered them a good set of fellows, and as well worth speaking to as any ones I had met with. The old saying, "them that don't work should not eat," don't apply to them, for they are rale workies, and know how to act genteel, too; for I assure you I was not more kindly, and hospitably, and liberally treated any where than just by these same people.

After supper I went to my lodgings for the night. Next morning I took another range round the town and returned to Boston.

Part of this evening I spent at Lieutenant Governor Armstrong's,* where I met a number of ladies and gentlemen. Part of it went off very pleasantly with my worthy landlord in his private rooms; and I do him the justice to say, that while he supplied his visiters with every thing that was nice, he had also picked out for himself as pretty a little bird as ever fluttered, and is in good keeping with everything about the establishment.

Having been invited to the theatre, I went over and sat a short time to be looked at. I was very genteel and quiet, and so I suppose I disappointed some of them, who expected to see a half horse half alligator sort of fellow.

This was my last night in Boston, and I am sure, if I never see the place again, I never can forget the kind and friendly manner in which I was treated by them. It ap-

* Samuel T. Armstrong, an eminent bookseller of Boston.

peared to me that every body was anxious to serve me, and make my time agreeable. And as a proof that comes home—when I called for my bill next morning, I was told there was no charge to be paid by me, and that he was very much delighted that I had made his house my home. I forgot to mention that they treated me so in Lowell—but it is true. This was, to me, at all events, proof enough of Yankee liberality; and more than they generally get credit for. In fact, from the time I entered New England, I was treated with the greatest friendship; and I hope never shall forget it; and I wish all who read this book, and who never were there, would take a trip among them. If they don't learn how to make money, they will know how to use it; and if they don't learn industry, they will see how comfortable every body can be that turns his hands to some employment.

Next day the stage called for me at seven o'clock, and I took my departure from Boston, and went to Providence in Rhode Island. Here I was invited to dine at two of the hotels, but declined both. In fact, I was tired out, and wanted a day or two to get rested; and my face being turned towards Washington and my business, I thought I had better *go ahead*.

We had, from Providence, what they call *a pretty considerable of a run,* and landed safely in New York that city of eternal din and confusion.

I spent that evening with some ladies and gentlemen, and rode out with —— ——, in his carriage, faster than I ever was driven by horse power, for twenty-five miles.

Next morning I took my leave of the city of New York, and arrived safely in Philadelphia.

Having promised Mr. Hoy of Camden to call and see
him on my return, and having fixed the time, I went
over accompanied by several gentlemen, to the Jersey
shore, where there were a great many people waiting to
receive me. They gave me the hand of friendship, and
appeared pleased that I had come over to see them. We
proceeded to Mr. Hoy's, and then I took a walk around
through Camden. On returning to Mr. Hoy's I took some
refreshments, and was called on for a toast, but begged
off, as I expected to be called on for one at dinner.

Some time after this we were asked in to dinner, and
heard some one say he had lost his pocket-book. And in
a few minutes a second cry was raised, that another man
had lost his pocket-book. I then felt for mine, but I felt
in vain—it was gone, with one hundred and sixty-eight
dollars in it. I told them there was another gentleman
that had his deposits removed, and it must be a Jackson
man who did it, as it was all on their own plan. But as I
was among my friends, I knew I was not just a broke man,
and therefore I shut pan on the subject, and fell to eating
my dinner. We had every thing that was good to eat, and
abundance of fine wine, so we soon forgot the ills of life.
After the table was cleared and some toasts drunk, they
toasted me in a very handsome manner, complimenting
me highly for the course I had taken as a public servant.
I returned my gratitude in a speech of about half an hour;
but which, as is said in certain advertisements, would be
too tedious to insert.

After spending a pleasant afternoon, I returned to Philadelphia in the horse-boat; the very one, I suppose, the
fellow told of when crossing over. He said they had put in
a couple of colts, and being very wild, they pitched ahead,

ran off with the boat down the river and never stopped
till they came up jam against the breakwater.

Next morning I was invited to go on to Baltimore in
the People's Line of steamboats. I accepted the proposal,
and started in the Ohio steamboat. What is a little remarkable is this, that the rail-road line had always heretofore beat the People's Line until that day, when we
passed them, and came into port sometime before them.
Whether this was because they had me on board or not,
I do not pretend to say. Some said, if I could tow a boat
up the Mississippi, it was no wonder I could help one
along on the Chesapeake bay.

Many of my friends met me on the wharf at Baltimore,
and escorted me to Barnum's, where there was a great
crowd of people. They called on me for a speech. I made
a great many apologies, but none seemed to fit the right
place, and I was compelled once more to play the orator.

As usual, when there is some speaking going on, there
is a good deal of eating and drinking; so I eat and drank
generously, and retired.

Several friends called on me, and requested me to visit
Major James P. Heath, member of Congress from Baltimore. I did so, and staid a short time at his house, and
then returned to uncle Davie's.

Next morning I took the stage for Washington. When
I arrived at the capitol, I found nothing new, more than
they had just got through the appropriation bill, and was
taking the vote to postpone Mr. Boone's resolution, setting the day of adjournment. I went in while the clerk
was calling the ayes and noes, and when he came to my
name, and I answered, every one was astonished to find
me at my post. "Did not I tell you," said I, "that I would

not vote on the appropriation bill, but when you came to any thing else, I was 'Charley on the spot?' "* I walked about the house, saw my friends, and sat out the Congress. When the House adjourned for good and all, I started for home, by the way of Philadelphia.

* Crockett delivered a speech in Congress on the appropriation bill, June 19, 1834, during the course of which he directed a humorous dig at Jackson and the President's followers in Congress:

"Sirs, I do not consider it good sense to be sitting here passing laws for Andrew Jackson to laugh at; it is not even good nonsense . . . out of those that the President has got about him, I have never seen but one honest countenance since I have been here, and he has just resigned."

Continuing Crockett declared indignantly:

"Sir, we have no Government but Andrew Jackson, without Secretaries; and, sir, he is surrounded by a set of imps of famine, that are as hungry as the flies that we have read in Aesop's Fables, that came after the fox and sucked his blood. Sir, they are a hungry swarm, and will lick up every dollar of the public money. . . .

"Sir, I still live with a hope of seeing better times. Let us all go home, and let the people live one year on glory, and it will bring them to their senses; and they will send us back here and teach us to make the gentleman in the white house take down his flag. Sir, the people will let him know that he is not the Government. I hope to live to see better times." (Speech on the Fortification Bill, *Register of Debates in Congress*, Part IV of Vol. X, June 19, 1834, p. 4, 586.)

CHAPTER TWENTY-ONE

I Am Presented with a Rifle

Did you, my good reader, ever witness a breaking up of Congress? If not, you had better come and see for yourself. The first thing that is done is, to be sure that Sunday shall be one of the last days. That is because we get paid for Sunday; and then, as they generally fix, at the end of long sessions, on Monday to break up, a good many can start on Saturday evening or Sunday morning, with two days' extra pay in hand, as they never calculate on much to be done on the last day of the session, except to send messages to the senate and president that they are ready to adjourn, &c., &c. We generally lounge or squabble the greater part of the session, and crowd into a few days of the last of the term three or four times the business done during as many preceding months. You may therefore guess at the deliberations of Congress, when you can't hear, for the soul of you, what's going on, nor no one

knows what it is, but three or four, and when it's no use
to try to know. Woe betide a bill that is opposed! It is
laid aside for further time, and that never comes. This is
considered, however, by some of the great men as good
legislation; to reject every claim, as if the American people
was a herd of scoundrels, and every petitioner a cheat, and
therefore they are doing the country service to reject
every thing. Most of these worthies are content to vote no,
and will not trouble themselves to investigate. I don't
know what they are made of, for to me nothing is more
delightful than to vote for a claim which, I think, is justly
due, and make them feel as if the government cared for
them and their concerns, and would pay what was justly
due. What do you think would a petitioner care about
going to fight for his country who had been dinging at the
doors of Congress, ever since the last war, for some claim
or other justly due him, but driven from post to pillar,
because he does not come within the spirit or letter of
some general law, or because if you pay him, you must
others like him? This an't the way with private people;
they must pay, or be called unjust, and be sued into the
bargain.

When I arrived in Philadelphia, I put up at the United
States, where I felt a kind of being at home.

Next morning I was informed that the rifle gun which
was to be presented to me by the young men of Philadelphia, was finished, and would be delivered that evening;
and that a committee had been appointed to wait on me
and conduct me to where I was to receive it. So, accordingly, in the evening the committee came, and I walked
with them to a room nearly fornent the old statehouse: it
was crowded full, and there was a table in the centre, with

the gun, a tomahawk, and butcher-knife, both of fine razor metal, with all the accoutrements necessary to the gun—the most beautiful I ever saw, or any body else; and I am now happy to add, as good as they are handsome. My friend, John M. Sanderson, Esq., who had the whole management of getting her made, was present, and delivered the gun into my hands. Upon receiving her, I addressed the company as follows:

"Gentlemen: I receive this rifle from the young men of Philadelphia, as a testimony of friendship, which I hope never to live to forget. This is a favorite article with me, and would have been my choice above all presents that could have been selected. I love a good gun, for it makes a man feel independent, and prepared either for war or peace.

"This rifle does honor to the gentleman that made it. I must say, long as I have been accustomed to handle a gun, I have never seen anything that could come near a comparison to her in beauty. I cannot think that ever such a rifle was made, either in this, or any other country; and how, gentlemen, to express my gratitude to you for your splendid present, I am at loss. This much, however, I will say, that myself and my sons will not forget you while we use this token of your kindne s for our amusement. If it should become necessary to use her in defence of the liberty of our country, in my time, I will do as I have done before; and if the struggle should come when I am buried in the dust, I will leave her in the hands of some who will honor your present, in company with your sons, in standing for our country's rights.

"Accept my sincere thanks, therefore, gentlemen, for your valuable present—one of which I will keep as a

testimony of your friendship, so long as I am in existence."

I then received the gun and accoutrements, and returned to the hotel, where I made an agreement with Mr.
Sanderson and Colonel Pulaski, to go with them the next
day to Jersey shore, at Camden, and try my gun.

Next morning we went out. I had been long out of
practice, so that I could not give her a fair trial. I shot
tolerable well, and was satisfied that when we became
better acquainted, the fault would be mine if the varmints did not suffer.

I was invited the next day to go up and spend the day
at the Fish House on the Schuylkill, where the fathers of
our country, in ancient days, used to assemble and spend
the day in taking their recreation and refreshments. It
has been a noted place ever since, and is as beautiful as
you can imagine. It is called the twenty-fifth state. They
have regular officers, and keep up the old customs with a
great deal of formality. We amused ourselves shooting,
and catching perch. We had a nice refreshment, and
abundance of the best to drink. Every gentleman took a
hand in cooking; and the day was truly spent in harmony
and peace.

The next morning was the Fourth of July, and I had
received an invitation, while at Washington, to take dinner in the first district, at the Hermitage, with the Whigs,
and had accepted the invitation.

At an early hour I was invited to the Musical Fund
Hall, where an oration was to be delivered; and went
with the honorable Messrs. Webster, Poindexter, Man-
gum, Ewing, and Robbins, senators, and Mr. Denny, of
the House of Representatives. We were conducted up

to a gallery in the first story of an immense building, crowded below to overflowing, with ladies and gentlemen.

After the address of the orator, the audience was also addressed by all the senators, and I was then called on. "A speech from Colonel Crockett," was the cry all over the house. I was truly embarrassed to succeed so many great men, and where I saw so many ladies; but I found no excuse would do, and so spoke.

I then returned to the hotel, where I was waited on in a short time by a committee, with a splendid carriage, and was conveyed to the Hermitage, where I met a large concourse of people; and when it was made known that I had arrived, I was received with loud and repeated cheers, and peals of cannon. I was conveyed to a large and cool shade, and introduced to a vast number of citizens, who all appeared glad to see me. I partook of cool drinks of various kinds, and amused myself among the people till near the dinner hour. We were then asked to walk out and take our seats on the stand, where the Declaration of Independence was read, and a most appropriate address was delivered by the orator of the day.

I was then called on by the crowd for a speech; but dinner was ready, and we agreed to postpone further speaking until after dinner.

The dinner, in elegance and variety, did honor to the person who prepared it. After the cloth was removed, and the regular toasts given, I was complimented with a toast.

I rose and requested the company to do me the favor to repair to the stand, and I would endeavor to address them from it, as the crowd was so great, it would be impossible for me to make them hear at the table, and if I had to speak, I desired to gratify all. When we got out,

I found a great many ladies surrounding the stand. I made my way to it among the crowd, who were loudly calling out for my speech, and addressed them.

I then thanked the people for their attention, and we repaired to the table, filled our glasses, and drank my toast.

By this time, Mr. Webster, Mr. Robbins, and Mr. Denny arrived, and each were severally toasted, and each made a speech. The whole of the day was delightfully spent; everybody seemed pleased, and I enjoyed myself much.

Shortly after this the committee returned with me, and we went to the Chesnut street theatre. Here I met a great concourse of people, all in a fine Fourth of July condition. Immediately upon its being announced that I had arrived, I was called on from all quarters for a speech. I rose, and made an apology that I was so hoarse, speaking so much, that I could hardly be heard. However, no excuse would be taken; so I was conveyed to the centre of the crowd, and made them a short address. They gave me two or three thunders like you hear on the stage, and then went on with the show.

I soon left them and returned to the hotel, and really was worn out with the scenes of the day, and making three off-hand speeches; and I have often thought since, that nothing could have induced me to have done so, if it had not been in Philadelphia, and on the Fourth of July. I was stimulated by being in sight of the old State-house, and Independence square, where the fathers of our country met, as it were, with halters on their necks, and subscribed their names to that glorious Declaration of Independence.

Next morning, I was introduced to the great powder-maker, Mr. Dupont, who said to me, that he had been examining my fine gun, and that he had wished to make me a present of half a dozen canisters of his best sportsman's powder. I thanked him, and he went off, and in a short time returned with one dozen, nicely boxed up and directed to me. I then made my arrangements to start the next morning.

While walking about that evening with a friend, we called in at a China importer's store. I was introduced to him; and after looking at his splendid collection for some time, he told me he had a wish to present me with a large pitcher. I thought the gentleman was joking, at first; but he assured me, that if I would accept it, he would pack it up in a box so that it could not break, and I could carry it home safely. I thanked him sincerely for his friendship. It was sent to me, and I carried it home and gave it to my wife, telling her that, when I was away, that pitcher should remind her that folks get thirsty, and the same spirit which prompted the gentleman to give, should make us use it. I am sorry I forgot his name.

Early next morning I set out for Pittsburg, by the fast line, and had a very pleasant trip over the mountains. I attracted much attention as I passed through Pennsylvania, where it was known who I was. About the middle of the State I met with an old man in a tavern, and asked him who was his representative in Congress. "Why," says he, "Dunlap." I told him that could not be, there was but one of that name in, and he was from Tennessee. "Well," says he, "it must be Crawford." No, I told him, there was no Crawford in the House. "Well, hang it, then, it must be George Chambers." "Ah, now you're right; I know

him well, he's a good fellow—walks the planks straight.
I hope you will re-elect him." "Well, I expect we will;
I know nothing against him, only he isn't on our side."
"What side are you on?" "Well, I'm for Jackson." "Why,"
said I, "I thought that was no side at all; he's *on top*." The
old man looked at me right hard. Says I, "Mister, what
makes you for Jackson?" "Why," says he, "he licked the
British at New Orleans, and paid off the national debt."
"Mister," says I, "who was the officers and soldiers that
fought at New Orleans besides General Jackson?" He
said he did not know. "Well," says I, "they ought to have
a part of the glory, any how—now tell me whose money
pays off the national debt?" "Why, I suppose, old Jackson's, as they keep so much talk about it." "Well, now,
my good old friend, suppose part of it was yours, and part
mine, and part everybody's else; and suppose he would
have been broke of his office if he had not paid out what
a law of Congress, made twenty years ago, provided for
paying, what is the glory of the whole of this?" He looked
kind of stumped. I bid him good bye, and told him that he
ought to read both sides.

I arrived in Pittsburg in the night, and early in the
morning went down to the wharf to inquire for a steamboat. I soon found Captain Stone, who commanded
the Hunter. He said he had been waiting a day, thinking that I would like to go with him. That was true,
and I found him all sorts of a clever man. We were to
start at ten o'clock. I returned to the tavern where I
had put up, and a great many gentlemen called to see
me, and, among others, Mr. Grant, brother-in-law of
Governor Carroll, of Tennessee. He invited me to walk
through the city, and to visit his house, which I did,

and he introduced me to a great many of the citizens. I returned, and prepared for a start.

My acquaintance in this place was very limited. I had been there before, but my name had not made such a noise then as now.

The marks of industry and enterprise are very visible in Pittsburg. It is a perfect workshop, and is increasing every year in extent, beauty, and population. The aqueduct, and other splendid works terminating the great canal from Philadelphia, speaks highly for Pennsylvania foresight and perseverence. What signifies the debt incurred by her? but it is no debt, in my mind. It is a noble, imperishing, and increasing investment for posterity; and they will, to remotest ages, bless the men who have sustained so much abuse by the pack out of office, and will consider them as the greatest benefactors of their State and of the nation. I say of the nation; for this canal is a new artery in the body politic, through which the life-blood of its future prosperity and union will flow for ever. Its present facilities have brought a part of the State of Ohio, in point of cost of transportation, within two days' drive with a wagon of the city of Philadelphia, and it will be lower still. Is not this national in its operation? Who can doubt it?

I had heard it said, particularly in New York, that this same canal never could get along, because their great western canal would carry all the produce and merchandize; and I took some pains to hear a little about it, and am fully persuaded such is not the fact, and never can be. I was informed that the trade on this Pennsylvania canal was four or five times what it was when the first year ended, and in a few years would be a profit to the

State; and to me it seems clear, that no one south of Pittsburg, in Ohio, and elsewhere, are going to send their merchandize way round by the New York canal, and run the risks of the lake, when they can put them snug into a boat at Philadelphia, and land them safe, without risk, in Pittsburg. I wish I could agree with the Pennsylvanians as well in other respects as I do on internal improvements. What will she not do for her inhabitants in a few years, when her twenty odd millions, invested in all her vast and various improvements, shall yield but a moderate profit! Her roads will all be paved; her rivers and creeks made navigable; her schools be free for high and low, and her inhabitants free from taxation!!! Reader, these events are sure to come.

And here, let me address a word to my own State. Go on with what little you have begun, and never rest until you have opened every facility to every part of our State. Though we are divided into east and west, we are all Tennessee. Give a "long pull, and a strong pull, and a pull altogether," and every difficulty will vanish. Give our inhabitants a chance among the rest of the States, and you'll not hear so much of Alabama, or Arkansas, or Texas.

Well, I've got a long slipe off from my steamboat, the Hunter, and I had better look up the captain. So off I starts, trunk, gun-case, old lady's pitcher, and all. "How's the water, Captain Stone?" "Why, colonel, the river is pretty considerable for a run, but the water is as cool as Presbyterian charity, and the old Monongahela is a leetle of the remains of what Abigail, the wife of old Nabal, carried as a present to David. Clear off the coal-dust out of your wizzand, and give us a yarn about your tower."

"Why, captain, may I be shot if you mightn't run with this same craft of yourn down, through, and out of Symmes's lower hole, and back again, afore I could get through half what I've seen; I've been clean away amongst the Yankees, where they call your name *Stunn*." "Me, Stunn! well, it's hard that as slick a fellow as me should go by such nick-names. Livin gingers! what d'ye suppose, colonel, they call me in Orlanes?" "I dare say, some hard name." "Only think of the parly vous; some call me Mr. Peer, and some, by jingo, call me Mr. Peter; and you can't beat it out of them. Only think of Sam Gun, the fireman; he took a spree with some of them Charlies, in Orlanes, and they begun to call him Mounsheer Fusil. Well, Sam bore it a good while; but at last he told Joe Head, the engineer, that the first fellow who miscalled his father's name, should have a tip of his daddle. 'Good,' says Joe; says he, 'Sam, only take care of their *caniffs*, as how they call them long knives.' Well, it wasn't long before Sam peeled the bark off of a parly's knowledge-box, and so Joe and him had it with a cabin full of them. So Sam he got off to the boat, but the calaboos men got Joe; so Joe he sends for me, and when they cum for me, they passed the word that Mr. Tate had sent for me. Well, off I goes to the police, and they axed me if I would go bail for Mounsheer Tate. 'No,' says I; 'don't know him.' 'Yes, but you do, captain,' said some one inside; and when I went in, who should it be but Joe Head! transmogrified into Mounsheer Tate!! Well, we got the matter explained, and they all laughed and drunk friends. Well, colonel, here's to you; I'm sure you didn't get anything better anywhere; and afore we quit, just tell me, did you see the sea-sarpint?" "No, indeed, I did not, although I spoke for him not to be out of the way." "Well, colonel, I wonder at them Yankee fellows, they are monstrous cute; but I suspect they don't know much about *snaking*. I think with me in the Hunter here, you with your rifle, and one of these 'long shore Spaniards with his lasso, we would give him a little of the hurricane tipp'd with thunder." "If we didn't catch him," says I, "we could scare him out of his skin, and that's all they want at the museum."

So we passed our time till we arrived opposite Wheeling. I walked up into the town, and was soon surrounded by many of the citizens, and in a short time was waited on by a committee, and invited to partake of a dinner that day at three o'clock. This kind invitation I was obliged to decline, lest I should lose my passage. So they treated me handsomely, and asked the captain, before he started, to run a short distance up the river, and as he came past they would give him a salute. He did so. I got on the hurricane deck, took off my hat, and returned their salute. They continued to cheer until we got out of hearing. All went on well, and we arrived at the mouth of Guyandotte, where we took on board Messrs. Hardin, Tompkins, and Beaty, three of the members of Congress from Kentucky. We went on pleasantly until we arrived at Cincinnati. Our boat was fine, and the Captain a clever fellow. It was night when we arrived; so, early next morning I called to see my two friends, Messrs. Smiths and families, spent a short time with them, and returned to the boat. By this time it was ascertained that I was on board, and a committee waited on me, and invited me to partake of a cold cut at three o'clock that day, and make them a speech. I agreed to do so.

I remained over night and took the packet boat next

morning for Louisville, where I arrived the day after.
My friends had provided for me at the Louisville hotel,
the finest public house I have been in west of the mountains. I was asked to make a speech to the people next
day, which I agreed to, as I had no hope of getting off in a
boat for a few days. It was published that I was to speak
on the next evening; so I was sent for in the morning to
visit Jeffersonville Springs, in Indiana, across the river.
I went, and found a number of ladies and gentlemen, and
after being introduced to the company, I was asked to
make a speech, to which I had but little objection, as I
wished to discuss the question of the President vetoing the
Wabash appropriation, and yet signing the Van Buren,
New York, Hudson river bill. This I did, and the people
appeared well pleased. I partook of some of the good
things of this life with them, exhorting all Jackson Van
Buren men to turn from the evil of their ways, and took
myself off for the other side of the river.

In the evening I attended at the court-house, and met
the largest concourse of people that ever has been assembled in Louisville since it has been settled. This I was
told by a gentleman who had resided there for upwards
of twenty years. The people all appeared to be excited
with curiosity or something else. I had no idea of attracting so much attention; but there I was in the thick of
them. I discovered there were a great many ladies amongst
the audience, and among them the celebrated Mrs. Drake.
A stand had been erected for me in the court-house yard,
on which I stood and addressed the crowd.

I then returned to the hotel, and in a short time a
committee of the young men waited on me and invited
me to a dinner on Thursday, as a testimony in favor of

my political course. I gave a conditional acceptance, and
no boat arriving, I attended and partook of them with a
splendid dinner. I was toasted, and made a speech, complimenting the young men for their zeal in the cause
of their country. If I had the powers of General Lafayette,
I would have written out all my speeches; but I have not,
and therefore omit this one. All passed off pleasantly,
and next day I took the steamboat Scotland, commanded
by Captain Buckner, a gentleman, every inch of him. After
a fine run, we arrived at Mills' Point on the 22d day of
July. Here I once more touched the soil of Tennessee,
and found my son William waiting to carry me home,
which was distant thirty-five miles.

When I landed and took out my fine gun, the folks
gathered round me to see the great curiosity. A large
fellow stepped up, and asked me why all the members did
not get such guns given them? I told him I got that gun
for being honest, in supporting my country instead of
bowing down and worshiping an idol. He looked at me
and said, that was very strong. "No stronger than true, my
friend," said I.

In a short time I set out for my own home: yes, my
own home, my own soil, my own humble dwelling, my
own family, my own hearts, my ocean of love and affection which neither circumstances nor time can dry up.
Here, like the wearied bird, let me settle down for awhile,
and shut out the world.

In the course of a few days, I determined to try my
new gun upon the living subject. I started for a hunt,
and shortly came across a fine buck. He fell at the distance
of one hundred and thirty steps. Not a bad shot, you will

say. I say, not a bad gun either. After a little practice with her, she came up to the eye prime, and I determined to try her at the first shooting-match for beef.

As this is a novelty to most of my readers, I will endeavor to give a description of this western amusement.

In the latter part of summer our cattle get very fat, as the range is remarkably fine; and some one, desirous of raising money on one of his cattle, advertises that on a particular day, and at a given place, a first-rate beef will be shot for.

When the day comes, every marksman in the neighborhood will meet at the appointed place, with his gun. After the company has assembled, a subscription paper is handed round, with the following heading:

"A. B. offers a beef worth twenty dollars, to be shot for, at twenty-five cents a shot." Then the names are put down by each person, thus:

D. C. puts in four shots, ... $1 00
E. F.   "   eight   " 2 00
G. H.   "   two   " 0 50

And thus it goes round, until the price is made up.

Two persons are then selected, who have not entered for shots, to act as judges of the match. Every shooter gets a board, and makes a cross in the centre of his target. The shot that drives the centre, or comes nearest to it, gets the *hide and tallow,* which is considered the first choice. The next nearest gets his choice of the hind quarters; the third gets the other hind quarter; the fourth takes choice of the fore quarters; the fifth the remaining quarter; and the sixth gets the lead in the tree against which we shoot.

The judges stand near the tree, and when a man fires they cry out, "Who shot?" and the shooter gives in his name; and so on, till all have shot. The judges then take all the boards, and go off by themselves, and decide what quarter each man has won. Sometimes one will get nearly all.

This is one of our homely amusements—enjoyed as much by us, and perhaps more, than most of your refined entertainments. Here each man takes a part, if he pleases, and no one is excluded, unless his improper conduct renders him unfit as an associate.

CHAPTER TWENTY-TWO

I Outwit a Yankee

I begin this chapter on the 8th day of July, 1835, at Home, Weakley county, Tennessee. I have just returned from a two weeks' electioneering canvass and I have spoken every day to large concourses of people with my competitor. I have him badly plagued, for he does not know as much about "the Government," the deposites, and the Little Flying Dutchman, whose life I wrote, as I can tell the people; and at times he is as much bothered as a fly in a tar pot to get out of the mess. A candidate is often stumped in making stump speeches. His name is Adam Huntsman; he lost a leg in an Indian fight, they say, during the last war, and the Government run him on the score of his military services. I tell him in my speech that I have great hopes of writing one more book, and that shall be the second fall of Adam, for he is on the Eve of an almighty thrashing. He relishes the joke about as much as a doctor does his own physic. I handle the administration without gloves, and I do believe I will double my competitor, if I have a fair shake, and he does not work like a mole in the dark. Jacksonism is dying here faster than it ever sprung up, and I predict that "the Government" will be the most unpopular man, in one year more, that ever had any pretensions to the high place he now fills. Four weeks from to-morrow will end the dispute in our elections, and if old Adam is not beaten out of his hunting shirt, my name isn't Crockett.

While on the subject of election matters, I will just relate a little anecdote about myself, which will show the people to the east, how we manage these things on the frontiers. It was when I first run for Congress; I was then in favor of the Hero, for he had chalked out his course so sleek in his letter to the Tennessee legislature, that, like Sam Patch, says I, "there can be no mistake in him," and so I went ahead. No one dreamt about the monster and the deposites at that time, and so, as I afterward found, many, like myself, were taken in by these fair promises, which were worth about as much as a flash in the pan when you have a fair shot at a fat bear.

But I am losing sight of my story. Well, I started off to the Cross Roads, dressed in my hunting shirt, and my rifle on my shoulder. Many of our constituents had assembled there to get a taste of the quality of the candidates at orating. Job Snelling, a gander-shanked Yankee, who had been caught somewhere about Plymouth Bay, and been shipped to the west with a cargo of codfish and rum, erected a large shantee, and set up shop for the occasion. A large posse of the voters had assembled before I arrived, and my opponent had already made considerable headway with his speechifying and his treating, when they spied me about a rifle shot from the camp, sauntering along as if I was not a party in business. "There comes Crockett," cried one. "Let us hear the colonel," cried another, and so I mounted the stump that had been cut down for the occasion, and began to bushwhack in the most approved style.

I had not been up long before there was such an uproar in the crowd that I could not hear my own voice, and some of my constituents let me know, that they could not listen to me on such a dry subject as the welfare of the nation, until they had something to drink, and that I must treat them. Accordingly I jumped down from the rostrum, and led the way to the shantee, followed by my constituents, shouting, "Huzza for Crockett," and "Crockett for ever!"

When we entered the shantee, Job was busy dealing out his rum in a style that showed he was making a good day's work of it, and I called for a quart of the best, but the crooked critur returned no other answer than by pointing to a board over the bar, on which he had chalked in large letters, *"Pay to-day and trust to-morrow."* Now that idea brought me up all standing; it was a sort of cornering in which there was no back out, for ready money in the west, in those times, was the shyest thing in all natur, and it was most particularly shy with me on that occasion.

The voters seeing my predicament, fell off to the other side, and I was left deserted and alone, as the Government will be, when he no longer has any offices to bestow. I saw, as plain as day, that the tide of popular opinion was against me, and that, unless I got some rum speedily, I should lose my election as sure as there are snakes in Virginny,—and it must be done soon, or even burnt brandy wouldn't save me. So I walked away from the shantee, but in another guess sort from the way I entered it, for on this occasion I had no train after me, and not a voice shouted, "Huzza for Crockett." Popularity sometimes depends on a very small matter indeed; in this particular it was worth a quart of New England rum, and no more.

Well, knowing that a crisis was at hand, I struck into the woods with my rifle on my shoulder, my best friend in time of need, and as good fortune would have it, I had not been out more than a quarter of an hour before I treed a fat coon, and in the pulling of a trigger, he lay dead at the root of the tree. I soon whipped his hairy jacket off his back, and again bent my steps towards the shantee, and walked up to the bar, but not alone, for this time I had half a dozen of my constituents at my heels. I threw down the coon skin upon the counter, and called for a quart, and Job, though busy in dealing out rum, forgot to point at his chalked rules and regulations, for he knew that a coon was as good a legal tender for a quart, in the west, as a New York shilling, any day in the year.

My constituents now flocked about me, and cried, "Huzza for Crockett," "Crockett for ever," and finding the tide had taken a turn, I told them several yarns, to get them in a good humor, and having soon dispatched the value of the coon, I went out and mounted the stump, without opposition, and a clear majority of the voters followed me to hear what I had to offer for the good of the nation. Before I was half through, one of my constituents moved that they would hear the balance of my speech, after they had washed down the first part with some more of Job Snelling's extract of cornstalk and molassess, and the question being put, it was carried unanimously. It wasn't considered necessary to tell the yeas and nays, so we adjourned to the shantee, and on the way I began to reckon that the fate of the nation pretty much depended upon my shooting another coon.

While standing at the bar, feeling sort of bashful while Job's rules and regulations stared me in the face, I cast down my eyes, and discovered one end of the coon skin sticking between the logs that supported the bar. Job had slung it there in the hurry of business. I gave it a sort of quick jerk, and it followed my hand as natural as if I had been the rightful owner. I slapped it on the counter, and Job, little dreaming that he was barking up the wrong tree, shoved along another bottle, which my constituents quickly disposed of with great good humor, for some of them saw the trick, and then we withdrew to the rostrum to discuss the affairs of the nation.

I don't know how it was, but the voters soon became dry again, and nothing would do, but we must adjourn to the shantee, and as luck would have it, the coon skin was still sticking between the logs, as if Job had flung it there on purpose to tempt me. I was not slow in raising it to the counter, the rum followed of course, and I wish I may be shot, if I didn't, before the day was over, get ten quarts for the same identical skin, and from a fellow, too, who in those parts was considered as sharp as a steel trap, and as bright as a pewter button.

This joke secured me my election, for it soon circulated like smoke among my constituents, and they allowed, with one accord, that the man who could get the whip hand of Job Snelling in fair trade, could outwit

Old Nick himself, and was the real grit for them in Congress. Job was by no means popular; he boasted of always being wide awake, and that any one who could take him in, was free to do so, for he came from a stock, that sleeping or waking had always one eye open, and the other not more than half closed. The whole family were geniuses. His father was the inventor of wooden nutmegs, by which Job said he might have made a fortune, if he had only taken out a patent and kept the business in his own hands; his mother Patience manufactured the first white oak pumpkin seeds of the mammoth kind, and turned a pretty penny the first season; and his aunt Prudence was the first to discover that corn husks, steeped into tobacco water, would make as handsome Spanish wrappers as ever came from Havana, and that oak leaves would answer all the purpose of filling, for no one could discover the difference except the man who smoked them, and then it would be too late to make a stir about it. Job, himself, bragged of having made some useful discoveries; the most profitable of which was the art of converting mahogany sawdust into cayenne pepper, which he said was a profitable and safe business; for the people have been so long accustomed to having dust thrown in their eyes, that there wasn't much danger of being found out.

The way I got to the blind side of the Yankee merchant, was pretty generally known before election day, and the result was, that my opponent might as well have whistled jigs to a milestone, as attempt to beat up for votes in that district. I beat him out and out, quite back into the old year, and there was scarce enough left of him, after the canvass was over, to make a small grease spot. He disappeared without even leaving a mark behind; and such will be the fate of Adam Huntsman, if there is a fair fight and no gouging.

After the election was over, I sent Snelling the price of the rum, but took good care to keep the fact from the knowledge of my constituents. Job refused the money, and sent me word, that it did him good to be taken in occasionally, as it served to brighten his ideas; but I afterwards learnt when he found out the trick that had been played upon him, he put all the rum I had ordered, in his bill against my opponent, who, being elated with the speeches he had made on the affairs of the nation, could not descend to examine into the particulars of a bill of a vender of rum in the small way.

CHAPTER TWENTY-THREE

I Resolve to Go to Texas

August 11, 1835. I am now at home in Weakley county. My canvass is over, and the result is known. Contrary to all expectation, I am beaten two hundred and thirty votes, from the best information I can get; and in this instance, I may say, bad is the best. My mantle has fallen upon the shoulders of Adam, and I hope he may wear it with becoming dignity, and never lose sight of the welfare of the nation, for the purpose of elevating a few designing politicians to the head of the heap. The rotten policy pursued by "the Government" cannot last long; it will either work its own downfall, or the downfall of the republic, soon, unless the people tear the seal from their eyes, and behold their danger time enough to avert the ruin.

I wish to inform the people of these United States what I had to contend against, trusting that the expose I shall make, will be a caution to the people not to repose too much power in the hands of a single man, though he should be "the greatest and the best." I had, as I have already said, Mr. Adam Huntsman for my competitor, aided by the popularity of both Andrew Jackson and Governor Carroll, and the whole strength of the Union Bank of Jackson. I have been told by good men, that some of the managers of the bank on the days of the election were heard say, that they would give twenty-five dollars a vote for votes enough to elect Mr. Huntsman. This is a pretty good price for a vote, and in ordinary times a round dozen might be got for the money.

I have always believed, since Jackson removed the deposites, that his whole object was to place the treasury where he could use it to influence elections; and I do believe he is determined to sacrifice every dollar of the treasury, to make the Little Flying Dutchman his successor.* If this is not my creed, I wish I may be shot. For

* The charter of the Bank of the United States was to expire in 1836, but when the friends of the Bank, Nicholas Biddle, Henry Clay, and Daniel Webster, sought to obtain its recharter in 1832, Jackson vetoed the bill. In the election of 1832, the bank question became the leading issue. After his reelection, Jackson, fearing the bank's power to bring on a panic, decided that the federal deposits should be withdrawn from its vaults. This was accomplished and the government funds were distributed among state banks.

How strongly Davy Crockett felt on the removal of the deposits is illustrated in a letter he wrote from Washington on January 8th, 1834 which went in part:

"I suppose you can see by the news papers that we are still engaged in discussing the great question of Jacksons kingly power exercised in the removil of the deposits and God only knows when this depate will end or what will be the result. . . . I consider the present time one that is marked with more danger than any period of our political history . . . you see our whole circulating medium deranged and our whole Commercial Community destroyed all to gratify the ambition of *King Andrew* the first becaus the united States Bank refused to lend its aid in upholding his corrupt party the truth is he is surrounded by a set of Imps of famin that is willing to destroy the best interest of the country to promote their own Interest I have spoken free but I write fourteen years since I have been a candidate, I never saw such means used to defeat any candidate, as were put in practice against me on this occasion. There was a disciplined band of judges and officers to hold the elections at almost every poll. Of late years they begin to find out that there's an advantage in this, even in the west. Some officers held the election, and at the same time had nearly all they were worth bet on the election. Such judges, I should take it, are like the handle of a jug, all on one side; and I am told it doesn't require much schooling to make the tally list correspond to a notch with the ballot box, provided they who make up the returns have enough loose tickets in their breeches pockets. I have no doubt that I was completely rascalled out of my election, and I do regret that duty to myself and to my country compels me to expose such villainy.

Well might Governor Poindexter exclaim—"Ah! my country, what degradation thou hast fallen into!" Andrew Jackson was, during my election canvass, franking the extra Globe with a prospectus in it to every postoffice in this district, and upon one occasion he had my mileage and pay as a member drawn up and sent to this district, to one of his minions, to have it published just a few days before the election. This is what I call small potatoes and a few of a hill. He stated that I had charged mileage for one thousand miles and that it was but seven hundred and fifty miles, and held out the idea that I had taken pay for the same mileage that Mr. Fitzgerald had taken, when it was well known that he charged thirteen hundred miles

the truth and the world will be convinsed I hope before it is too late."
(Original manuscript is in the Tennessee Historical Society.)
The "Flying Dutchman" was Martin Van Buren.

from here to Washington, and he and myself both live in the same county. It is somewhat remarkable how this fact should have escaped the keen eye of "the Government."

The general's pet, Mr. Grundy, charged for one thousand miles from Nashville to Washington, and it was sanctioned by the Legislature, I suppose because he would huzza! for Jackson; and because I think proper to refrain from huzzaing until he goes out of office, when I shall give a screamer, that will be heard from the Mississippi to the Atlantic, or my name's not Crockett—for this reason he came out openly to electioneer against me. I now say, that the oldest man living never heard of the President of a great nation to come down to open electioneering for his successor. It is treating the nation as if it was the property of a single individual, and he had the right to bequeath it to whom he pleased—the same as a patch of land for which he had the patent. It is plain to be seen that the poor superannuated old man is surrounded by a set of horse leeches, who will stick to him while there is a drop of blood to be got, and their maws are so capacious that they will never get full enough to drop off. The Land office, the Post office, and the Treasury itself may all be drained, and we shall still find them craving for more. They use him to promote their own private interests, and for all his sharp sight, he remains as blind as a dead lion to the jackals who are tearing him to pieces. In fact, I do believe he is a perfect tool in their hands, ready to be used to answer any purpose to promote either their interest or gratify their ambition.

I came within two hundred and thirty votes of being elected, notwithstanding I had to contend against "the greatest and the best," with the whole power of the

Treasury against me. The Little Flying Dutchman will no doubt calculate upon having a true game cock in Mr. Huntsman, but if he doesn't show them the white feather before the first session is over, I agree never to be set down for a prophet, that's all. I am gratified that I have spoken the truth to the people of my district regardless of consequences. I would not be compelled to bow down to the idol for a seat in Congress during life. I have never known what it was to sacrifice my own judgment to gratify any party, and I have no doubt of the time being close at hand when I will be rewarded for letting my tongue speak what my heart thinks. I have suffered myself to be polit-ically sacrificed to save my country from ruin and dis-grace, and if I am never again elected, I will have the gratification to know that I have done my duty. Thus much I say in relation to the manner in which my down-fall was effected, and in laying it before the public, "I take the responsibility." I may add in the words of the man in the play, "Crockett's occupation's gone."

Two weeks and more have elapsed since I wrote the foregoing account of my defeat, and I confess the thorn still rankles, not so much on my own account as the nation's, for I had set my heart on following up the travel-ing deposites until they should be fairly gathered to their proper nest, like young chickens, for I am aware of the vermin that are on the constant look out to pounce upon them, like a cock at a blackberry, which they would have done long since, if it had not been for a few such men as Webster, Clay, and myself. It is my parting advice, that this matter be attended to without delay, for before long the little chickens will take wing, and even

the powerful wand of the magician of Kinderhook will
be unable to point out the course they have flown.

As my country no longer requires my services, I have
made up my mind to go to Texas. My life has been
one of danger, toil, and privation, but these difficulties
I had to encounter at a time when I considered it nothing more than right good sport to surmount them; but
now I start anew upon my own hook, and God only grant
that it may be strong enough to support the weight
that may be hung upon it. I have a new row to hoe, a
long and rough one, but come what will I'll go ahead.

A few days ago I went to a meeting of my constituents.
My appetite for politics was at one time just about as
sharp set as a saw mill, but late events have given me something of a surfeit, more than I could well digest; still
habit they say is second natur, and so I went, and gave
them a piece of my mind touching "the Government" and
the succession, by way of a codicil to what I have often
said before.

I told them to keep a sharp lookout for the deposites,
for it requires an eye as insinuating as a dissecting knife
to see what safety there is in placing one million of the
public funds in some little country shaving shop with no
more than one hundred thousand dollars capital. This
bank, we will just suppose, without being too particular,
is in the neighborhood of some of the public lands, where
speculators, who have every thing to gain and nothing to
lose, swarm like crows about carrion. They buy the
United States' land upon a large scale, get discounts
from the aforesaid shaving shop, which are made upon a
large scale also upon the United States' funds; they
pay the whole purchase money with these discounts, and

get a clear title to the land, so that when the shaving shop comes to make a Flemish account of her transactions, "the Government" will discover that he has not only lost the original deposite, but a large portion of the public lands to boot. So much for taking the responsibility.

I told them that they were hurrying along a broad M'Adamized road to make the Little Flying Dutchman the successor, but they would no sooner accomplish that end than they would be obliged to buckle to, and drag the Juggernaut through many narrow and winding and out-of-the-way paths, and hub deep in the mire. That they reminded me of the Hibernian, who bet a glass of grog with a hod carrier that he could not carry him in his hod up a ladder to the third story of a new building. He seated himself in the hod, and the other mounted the ladder with his load upon his shoulder. He ascended to the second story pretty steadily, but as he approached the third his strength failed him, he began to totter, and Pat was so delighted at the prospect of winning his bet, that he clapped his hands and shouted, "By the powers, the grog's mine," and he made such a stir in the hod, that I wish I may be shot if he didn't win it, but he broke his neck in the fall. And so I told my constituents that they might possibly gain the victory, but in doing so, they would ruin their country.

I told them, moreover, of my services, pretty straight up and down, for a man may be allowed to speak on such subjects when others are about to forget them; and I also told them of the manner in which I had been knocked down and dragged out, and that I did not consider it a fair fight any how they could fix it. I put the ingredients in the cup pretty strong I tell you, and I concluded my speech by telling them that I was done with politics for the present, and that they might all go to hell, and I would go to Texas.*

When I returned home I felt a sort of cast down at the change that had taken place in my fortunes, and sorrow, it is said, will make even an oyster feel poetical. I never tried my hand at that sort of writing, but on this particular occasion such was my state of feeling, that I began to fancy myself inspired, so I took pen in hand, and as usual I went ahead. When I had got fairly through, my poetry looked as zigzag as a worm fence; the lines wouldn't tally no how; so I showed them to Peleg Longfellow, who has a first rate reputation with us for that sort of writing, having some years ago made a carrier's address for the Nashville Banner, and Peleg lopped off some lines, and stretched out others; but I wish I may be shot if I don't rather think he has made it worse than it was when I placed it in his hands. It being my first, and, no doubt, last piece of poetry, I will print it in this place, as it will serve to express my feelings on leaving my home, my neighbors, and friends and country, for a strange land, as fully as I could in plain prose.

Farewell to the mountains whose mazes to me
Were more beautiful far than Eden could be;
No fruit was forbidden, but Nature had spread

---

* Crockett had evidently decided to go to Texas even before he was defeated for reelection to Congress. In a letter from Washington, December 25, 1834, he wrote to his friend, Charles Shultz: "I have almost given up the Ship as lost; I have gone so far as to declare that if *he, martin vanburen,* is elected that I will leave the united States—for I never will live under his Kingdom; before I will submit to his Government I will go to the wildes of Texas—I will consider that government a paradise to what this will be. . . ." (The Magazine of History, vol. XXV, July, 1917, pp. 75-76)

Her bountiful board, and her children were fed.
The hills were our garners—our herds wildly grew,
And Nature was shepherd and husbandman too.
I felt like a monarch, yet thought like a man,
As I thanked the Great Giver, and worshiped his plan.

The home I forsake where my offspring arose;
The graves I forsake where my children repose.
The home I redeemed from the savage and wild:
The home I have loved as a father his child;
The corn that I planted, the fields that I cleared,
The flocks that I raised, and the cabin I reared;
The wife of my bosom—Farewell to ye all!
In the land of the stranger I rise or I fall.

Farewell to my country!—I fought for thee well,
When the savage rushed forth like the demons from hell.
In peace or in war I have stood by thy side—
My country, for thee I have lived—would have died!
But I am cast off—my career now is run
And I wander abroad like the prodigal son—
Where the wild savage roves, and the broad prairies spread,
The fallen—despised—will again go ahead!

CHAPTER TWENTY-FOUR

The Puppet Show at Little Rock

In my last chapter I made mention of my determination to cut and quit the States until such time as honest and independent men should again work their way to the head of the heap; and as I should probably have some idle time on hand before that state of affairs shall be brought about, I promised to give the Texians a helping hand on the high road to freedom. Well, I was always fond of having my spoon in a mess of that kind, for if there is anything in this world particularly worth living for, it is freedom; anything that would render death to a brave man particularly pleasant, it is freedom.

I am now on my journey, and have already tortled along as far as Little Rock, on the Arkansas, about one hundred and twenty-five miles from the mouth. I had promised to write another book, expecting, when I made that promise, to write about politics, and use up "the

Government," his successor, the removal of the deposites, and so on, matters and things that come as natural to me as bear hunting; but being rascalled out of my election, I am taken all aback, and I must now strike into a new path altogether. Still I will redeem my promise and make a book, and it shall be about my adventures in Texas, hoping that my friends, Messrs. Webster, and Clay, and Biddle, will keep a sharp lookout upon "the Government" during my absence—I am told that every author of distinction writes a book of travels now-a-days.

My thermometer stood somewhat below the freezing point as I left my wife and children; still there was some thawing about the eyelids, a thing that had not taken place since I first ran away from my father's house when a thoughtless vagabond boy. I dressed myself in a clean hunting shirt, put on a new fox-skin cap with the tail hanging behind, took hold of my rifle Betsey, which all the world knows was presented to me by the patriotic citizens of Philadelphia, as a compliment for my unflinching opposition to the tyrannic measures of "the Government," and thus equipped, I started off with a heavy heart for Mill's Point, to take steamboat down the Mississippi, and go ahead in a new world.

While walking along, and thinking whether it was altogether the right grit to leave my poor country at a time she most needed my services, I came to a clearing, and I was slowly rising a slope, when I was startled by loud, profane, and boisterous voices, (as loud and profane as have been heard in the White House of late years,) which seemed to proceed from a thick covert of undergrowth, about two hundred yards in advance of me, and about one hundred to the right of my road.

"You kin, kin you?"

"Yes, I kin, and am able to do it! Boo-oo-oo!—O! wake snakes, and walk your chalks! Brimstone and —— fire! Don't hold me, Nick Stoval! The fight's made up, and let's go at it. —— my soul if I don't jump down his throat and gallop every chitterling out of him, before you can say 'quit!' "

"Now, Nick, don't hold him! Jist let the wild cat come, and I'll tame him. Ned will see me a fair fight—won't you, Ned?"

"Oh! yes, I'll see you a fair fight; blast my old shoes if I don't."

"That's sufficient, as Tom Haynes said, when he saw the elephant. Now let him come."

Thus they went on, with countless oaths interspersed, which I dare not even hint at, and with much that I could not distinctly hear.

In mercy's name! thought I, what a band of ruffians is at work here! I quickened my gait, and had come nearly opposite to the thick grove whence the noise proceeded, when my eye caught indistinctly, through the foliage of the dwarf oaks and hickories that intervened, glimpses of a man or men, who seemed to be on a violent struggle; and I could occasionally catch those deep-drawn, emphatic oaths, which men in conflict utter, when they deal blows. I hurried to the spot, but before I reached it, I saw the combatants come to the ground, and after a short struggle, I saw the uppermost one (for I could not see the other) make a heavy plunge with both his thumbs, and at the same instant I heard a cry in the accent of keenest torture, "Enough! my eye is out!"

I stood completely horror-struck for a moment. The

accomplices in the brutal deed had all fled at my approach; at least I supposed so, for they were not to be seen.

"Now, blast your corn-shucking soul," said the victor, a lad of about eighteen, as he rose from the ground, "come cuttin' your shines 'bout me agin, next time I come to the Court House, will you? Get your owl-eye in agin, if you can."

At this moment he saw me for the first time. He looked as though he couldn't help it, and was for making himself particularly scarce, when I called to him, "Come back, you brute, and assist me in relieving the poor crittur you have ruined for ever."

Upon this rough salutation, he sort of collected himself, and with a taunting curl of the nose he replied, "You needn't kick before you're spurr'd. There ain't nobody there, nor hain't been, nother. I was jist a seein' how I could a fout." So saying, he bounded to his plough, which stood in the corner of the fence about fifty yards from the battle ground.

Now would any man in his senses believe that a rational being could make such a darned fool of himself? but I wish I may be shot, if his report was not as true as the last post-office report, every word, and a little more satisfactory. All that I had heard and seen was nothing more nor less than what is called a rehearsal of a knock-down and drag-out fight, in which the young man had played all the parts, for his own amusement, and by way of keeping his hand in. I went to the ground from which he had risen, and there were the prints of his two thumbs, plunged up to the balls in the mellow earth, about the distance of a man's eyes apart, and the ground around was broken up, as if two stags had been engaged upon it.

As I resumed my journey I laughed outright at this adventure, for it reminded me of Andrew Jackson's attack upon the United States Bank. He had magnified it into a monster, and then began to rip and tear, and swear and gouge, until he thought he had the monster on its back; and when the fight was over, and he got up to look about for his enemy, he could find none for the soul of him, for his enemy was altogether in his heated imagination. These fighting characters are never at peace, unless they have something to quarrel with, and rather than have no fight at all, they will trample on their own shadows.

The day I arrived at Little Rock, I no sooner quit the steamer than I streaked it straight ahead for the principal tavern, which is nothing to boast of, no how, unless a man happens to be like the member of Congress from the south, who was converted to Jacksonism, and then made a speech as long as the longitude about his political honesty. Some men, it seems, take a pride in saying a great deal about nothing—like windmills, their tongues must be going whether they have any grist to grind nor not. This is all very well in Congress, where every member is expected to make a speech, to let his constituents know that some things can be done as well as others; but I set it down as being rather an imposition upon good nature to be compelled to listen, without receiving the consideration of eight dollars per day, besides mileage, as we do in Congress. Many members will do nothing else for their pay but listen, day in and day out, and I wish I may be shot, if they do not earn every penny of it, provided they don't sleep, or Benton or little Isaac Hill will spin their yarns but once in a week. No man who has not tried it can imagine what dreadful hard work it is to listen. Splitting gum logs in the dog days is child's play to it. I've tried both, and give the preference to the gum logs.

Well, as I said, I made straight for the tavern, and as I drew nigh, I saw a considerable crowd assembled before the door. So, thought I, they have heard that Colonel Crockett intended to pay a visit to their settlement, and they have already got together to receive him in due form. I confess I felt a little elated at the idea, and commenced ransacking the lumber room of my brain, to find some one of my speeches that I might furbish up for the occasion; and then I shouldered my Betsey, straightened myself, and walked up to the door, charged to the muzzle and ready to let fly.

But, strange as it may seem, no one took any more notice of me, than if I had been Martin Van Buren, or Dick Johnson, the celebrated wool grower. This took me somewhat aback, and I inquired what was the meaning of the gathering; and I learnt that a traveling showman had just arrived, and was about to exhibit for the first time the wonderful feats of Harlequin, and Punch, and Judy, to the impatient natives. It was drawing towards nightfall, and expectation was on tip-toe: the children were clinging to their mothers' aprons, with their chubby faces dimpled with delight, and asking, "What is it like? When will it begin?" and similar questions, while the women, as all good wives are in duty bound to do, appealed to their husbands for information; but the call for information was responded to in this instance, as is sometimes the case in Congress; their husbands understood the mater about as well as "the government" did the post-office accounts.

The showman at length made his appearance, with a countenance as wo-begone as that of "the government" when he found his batch of dirty nominations rejected by the Senate, and mentioned the impossibility that any performance should take place that evening, as the lame fiddler had overcharged his head, and having but one leg at best, it did not require much to destroy his equilibrium. And, as all the world knows, a puppet show without a fiddle is like roast pork and no apple sauce. This piece of intelligence was received with a general murmur of dissatisfaction; and such was the indignation of his majesty, the sovereign people, at being thwarted in his rational amusements, that according to the established custom in such cases made and provided, there were some symptoms of a disposition to kick up a row, break the show, and finish the amusements of the day by putting Lynch's law in practice upon the poor showman. There is nothing like upholding the dignity of the people, and so Lieut. Randolph thought, when with his cowardly and sacrilegious hand he dared to profane the anointed nose of "the government," and bring the whole nation into contempt. If I had been present, may disgrace follow my career in Texas, if I wouldn't have become a whole hog Jackson man upon the spot, for the time being, for the nose of "the government" should be held more sacred than any other member, that it may be kept in good order to smell out all the corruption that is going forward—not a very pleasant office, and by no means a sinecure.

The indignant people, as I have already said, were

about to exercise their reserved rights upon the unlucky
showman, and Punch and Judy too, when, as good fortune
would have it, an old gentleman drove up to the tavern
door in a sulky, with a box of books and pamphlets of his
own composition— (for he was an author, like myself) —
thus being able to vouch for the moral tendency of every
page he disposed of. Very few booksellers can do the same,
I take it. His linen and flannels, which he had washed in
the brooks by the wayside, were hanging over the back of
the crazy vehicle to dry, while his own snuffy countenance
had long bid defiance to sun, wind, and water, to bleach it.

His jaded beast stopped instinctively upon seeing a
crowd, while the old man remained seated for some moments before he could recall his thoughts from the world
of imagination, where they were gleaning for the benefit
of mankind. He looked, it must be confessed, more like a
lunatic than a moral lecturer; but being conscious of his
own rectitude, he could not conceive how his outward
Adam could make him ridiculous in the eyes of another;
but a fair outside is everything to the world. The tulip
flower is highly prized, although indebted for its beauty
to the corruption engendered at the root; and so it is
with man.

We occasionally meet with one possessing sufficient
philosophy to look upon life as a pilgrimage, and not as
a mere round of pleasure:—who, treating this world as
a place of probation, is ready to encounter suffering,
and not expecting the sunshine of prosperity, escapes
being overclouded by disappointment. Such is the character of the old preacher, whose ridiculous appearance in
the eyes of the thoughtless and ignorant is only exceeded
by the respect and veneration of those who are capable of

estimating his real worth. I learnt that he was educated for the church, but not being able to obtain a living, he looked upon the whole earth as his altar, and all mankind as his flock. He was penniless, and therefore had no predilection for this or that section of the globe, for wherever he might be, his journey of probation still continued, and in every spot he found that human nature was the same. His life was literally that of a pilgrim. He was an isolated being, though his heart overflowed with the milk of human kindness; for being indiscriminate in his affection, very few valued it. He who commences the world with a general love for mankind, and suffers his feelings to dictate to his reason, runs a great hazard of reaping a plentiful harvest of ingratitude, and of closing a tedious existence in misanthropy. But it was not so with the aged preacher.

Being unable to earn his bread as an itinerant lecturer, —for in those cases it is mostly poor preach and worse pay —he turned author and wrote histories which contained but little information, and sermons which, like many others, had nothing to boast of, beyond being strictly orthodox. He succeeded in obtaining a sulky, and a horse to drag it, by a plea of mercy, which deprived the hounds of their food, and with these he traveled over the western states, to dispose of the product of his brain; and when poverty was deprived of the benefit of his labor, in the benevolence of his heart he would deliver a moral lecture, which had the usual weight of homilies on this subject. A lecture is the cheapest thing that a man can bestow in charity, and many of our universal philanthropists have made the discovery.

The landlord now made his appearance, and gave a hearty welcome to the reverend traveler, and shaking

him by the hand, added, that he never came more opportunely in all his life.

"Opportunely!" exclaimed the philosopher.

"Yes," rejoined the other; "you have a heart and head
that labor for the benefit of us poor mortals."

"Oh! true, an excellent market for my pamphlets,"
replied the other, at the same time beginning to open the
trunk that lay before him.

"You misunderstand me," added the landlord. "A
poor showman with a sick wife and five children has
arrived from New Orleans ——"

"I will sell my pamphlets to relieve their wants, and
endeavor to teach them resignation."

"He exhibits to-night in my large room: you know
the room, sir—I let him have it gratis."

"You are an honest fellow. I will witness his show,
and add my mite to his assistance."

"But," replied the innkeeper, "the lame fiddler is
fond of the bottle, and is now snoring in the hayloft."

"Degrading vice!" exclaimed the old man, and taking
"God's Revenge against Drunkenness" from the trunk,
and standing erect in the sulky, he commenced reading to
his astonished audience. The innkeeper interrupted
him by observing that the homily would not fill the
empty purse of the poor showman, and unless a fiddler
could be obtained, he must depend on charity, or go
supperless to bed. And moreover, the people, irritated at
their disappointment, had threatened to tear the show
to pieces.

"But what's to be done?" demanded the parson.

"Your reverence shakes an excellent bow," added the
innkeeper, in an insinuating tone.

"I!" exclaimed the parson; "I fiddle for a puppet show!"

"Not for the puppet show, but for the sick wife and five hungry children."

A tear started into the eyes of the old man, as he added in an under tone, "If I could be concealed from the audience——"

"Nothing easier," cried the other; "we will place you behind the scenes, and no one will ever dream that you fiddled at a puppet show."

The matter being thus settled, they entered the house, and shortly afterward the sound of a fiddle squeaking like a giggling girl, tickled into ecstasies, restored mirth and good humor to the disappointed assemblage, who rushed in, helter-skelter, to enjoy the exhibition.

All being seated, and silence restored, they waited in breathless expectation for the rising of the curtain. At length Harlequin made his appearance, and performed astonishing feats of activity on the slack rope; turning somersets backward and forward, first on this side, and then on that, with as much ease as if he had been a politician all his life,—the parson sawing vigorously on his fiddle all the time. Punch followed, and set the audience in a roar with his antic tricks and jests; but when Judy entered with her broomstick the burst of applause was as great as ever I heard bestowed upon one of Benton's slang-whang speeches in Congress,* and I rather think quite as well merited.

* Thomas Hart Benton, United States Senator from Missouri, was one of the most vigorous oratorical supporters of Jackson of the period, and his anti-Bank speeches won wide popular endorsement. "Benton's mint drops" which Davy mentions frequently were gold coins which returned to circulation after Benton had changed the ratio between gold and silver from 15 to 1 to 16 to 1.

As the plot thickened, the music of the parson became more animated; but unluckily in the warmth of his zeal to do justice to his station, his elbow touched the side scene, which fell to the floor, and exposed him, working away in all the ecstasies of little Isaac Hill, while reading one of his long orations about things in general to empty benches. No ways disconcerted by the accident, the parson seized upon it as a fine opportunity of conveying a lesson to those around him, at the same time that he might benefit a fellow mortal. He immediately mounted the chair upon which he was seated, and addressed the audience to the following effect:

"Many of you have come here for amusement, and others no doubt to assist the poor man, who is thus struggling to obtain a subsistence for his sick wife and children. Lo! the moral of a puppet show! But is this all? Has he not rendered unto you your money's worth? This is not charity. If you are charitably inclined, here is an object fully deserving of it."

He preached upon this text for full half an hour, and concluded with taking his hat to collect assistance from his hearers for the friendless showman and his family.

The next morning, when his sulky was brought to the door, the showman and his wife came out to thank their benefactor. The old man placed his trunk of pamphlets before him, and proceeded on his pilgrimage, the little children following him through the village with bursts of gratitude.

CHAPTER TWENTY-FIVE

Betsey Wins Me a Shooting Match

The public mind having been quieted by the exhibition of the puppet show, and allowed to return to its usual channel, it was not long before the good people of Little Rock began to inquire what distinguished stranger had come among them; and learning that it was neither more nor less than the identical Colonel Crockett, the champion of the fugitive deposites, than straight they went ahead at getting up another tempest in a teapot; and I wish I may be shot, if I wasn't looked upon as almost as great a sight as Punch and Judy.

Nothing would answer, but I must accept of an invitation to a public dinner. Now as public dinners have become so common, that it is enough to take away the appetite of any man, who has a proper sense of his own importance, to sit down and play his part in the humbug business, I had made up my mind to write a letter declin-

ing the honour, expressing my regret, and winding up
with a flourish of trumpets about the patriotism of the
citizens of Little Rock, and all that sort of thing; when
the landlord came in, and says he, "Colonel, just oblige
me by stepping into the back yard a moment."

I followed the landlord in silence, twisting and turning
over in my brain, all the while, what I should say in my
letter to the patriotic citizens of Little Rock, who were
bent on eating a dinner for the good of their country;
when he conducted me to a shed in the yard, where I
beheld, hanging up, a fine fat cub bear, several haunches
of venison, a wild turkey as big as a young ostrich, and
small game too tedious to mention. "Well, Colonel, what
do you think of my larder?" says he. "Fine!" says I. "Let us
liquor." We walked back to the bar. I took a horn, and
without loss of time I wrote to the committee, that I
accepted of the invitation to a public dinner with pleasure,
—that I would be always found ready to serve my country,
either by eating or fasting; and that the honor the
patriotic citizens of Little Rock had conferred upon me,
rendered it the proudest moment of my eventful life. The
chairman of the committee was standing by while I wrote
the letter, which I handed to him; and so this important
business was soon settled.

As there was considerable time to be killed, or got rid
of in some way, before the dinner could be cooked, it
was proposed that we should go beyond the village, and
shoot at a mark, for they had heard I was a first-rate
shot, and they wanted to see for themselves, whether
fame had not blown her trumpet a little too strong in
my favor: for since she had represented "the Government" as being a first-rate statesman, and Colonel Benton

as a first rate orator, they could not receive such reports without proper allowance, as Congress thought of the Post Office report.

Well, I shouldered my Betsey, and she is just about as beautiful a piece as ever came out of Philadelphia, and I went out to the shooting ground, followed by all the leading men in Little Rock, and that was a clear majority of the town, for it is remarkable, that there are always more leading men in small villages than there are followers.

I was in prime order. My eye was as keen as a lizard, and my nerves were as steady and unshaken as the political course of Henry Clay; so at it we went, the distance, one hundred yards. The principal marksmen, and such as had never been beat, led the way, and there was some pretty fair shooting, I tell you. At length it came to my turn. I squared myself, raised my beautiful Betsey to my shoulder, took deliberate aim, and smack I sent the bullet right into the centre of the bull's eye. "There's no mistake in Betsey," said I, in a sort of careless way, as they were all looking at the target, sort of amazed, and not at all over pleased.

"That's a chance shot, Colonel," said one who had the reputation of being the best marksman in those parts.

"Not as much chance as there was," said I, "when Dick Johnson took his darkie for better for worse. I can do it five times out of six any day in the week." This I said in as confident a tone as "the Government" did, when he protested that he forgave Colonel Benton for shooting him, and he was now the best friend he had in the world. I knew it was not altogether as correct as it might be, but when a man sets about going the big figure, halfway measures won't answer no how; and "the greatest and the best" had set me the example, that swaggering will answer a good purpose at times.

They now proposed that we should have a second trial; but knowing that I had nothing to gain and every thing to lose, I was for backing out and fighting shy; but there was no let-off, for the cock of the village, though whipped, determined not to stay whipped; so to it again we went. They were now put upon their mettle, and they fired much better than the first time; and it was what might be called pretty sharp shooting. When it came to my turn, I squared myself, and turning to the prime shot, I gave him a knowing nod, by way of show-ing my confidence; and says I, "Look out for the bull's eye, stranger." I blazed away, and I wish I may be shot if I didn't miss the target. They examined it all over, and could find neither hair nor hide of my bullet, and pro-nounced it a dead miss; when says I, "Stand aside and let me look, and I warrant you I get on the right trail of the critter." They stood aside, and I examined the bull's eye pretty particular, and at length cried out, "Here it is; there is no snakes if it ha'n't followed the very track of the other." They said it was utterly impossible, but I insisted on their searching the hole, and I agreed to be stuck up as a mark myself, if they did not find two bullets there. They searched for my satisfaction, and sure enough it all come out just as I had told them; for I had picked up a bullet that had been fired, and stuck it deep into the hole, without any one perceiving it. They were all perfectly satisfied, that fame had not made too great a flourish of trumpets when speaking of me as a marksman; and they all said they had enough of shooting for that day, and they moved, that we adjourn to the tavern and liquor.

We had scarcely taken drinks round before the landlord announced that dinner was ready, and I was escorted into the dining room by the committee, to the tune of "See the conquering hero comes," played upon a drum, which had been beaten until it got a fit of the sullens, and refused to send forth any sound; and it was accompanied by the wheazing of a fife that was sadly troubled with a spell of the asthma. I was escorted into the dining room, I say, somewhat after the same fashion that "the Government" was escorted into the different cities when he made his northern tour; the only difference was, that I had no sycophants about me, but true hearted hospitable friends, for it was pretty well known that I had, for the present, abandoned all intention of running for the Presidency against the Little Flying Dutchman.

The dinner was first rate. The bear meat, the venison, and wild turkey would have tempted a man who had given over the business of eating altogether; and every thing was cooked to the notch precisely. The enterprising landlord did himself immortal honor on this momentous occasion; and the committee, thinking that he merited public thanks for his patriotic services, handed his name to posterity to look at in the lasting columns of the Little Rock Gazette; and when our children's children behold it, they will think of the pure patriots who sat down in good fellowship to feast on the bear meat and venison; and the enthusiasm the occasion is calculated to awaken will induce them to bless the patriot who, in a cause so glorious, spared no pains in cooking the dinner and serving it in a becoming manner. And this is fame!

The fragments of the meats being cleared off, we went through the customary evolution of drinking thirteen regular toasts, after every one of which our drum with the loose skin grumbled like an old horse with an empty stomach; and our asthmatic fife squeaked, like a stuck pig, a spirit-stirring tune, which we put off christening until we should come to prepare our proceedings for posterity. The fife appeared to have but one tune in it; possibly it might have had more, but the poor fifer, with all his puffing and blowing, his too-too-tooing, and shaking his head and elbow, could not, for the body and soul of him, get more than one out of it. If the fife had had an extra tune to its name, sartin it wouldn't have been quite so hide bound on such an occasion, but have let us have it, good, bad, or indifferent. We warn't particular by no means.

Having gone through with the regular toasts, the president of the day drank, "Our distinguished guest, Col. Crockett," which called forth a prodigious clattering all around the table, and I soon saw that nothing would do, but I must get up and make them a speech. I had no sooner elongated my outward Adam, than they at it again, with renewed vigor, which made me sort of feel that I was still somebody, though no longer a member of Congress.

In my speech I went over the whole history of the present administration; took a long shot at the flying deposites, and gave an outline, a sort of charcoal sketch, of the political life of "the Government's" heir-presumptive. I also let them know how I had been rascalled out of my election, because I refused to bow down to the idol; and as I saw a number of young politicians around the table, I told them, that I would lay down a few rules for their guidance, which, if properly attended to, could not fail to lead them on the highway to distinction and public honor. I told them, that I was an old hand at the business, and as I was about to retire for a time, I would give them a little instruction gratis, for I was up to all the tricks of the trade, though I had practiced but few.

"Attend all public meetings," says I, "and get some friends to move that you take the chair; if you fail in this attempt, make a push to be appointed secretary; the proceedings of course will be published, and your name is introduced to the public. But should you fail in both undertakings, get two or three acquaintances, over a bottle of whiskey, to pass some resolutions, no matter on what subject; publish them even if you pay the printer—it will answer the purpose of breaking the ice, which is the main point in these matters. Intrigue until you are elected an officer of the militia; this is the second step towards promotion, and can be accomplished with ease, as I know an instance of an election being advertised, and no one attending, the innkeeper at whose house it was to be held, having a military turn, elected himself colonel of his regiment." Says I, "You may not accomplish your ends with as little difficulty, but do not be discouraged—Rome wasn't built in a day.

"If your ambition or circumstances compel you to serve your country, and earn three dollars a day, by becoming a member of the legislature, you must first publicly avow that the constitution of the state is a shackle upon free and liberal legislation; and is, therefore, of as little use in the present enlightened age, as an old almanac of the year in which the instrument was framed. There is policy in this measure, for by making the constitution a mere dead letter, your headlong proceedings will be attributed to a bold and unshackled mind; whereas, it might otherwise be thought they arose from sheer mulish ignorance. 'The Government' has set the example in his attack upon the constitution of the United States, and who should fear to follow where 'the Government' leads?

"When the day of election approaches, visit your constituents far and wide. Treat liberally, and drink freely, in order to rise in their estimation, though you fall in your own. True, you may be called a drunken dog by some of the clean shirt and silk stocking gentry, but the real rough necks will style you a jovial fellow, their votes are certain, and frequently count double. Do all you can to appear to advantage in the eyes of the women. That's easily done—you have but to kiss and slabber their children, wipe their noses, and pat them on the head; this cannot fail to please their mothers, and you may rely on your business being done in that quarter.

"Promise all that is asked," said I, "and more if you can think of any thing. Offer to build a bridge or a church, to divide a county, create a batch of new offices, make a turnpike, or any thing they like. Promises cost nothing, therefore deny nobody who has a vote or sufficient influence to obtain one.

"Get up on all occasions, and sometimes on no occasion at all, and make long-winded speeches, though composed of nothing else than wind—talk of your devotion to your country, your modesty and disinterestedness, or on any such fanciful subject. Rail against taxes of all kinds, office-holders, and bad harvest weather; and wind up with a flourish about the heroes who fought and bled for our liberties in the times that tried men's souls. To be sure you run the risk of being considered a bladder of wind, or an empty barrel, but never mind that, you will find enough of the same fraternity to keep you in countenance.

"If any charity be going forward, be at the top of it, provided it is to be advertised publicly; if not, it isn't worth your while. None but a fool would place his candle under a bushel on such an occasion.

"These few directions," said I, "if properly attended to, will do your business; and when once elected, why a fig for the dirty children, the promises, the bridges, the churches, the taxes, the offices, and the subscriptions, for it is absolutely necessary to forget all these before you can become a thorough-going politician, and a patriot of the first water."

My speech was received with three times three, and all that; and we continued speechifying and drinking until nightfall, when it was put to vote, that we would have the puppet show over again, which was carried *nem. con.* The showman set his wires to work, just as "the Government" does the machinery in his big puppet show; and we spent a delightful and rational evening. We raised a subscription for the poor showman; and I went to bed, pleased and gratified with the hospitality and kindness of the citizens of Little Rock. There are some first-rate men there, of the real half-horse half-alligator breed, with a sprinkling of the steamboat, and such as grow nowhere on the face of the universal earth, but just about the back bone of North America.

CHAPTER TWENTY-SIX

I Meet a Curious Innkeeper

The day after our public dinner I determined to leave
my hospitable friends at Little Rock, and cross Arkansas
to Fulton on the Red River, a distance of about one hundred and twenty miles. They wanted me to stay longer;
and the gentleman who had the reputation of being the
best marksman in those parts was most particularly anxious that we should have another trial of skill; but says
I to myself "Crockett, you've had just about glory enough
for one day, so take my advice and leave well enough
alone." I declined shooting, for there was nothing at all to
be gained by it, and I might possibly lose some little of
the reputation I had acquired. I have always found that
it is a very important thing for a man who is fairly going
ahead, to know exactly how far to go, and when to stop.
Had "the Government" stopped before he meddled with

the constitution, the deposites, and "taking the responsibility," he would have retired from office with almost as
much credit as he entered upon it, which is as much as
any public man can reasonably expect. But the General is
a whole team, and when fairly started, will be going ahead;
and one might as well attempt to twist a streak of lightning into a true lover's knot as to stop him.

Finding that I was bent on going, for I became impatient to get into Texas, my kind friends at Little Rock
procured me a good horse to carry me across to Red River.
There are no bounds to the good feeling of the pioneers
of the west; they consider nothing a trouble that will confer a favor upon a stranger that they chance to take a fancy
to: true, we are something like chesnut burs on the outside, rather prickly if touched roughly, but there's good
fruit within.

My horse was brought to the door of the tavern, around
which many of the villagers was assembled. The drum and
fife were playing what was intended for a lively tune, but
the skin of the drum still hung as loose as the hide of a fat
man far gone in a consumption; and the fife had not yet
recovered from the asthma. The music sounded something
like a fellow singing, "Away with melancholy," on the way
to the gallows. I took my leave of the landlord, shook
hands with the showman, who had done more than an
average business, kissed his wife, who had recovered, and
bidding farewell to all my kind hearted friends, I mounted
my horse and left the village, accompanied by four or five
gentlemen. The drum and fife now appeared to exert
themselves, and made more noise than usual, while the
crowd sent forth three cheers to encourage me on my way.

I tried to raise some recruits for Texas* among my companions, but they said they had their own affairs to attend to, which would keep them at home for the present, but no doubt they would come over and see us as soon as the disturbances should be settled. They looked upon Texas as being part of the United States, though the Mexicans did claim it; and they had no doubt the time was not very distant when it would be received into the glorious Union.

My companions did not intend seeing me farther on my way than the Washita river, near fifty miles. Conversation was pretty brisk, for we talked about the affairs of the nation and Texas; subjects that are by no means to be exhausted, if one may judge by the long speeches made in Congress, where they talk year in and year out, and it would seem that as much still remains to be said as ever. As we drew nigh to the Washita, the silence was broken alone by our own talk and the clattering of our horses' hoofs, and we imagined ourselves pretty much the only travelers, when we were suddenly somewhat startled by the sound of music. We checked our horses, and listened, and the music continued. "What can all that mean?" says I. "Blast my old shoes if I know, Colonel," says one of the party. We listened again, and we now heard, "Hail Columbia, happy land!" played in first rate style. "That's fine," says I. "Fine as silk, Colonel, and a leetle finer," says the other; "but hark, the tune's changed." We took another spell of listening, and

* Between 1821 and 1835, 25,000 Texans, mostly from the United States, had migrated to the province under the stimulus of a liberal Mexican land policy. In 1829 this liberal policy was changed, and conflict broke out between the Texans and the Mexican government. An open revolt of the Texans against the Mexican government began in 1835.

now the musician struck up in a brisk and lively manner, "Over the water to Charley." "That's mighty mysterious," says one; "Can't cipher it out no how," says another; "A notch beyant my measure," says a third. "Then let us go ahead," says I, and off we dashed at a pretty rapid gait, I tell you—by no means slow.

As we approached the river, we saw to the right of the road a new clearing on a hill, where several men were at work, and they running down the hill like wild Indians, or rather, like the office-holders in pursuit of the deposites. There appeared to be no time to be lost, so they ran, and we cut ahead for the crossing. The music continued in all this time stronger and stronger, and the very notes appeared to speak distinctly, "Over the water to Charley."

When we reached the crossing, we were struck all of a heap, at beholding a man seated in a sulky in the middle of the river, and playing for life on a fiddle. The horse was up to his middle in the water, and it seemed as if the flimsy vehicle was ready to be swept away by the current. Still the fiddler fiddled on composedly, as if his life had been insured, and he was nothing more than a passenger. We thought he was mad, and shouted to him. He heard us and stopped his music. "You have missed the crossing," shouted one of the men from the clearing. "I know I have," returned the fiddler. "If you go ten feet farther you will be drowned." "I know I shall," returned the fiddler. "Turn back," said the man. "I can't," said the other. "Then how the devil will you get out?" "I'm sure I don't know: come you and help me."

The men from the clearing, who understood the river, took our horses and rode up to the sulky, and after some difficulty succeeded in bringing the traveler safe to shore, when we recognised the worthy parson who had fiddled for us at the puppet show at Little Rock. They told him that he had had a narrow escape, and he replied that he had found that out an hour ago. He said he had been fiddling to the fishes for a full hour, and had exhausted all the tunes that he could play without notes. We then asked him what could have induced him to think of fiddling at a time of such peril; and he replied, that he had remarked in his progress through life, that there was nothing in univarsal natur so well calculated to draw people together as the sound of a fiddle; and he knew that he might bawl until he was hoarse for assistance, and no one would stir a peg; but they would no sooner hear the scraping of his catgut, than they would quit all other business, and come to the spot in flocks. We laughed heartily at the knowledge the parson showed of human natur. And he was right.

Having fixed up the old gentleman's sulky right and tight, and after rubbing down his poor jaded animal, the company insisted on having a dance before we separated. We all had our flasks of whiskey; we took a drink all round, and though the parson said he had about enough fiddling for one day, he struck up with great good humor; at it we went and danced straight fours for an hour and better. We all enjoyed ourselves very much, but came to the conclusion that dancing wasn't altogether the thing without a few petticoats to give it variety.

The dance being over, our new friends pointed out the right fording, and assisted the parson across the river. We took another drink all around, and after shaking each other cordially by the hand, we separated, wishing

each other all the good fortune that the rugged lot that
has been assigned us will afford. My friends retraced
the road to Little Rock, and I pursued my journey; and
as I thought of their disinterested kindness to an entire
stranger, I felt that the world is not quite as heartless
and selfish as some grumblers would have us think.

The Arkansas is a pretty fine territory, being about
five hundred and fifty miles in length from east to west,
with a mean width of near two hundred, extending over
an area of about one hundred thousand square miles.
The face of the country from its great extent is very
much diversified. It is pretty well watered, being inter-
sected by the Arkansas river, and branches of the Red,
Washita, and White rivers. The Maserne mountains,
which rise in Missouri, traverse Arkansas, and extend
into Texas. That part of the Territory to the southeast
of the Masernes is for the most part low, and in many
places liable to be overflowed annually. To the north-
west of the mountains, the country presents generally
an open expanse of prairie without wood, except near the
borders of the streams. The seasons of the year partake of
those extremes of heat and cold, which might be expected
in so great an extent, and in a country which affords so
much difference of level. The summers are as remarkable
as the winters for extreme of temperature. The soil
exhibits every variety, from the most productive to the
most sterile. The forest trees are numerous and large;
such as oak, hickory, sycamore, cotton-wood, locust, and
pine. The cultivated fruit trees are the apple, pear, peach,
plum, nectarine, cherry, and quince; and the various
kinds of grains, such as wheat, rye, oats, barley, and Indian
corn, succeed amazing well. Cotton, Indian corn, flour,

peltry, salted provisions, and lumber, are the staples of this
territory. Arkansas was among the most ancient settlements of the French in Louisiana. That nation had a hunting and trading post on the Arkansas river, as early as the
beginning of the eighteenth century. Arkansas, I rather
reckon, will be admitted as a state into the Union during
the next session of Congress; and if the citizens of Little
Rock are a fair sample of her children, she cannot fail to
go ahead.

I kept in company with the parson until we arrived at
Greenville, and I do say, he was just about as pleasant
an old gentleman to travel with, as any man who wasn't
too darned particular, could ask for. We talked about
politics, religion, and nature, farming, and bear hunting,
and the many blessings that an all bountiful Providence
has bestowed upon our happy country. He continued to
talk upon this subject, traveling over the whole ground
as it were, until his imagination glowed, and his soul became full to overflowing; and he checked his horse, and
I stopped mine also, and a stream of eloquence burst forth
from his aged lips, such as I have seldom listened to: it
came from the overflowing fountain of a pure and grateful
heart. We were alone in the wilderness, but as he proceeded, it seemed to me as if the tall trees bent their tops
to listen;—that the mountain stream laughed out joyfully as it bounded on like some living thing; that the
fading flowers of autumn smiled, and sent forth fresher
fragrance, as if conscious that they would revive in spring,
and even the sterile rocks seemed to be endued with some
mysterious influence. We were alone in the wilderness,
but all things told me that God was there. The thought
renewed my strength and courage. I had left my country,

felt somewhat like an outcast, believed that I had been neglected and lost sight of: but I was now conscious that there was still one watchful Eye over me; no matter whether I dwelt in the populous cities, or threaded the pathless forest alone; no matter whether I stood in the high places among men, or made my solitary lair in the untrodden wild, that Eye was still upon me. My very soul leaped joyfully at the thought; I never felt so grateful in all my life; I never loved my God so sincerely in all my life. I felt that I still had a friend.

When the old man finished, I found that my eyes were wet with tears. I approached and pressed his hand, and thanked him, and says I, "Now let us take a drink." I set him the example, and he followed it, and in a style too that satisfied me, that if he had ever belonged to the Temperance society, he had either renounced membership, or obtained a dispensation. Having liquored, we proceeded on our journey, keeping a sharp look-out for mill-seats and plantations as we rode along.

I left the worthy old man at Greenville, and sorry enough I was to part with him, for he talked a great deal, and he seemed to know a little about everything. He knew all about the history of the country; was well acquainted with all the leading men: knew where all the good lands lay in most of the western states, as well as the cutest clerk in the Land Office; and had traced most of the rivers to their sources. He was very cheerful and happy, though to all appearances very poor. I thought that he would make a first-rate agent for taking up lands, and mentioned it to him; he smiled, and pointing above, said, "My wealth lies not in this world."

I mounted my horse and pushed forward on my road

to Fulton. When I reached Washington, a village a few miles from the Red river, I rode up to the Black Bear tavern, when the following conversation took place between me and the landlord, which is a pretty fair sample of the curiosity of some folks:—

"Good morning, mister—I don't exactly recollect your name now," said the landlord as I alighted.

"It's of no consequence," said I.

"I'm pretty sure I've seen you somewhere."

"Very likely you may, I've been there frequently."

"I was sure 'twas so; but strange I should forget your name," says he.

"It is indeed somewhat strange that you should forget what you never knew," says I.

"It is unaccountable strange. It's what I'm not often in the habit of, I assure you. I have, for the most part, a remarkably detentive memory. In the power of people that pass along this way, I've scarce ever made, as the doctors say, a *slapsus slinkum* of this kind afore."

"Eh heh!" I shouted, while the critter continued.

"Traveling to the western country, I presume, mister?"

"Presume anything you please, sir," said I; "but don't trouble me with your presumptions."

"O Lord, no, sir—I won't do that, I've no ideer of that—not the least ideer in the world," says he; "I suppose you've been to the westward afore now?"

"Well, suppose I have?"

"Why, on that supposition, I was going to say you must be pretty well—that is to say, you must know something about the place."

"Eh heh!" I ejaculated, looking sort of mazed full in his face. The tarnal critter still went ahead.

"I take it you're a married man, mister?"

"Take it as you will, that is no affair of mine," says I.

"Well, after all, a married life is the most happiest way of living; don't you think so, mister?"

"Very possible," says I.

"I conclude you have a family of children, sir?"

"I don't know what reason you have to conclude so."

"Oh, no reason in the world, mister, not the least," says he; "but I thought I might just take the liberty to make the presumption, you know; that's all, sir. I take it, mister, you're a man about my age?"

"Eh heh!"

"How old do you call yourself, if I may be so bold?"

"You're bold enough, the devil knows," says I; and as I spoke rather sharp, the varment seemed rather staggered, but he soon recovered himself, and came up to the chalk again.

"No offense I hope—I—I—I—wouldn't be thought uncivil, by any means; I always calculate to treat everybody with civility."

"You have a very strange way of showing it."

"True, as you say, I ginerally take my own way in these ere matters. Do you practice law, mister, or farming, or mechanicals?"

"Perhaps so," says I.

"Ah, I judge so; I was pretty certain it must be the case. Well, it's as good business as any there is followed now-a-days."

"Eh heh!" I shouted, and my lower jaw fell in amazement at his perseverance.

"I take it you've money at interest, mister?" continued

the varment, without allowing himself time to take breath.

"Would it be of any particular interest to you to find out?" says I.

"Oh, not at all, not the least in the world, sir; I'm not at all inquisitive about other people's matters; I minds my own business—that's my way."

"And a very odd way you have of doing it, too."

"I've been thinking what persuasion you're of— whether you're a Unitarian or Baptist, or whether you belong to the Methodisses."

"Well, what's the conclusion?"

"Why, I have concluded that I'm pretty near right in my conjectures. Well, after all, I'm inclined to think they're the nearest right of any persuasion—though some folks think differently."

"Eh heh!" I shouted again.

"As to pollyticks, I take it, you—that is to say, I suppose you——"

"Very likely."

"Ah! I could have sworn it was so from the moment I saw you. I have a knack at finding out a man's sentiments. I dare say, mister, you're a justice in your own country?"

"And if I may return the compliment, I should say you're a just ass everywhere." By this time I began to get weary of his impertinence, and led my horse to the trough to water, but the darned critter followed me up.

"Why, yes," said he, "I'm in the commission of the peace, to be sure—and an officer in the militia—though, between you and I, I wouldn't wish to boast of it."

My horse having finished drinking, I put one foot in

the stirrup, and was preparing to mount. "Any more inquiries to make?" said I.

"Why, no, nothing to speak on," said he. "When do you return, mister?"

"About the time I come back," said I; and leaping into the saddle, galloped off. The pestiferous varment bawled after me, at the top of his voice,—

"Well, I shall look for ye, then. I hope you won't fail to call."

Now, who in all natur do you reckon the critter was, who afforded so fine a sample of the impertinent curiosity that some people have to pry into other people's affairs?

I knew him well enough at first sight, though he seemed to have forgotten me. It was no other than Job Snelling, the manufacturer of cayenne pepper out of mahogany sawdust, and upon whom I played the trick with the coon skin. I pursued my journey to Fulton, and laughed heartily to think what a swither I had left poor Job in, at not gratifying his curiosity; for I knew he was one of those fellows who would peep down your throat just to ascertain what you had eaten for dinner.

When I arrived at Fulton, I inquired for a gentleman to whom my friends at Little Rock had given me a letter of introduction. I was received in the most hospitable manner; and as the steamboat did not start for Natchitoches until the next day, I spent the afternoon in seeing all that was to be seen. I left the horse with the gentleman, who promised to have him safely returned to the owner; and I took the steamboat, and started on my way down the Red river, right well pleased with my reception at Fulton.

CHAPTER TWENTY-SEVEN

I Take On a Red River Gambler

There was a considerable number of passengers on board the boat, and our assortment was somewhat like the Yankee merchant's cargo of notions, pretty particularly miscellaneous, I tell you. I moved through the crowd from stem to stern, to see if I could discover any face that was not altogether strange to me; but after a general survey, I concluded that I had never seen one of them before. There were merchants, and emigrants, and gamblers, but none who seemed to have embarked in the particular business that for the time being occupied my mind—I could find none who were going to Texas. All seemed to have their hands full enough of their own affairs, without meddling with the cause of freedom. The greater share of glory will be mine, thought I, so go ahead, Crockett.

I saw a small cluster of passengers at one end of the boat, and hearing an occasional burst of laughter, thinks

I, there's some sport started in that quarter, and having nothing better to do, I'll go in for my share of it. Accordingly I drew nigh to the cluster, and seated on the chest was a tall, lank, sea-sarpent looking blackleg, who had crawled over from Natchez under the hill, and was amusing the passengers with his skill at thimblerig; at the same time he was picking up their shillings just about as expeditiously as a hungry gobbler would a pint of corn. He was doing what might be called an average business in a small way, and lost no time in gathering up the fragments.

I watched the whole process for some time, and found that he had adopted the example set by the old tempter himself, to get the weathergage of us poor weak mortals. He made it a point to let his victims win always the first stake, that they might be tempted to go ahead; and then, when they least suspected it, he would come down upon them like a hurricane in a cornfield, sweeping all before it.

I stood looking on, seeing him pick up the chicken feed from the green horns, and thought if men are such darned fools as to be cheated out of their hard earnings by a fellow who has just brains enough to pass a pea from one thimble to another, with such sleight of hand, that you could not tell under which he had deposited it, it is not astonishing that the magician of Kinderhook should play thimblerig upon the big figure, and attempt to cheat the whole nation. I thought that "the Government" was playing the same game with the deposites, and with such address, too, that before long it will be a hard matter to find them under any of the thimbles where it is supposed they have been originally placed.

The thimble conjurer saw me looking on, and eyeing

me as if he thought I would be a good subject, said carelessly, "Come, stranger, won't you take a chance?" the
whole time passing the pea from one thimble to the other,
by way of throwing out a bait for the gudgeons to bite
at. "I never gamble, stranger," says I, "principled against
it; think it a slippery way of getting through the world at
best." "Them are my sentiments to a notch," says he;
"but this is not gambling by no means. A little innocent
pastime, nothing more. Better take a hack by way of trying
your luck at guessing." All this time he continued working
with his thimbles; first putting the pea under one, which
was plain to be seen, and then uncovering it, would show
that the pea was there; he would then put it under the
second thimble, and do the same, and then under the
third; all of which he did to show how easy it would be to
guess where the pea was deposited, if one would only keep
a sharp look-out.

"Come, stranger," says he to me again, "you had better
take a chance. Stake a trifle, I don't care how small, just
for the fun of the thing."

"I am principled against betting money," says I, "but I
don't mind going in for drinks for the present company,
for I'm as dry as one of little Isaac Hill's regular set of
speeches."

"I admire your principles," says he, "and to show
that I play with these here thimbles just for the sake of
pastime, I will take that bet, though I am a whole hog
temperance man. Just say when, stranger."

He continued all the time slipping the pea from one
thimble to another; my eye was as keen as a lizard's,
and when he stopped, I cried out, "Now; the pea is under
the middle thimble." He was going to raise it to show

that it wasn't there, when I interfered, and said, "Stop, if you please," and raised it myself, and sure enough the pea was there; but it mought have been otherwise if he had had the uncovering of it.

"Sure enough you've won the bet," says he. "You've a sharp eye, but I don't care if I give you another chance. Let us go fifty cents this bout; I'm sure you'll win."

"Then you're a darned fool to bet, stranger," says I; "and since that is the case, it would be little better than picking your pocket to bet with you; so I'll let it alone."

"I don't mind running the risk," said he.

"But I do," says I; "and since I always let well enough alone, and I have had just about glory enough for one day, let us all go to the bar and liquor."

This called forth a loud laugh at the thimble conjurer's expense; and he tried hard to induce me to take just one chance more, but he mought just as well have sung psalms to a dead horse, for my mind was made up; and I told him, that I looked upon gambling as about the dirtiest way that a man could adopt to get through this dirty world; and that I would never bet any thing beyond a quart of whisky upon a rifle shot, which I considered a legal bet, and gentlemanly and rational amusement. "But all this cackling," says I, "makes me very thirsty, so let us adjourn to the bar and liquor."

He gathered up his thimbles, and the whole company followed us to the bar, laughing heartily at the conjurer; for, as he had won some of their money, they were sort of delighted to see him beaten with his own cudgel. He tried to laugh too, but his laugh wasn't at all pleasant and rather forced. The barkeeper placed a big-bellied bottle before us; and after mixing our liquor, I was

called on for a toast, by one of the company, a chap just
about as rough hewn as if he had been cut out of a gum
log with a broad-axe, and sent into the market without
even being smoothed off with a jack plane; one of them
chaps who, in their journey through life, are always
ready for a fight or a frolic, and don't care the toss of a
copper which.

"Well, gentlemen," says I, "being called upon for a
toast, and being in a slave-holding state, in order to
avoid giving offence and running the risk of being
lynched, it may be necessary to premise that I am neither
an abolitionist nor a colonizationist, but simply Colonel
Crockett of Tennessee, now bound for Texas." When
they heard my name, they gave three cheers for Colonel
Crockett; and silence being restored, I continued, "Now,
gentlemen, I will offer you a toast, hoping, after what I
have stated, that it will give offence to no one present;
but should I be mistaken, I must imitate the 'old Roman,'
and take the responsibility. I offer, gentlemen, The abolition of slavery: let the work first begin in the two houses
of Congress. There are no slaves in the country more
servile than the party slaves in Congress. The wink or the
nod of their masters is all-sufficient for the accomplish-
ment of the most dirty work."

They drank the toast in a style that satisfied me that
the little Magician might as well go to a pigsty for wool,
as to beat round in that part for voters: they were all
either for Judge White or Old Tippecanoe. The thimble
conjurer having asked the barkeeper how much there
was to pay, was told that there were sixteen smallers,
which amounted to one dollar. He was about to lay down
the blunt, but not in Benton's metallic currency, which I

find has already become as shy as honesty with an office-holder, but he planked down one of Biddle's notes, when I interfered, and told him that the barkeeper had made a mistake.

"How so?" demanded the barkeeper.

"How much do you charge," said I, "when you retail your liquor?"

"A fip a glass."

"Well, then," says I, "as Thimblerig here, who belongs to the temperance society, took it in wholesale, I reckon you can afford to let him have it at half price?"

Now, as they had all noticed that the conjurer went what is called the heavy wet, they laughed outright, and we heard no more about temperance from that quarter. When we returned to the deck, the blackleg set to work with his thimbles again, and bantered me to bet; but I told him that it was against my principle, and as I had already reaped glory enough for one day, I would just let well enough alone for the present. If the "old Roman" had done the same in relation to the deposites and "the monster," we should have escaped more difficulties than all the cunning of the Little Flying Dutchman, and Dick Johnson to boot, will be able to repair. I shouldn't be astonished if the new Vice President's head should get wool gathering before they have half unraveled the knotted and twisted thread of perplexities that the old General has spun,—in which case his charming spouse will no doubt be delighted, for then they will be all in the family way. What a handsome display they will make in the White House! No doubt the first act of Congress will be to repeal the duties on Cologne and Lavender waters, for they will be in great demand about the Palace, particularly in the dog days.

One of the passengers hearing that I was on board of the boat, came up to me and began to talk about the affairs of the nation, and said a good deal in favor of "the Magician," and wished to hear what I had to say against him. He talked loud, which is the way with all politicians educated in the Jackson school; and by his slang-whanging drew a considerable crowd around us. Now, this was the very thing I wanted, as I knew I should not soon have another opportunity of making a political speech; he no sooner asked to hear what I had to say against his candidate, than I let him have it, strong and hot as he could take, I tell you.

"What have I to say against Martin Van Buren? He is an artful, cunning, intriguing, selfish, speculating lawyer, who, by holding lucrative offices for more than half his life, has contrived to amass a princely fortune, and is now seeking the Presidency, principally for sordid gain, and to gratify the most selfish ambition. His fame is unknown to the history of our country, except as a most adroit political manager and successful office hunter. He never took up arms in defence of his country, in her days of darkness and peril. He never contributed a dollar of his surplus wealth to assist her in her hours of greatest want and weakness. Office and money have been the gods of his idolatry; and at their shrines has the ardent worship of his heart been devoted, from the earliest days of his manhood to the present moment. He can lay no claim to pre-eminent services as a statesman; nor has he ever given any evidences of superior talent, except as a political electioneerer and intriguer. As a politician, he is 'all things to all men.'

He is for internal improvement, and against it; for the tariff, and against it; for the bank monopoly, and against it; for the abolition of slavery, and against it; and for anything else, and against anything else, just as he can best promote his popularity, and subserve his own private interest. He is so totally destitute of moral courage, that he never dares to give an opinion upon any important question until he first finds out whether it will be popular, or not. He is celebrated as the 'Little Non-Committal Magician,' because he enlists on no side of any question, until he discovers which is the strongest party; and then always moves in so cautious, sly, and secret a manner, that he can change sides at any time, as easily as a juggler or a magician can play off his arts of leger-de-main.

"Who is Martin Van Buren? He is the candidate of the office-holders, and office expectants, who nominated him for the Presidency at a convention assembled in the city of Baltimore, in May last. The first account we have of his political life is while he was a member of the Senate of New York, at the time when Mr. Clinton was nominated as the federal candidate for the presidency, in opposition to Mr. Madison. The support he then gave Mr. Clinton afforded abundant evidence of that spirit of opposition to the institutions of his country, which was prominently developed in the conduct of those with whom he was united. Shortly after the success of Mr. Madison, and during the prosecution of the war, Rufus King, of New York, (for whom Mr. Van Buren voted,) was elected to the Senate of the United States, avowedly opposed to the administration. Upon his entrance into that body, instead of devoting his energies to maintain the war, he commenced a tirade of abuse against the administration for having attempted relief to the oppressed seamen of our gallant navy, who had been compelled by British violence to arm themselves against their country, their firesides, and their friends. Thus Martin Van Buren countenanced by his vote in the Senate of New York, an opposition to that war, which, a second time, convinced Great Britain that Americans could not be awed into bondage and subjection.

"Subsequent to this time, Mr. Van Buren became himself a member of the United States Senate, and, while there, *opposed* every proposition to improve the west, or to add to her numerical strength.

"He voted *against* the continuance of the national road through Ohio, Indiana, Illinois, and *against* appropriations for its preservation.

"He voted *against* the graduation of the price of the public lands.

"He voted *against* ceding the refuse lands to the States in which they lie.

"He voted *against* making donations of the lands to actual settlers.

"He again voted *against* ceding the refuse lands, not worth twenty-five cents per acre, to the new States for purposes of education and internal improvement.

"He voted *against* the bill providing 'settlement and pre-emption rights' to those who had assisted in opening and improving the western country, and thus deprived many an honest poor man of a home.*

* While in Congress, Davy Crockett was an eloquent champion of the rights of the actual settlers on the western lands. In a moving speech, delivered in the House of Representatives on January 5, 1829, Crockett spoke up for the settlers. Here are some excerpts from the speech as reported by the *Register of Debates, United States Congress.* "The persons in whose behalf he pleaded were the hardy sons of the

"He voted *against* donations of land to Ohio, to prose-
cute the Miami Canal; and, although a member of the
Senate, he was not present when the vote was taken upon
the engrossment of the bill giving land to Indiana for
her Wabash and Erie Canal, and was known to have
opposed it in all its stages.

"He voted *in favor* of erecting toll gates on the national
road; thus demanding a tribute from the west for the
right to pass upon her own highways, constructed out of
her own money—a thing never heard of before.

"After his term of service had expired in the Senate,
he was elected Governor of New York, by a plurality

soil; men who had entered the country when it lay in a state of native
wilderness; men who had broken the cane, and opened in the wilderness a home for their wives and children. . . . They had mingled the
sweat of their brows with the soil they occupied, and by the hand of
hard and persevering toil had earned the little comforts they possessed.
Was it fair for the General Government to take away these humble
cottages from them? . . . Give it to them, and you will bind them to
their Government by an indissoluble tie. Nothing makes a people love
their Government like such acts of parental kindness. Sir, these people,
though poor, are of inestimable value in a free republic. They are
the bone and sinew of the land; they are its strength and its bulwark;
they are its main reliance in the hour of danger, and the first to breast
the onset of an enemy. Will you take away their little all and give it to
the Legislature to speculate upon? Or will you make to each of these
meritorious citizens the donation of his humble piece of land, where
he has at last found a refuge from the pursuit of more successful warrant holders? . . . . Let it be their own. While they bedew it with the
sweat of their faces, let them at least have the consolation of knowing
that they may leave it to their own children, and not have it squandered
on the sons of a stranger. . . .

"Some of them are widows, whose husbands fell while fighting your
battles on the frontiers. None of them are rich, but they are an honest,
industrious, hardy, persevering, kind-hearted people. I know them—
I know their situation. I have shared the hospitality of their cottages,
and been honored by their confidence with a seat in this assembly; and
base and ungrateful, indeed, must I be, when I cease to remember it.
No, sir, I cannot forget it; and if their little all is to be wrested from
them, for the purposes of State speculation; if a swindling machine is
to be set up to strip them of what little the surveyors, and the colleges,
and the warrant holders, have left them, it shall never be said that I
sat by in silence, and refused, however humbly, to advocate their cause."

of votes. He was afterwards sent to England as minister plenipotentiary, and upon his return was elected Vice President of the United States, which office he now holds, and from which the office-holders are seeking to transfer him to the Presidency."

My speech was received with great applause, and the politician, finding that I was better acquainted with his candidate than he was himself, for I wrote his life, shut his fly trap, and turned on his heel without saying a word. He found that he had barked up the wrong tree. I afterward learnt that he was a mail contractor in those parts, and that he also had large dealings in the land office, and therefore thought it necessary to chime in with his penny whistle, in the universal chorus. There's a large band of the same description, but I'm thinking Uncle Sam will some day find out that he has paid too much for the piper.

CHAPTER TWENTY-EIGHT

Thimblerig's Story

After my speech, and setting my face against gambling, poor Thimblerig was obliged to break off conjuring for want of customers, and call it half a day. He came and entered into conversation with me, and I found him a good-natured, intelligent fellow, with a keen eye for the main chance. He belonged to that numerous class, that it is perfectly safe to trust as far as a tailor can sling a bull by the tail—but no farther. He told me that he had been brought up a gentleman; that is to say, he was not instructed in any useful pursuit by which he could obtain a livelihood, so that when he found he had to depend upon himself for the necessaries of life, he began to suspect, that dame nature would have conferred a particular favor if she had consigned him to the care of any one else. She had made a very injudicious choice when she selected him to sustain the dignity of a gentleman.

The first bright idea that occurred to him as a speedy means of bettering his fortune, would be to marry an heiress. Accordingly, he looked about himself pretty sharp, and after glancing from one fair object to another, finally, his hawk's eye rested upon the young and pretty daughter of a wealthy planter. Thimblerig run his brazen face with his tailor for a new suit, for he abounded more in that metallic currency than he did in either Benton's mint drops or in Biddle's notes; and having the gentility of his outward Adam thus endorsed by his tailor —an important endorsement, by-the-way, as times go—he managed to obtain an introduction to the planter's daughter.

Our worthy had the principle of going ahead strongly developed. He was possessed of considerable address, and had brass enough in his face to make a wash-kettle: and having once got access to the planter's house, it was no easy matter to dislodge him. In this he resembled those politicians who commence life as office-holders; they will hang on, tooth and nail, and even when death shakes them off, you'll find a commission of some kind crumpled up in their clenched fingers. Little Van appears to belong to this class—there's no beating his snout from the public crib. He'll feed there while there's a grain of corn left, and even then, from long habit, he'll set to work and gnaw at the manger.

Thimblerig got the blind side of the planter, and everything, to outward appearances, went on swimmingly. Our worthy boasted to his cronies that the business was settled, and that in a few weeks he should occupy the elevated station in society that nature had designed him to adorn. He swelled like the frog in the fable, or, rather, like

Johnson's wife, of Kentucky, when the idea occurred to her of figuring away at Washington. But there's many a slip 'twixt the cup and the lip, says the proverb, and suddenly Thimblerig discontinued his visits at the planter's house. His friends inquired of him the meaning of this abrupt termination of his devotions.

"I have been treated with disrespect," replied the worthy, indignantly.

"Disrespect! in what way?"

"My visits, it seems, are not altogether agreeable."

"But how have you ascertained that?"

"I received a hint to that effect; and I can take a hint as soon as another."

"A hint!—and have you allowed a hint to drive you from the pursuit? For shame. Go back again."

"No, no, never! a hint is sufficient for a man of my gentlemanly feelings. I asked the old man for his daughter."

"Well, what followed? what did he say?"

"Didn't say a word."

"Silence gives consent all the world over."

"So I thought. I then told him to fix the day."

"Well, what then?"

"Why, then, he kicked me down stairs, and ordered his slaves to pump upon me. That's hint enough for me, that my visits are not properly appreciated; and blast my old shoes if I condescend to renew the acquaintance, or notice them in any way until they send for me."

As Thimblerig's new coat became rather too seedy to play the part of a gentleman much longer in real life, he determined to sustain that character upon the stage, and accordingly joined a company of players. He began, according to custom, at the top of the ladder, and was regularly hissed and pelted through every gradation until he found himself at the lowest rowel. "This," said he, "was a dreadful check to proud ambition;" but he consoled himself with the idea of peace and quietness in his present obscure walk; and though he had no prospect of being elated by the applause of admiring multitudes, he no longer trod the scene of mimic glory in constant dread of becoming a target for rotten eggs and oranges. "And there was much in that," said Thimblerig. But this calm could not continue for ever.

The manager, who, like all managers who pay salaries regularly, was as absolute behind the scenes as the "old Roman" is in the White House, had fixed upon getting up an eastern spectacle, called the Cataract of the Ganges. He intended to introduce a fine procession, in which an elephant was to be the principal feature. Here a difficulty occurred. What was to be done for an elephant? Alligators were plenty in those parts, but an elephant was not to be had for love or money. But an alligator would not answer the purpose, so he determined to make a pasteboard elephant as large as life, and twice as natural. The next difficulty was to find members of the company of suitable dimensions to perform the several members of the pasteboard star. The manager cast his eye upon the long, gaunt figure of the unfortunate Thimblerig, and cast him for the hinder legs, the rump, and part of the back of the elephant. The poor player expostulated, and the manager replied, that he would appear as a star on the occasion, and would no doubt receive more applause than he had during his whole career. "But I shall not be seen," said the player. "All the better," replied the manager, "as in that case you will have nothing to apprehend from eggs and oranges."

Thimblerig, finding that mild expostulation availed nothing, swore that he would not study the part, and accordingly threw it up in dignified disgust. He said that it was an outrage upon the feelings of the proud representative of Shakespeare's heroes, to be compelled to play pantomine in the hinder parts of the noblest animal that ever trod the stage. If it had been the fore quarters of the elephant, it might possibly have been made a speaking part; at any rate, he might have snorted through the trunk, if nothing more; but from the position he was to occupy, damned the word could he utter, or even roar with propriety. He therefore positively refused to act, as he considered it an insult to his reputation to tread the stage in such a character; and he looked upon the whole affair as a profanation of the legitimate drama. The result was, our worthy was discharged from the company, and compelled to commence hoeing another row.

He drifted to New Orleans, and hired himself as marker to a gambling table. Here he remained but a few months, for his idea of arithmetic differed widely from those of his employer, and accordingly they had some difficulty in balancing their cash account; for when his employer, in adding up the receipts, made it nought and carry two, Thimblerig insisted that it should be nought and carry one; and in order to prove that he was correct, he carried himself off, and left nothing behind him.

He now commenced professional blackleg on his own hook, and took up his quarters in Natchez under the hill. Here he remained, doing business in a small way, until Judge Lynch commenced his practice in that quarter, and made the place too hot for his comfort. He shifted his habitation, but not having sufficient capital to go the big figure, he practised the game of thimblerig until he acquired considerable skill, and then commenced passing up and down the river in the steamboats; and managed, by close attention to business, to pick up a decent livelihood in the small way, from such as had more pence in their pockets than sense in their noddles.

I found Thimblerig to be a pleasant talkative fellow. He communicated the foregoing facts with as much indifference as if there had been nothing disgraceful in his career; and at times he would chuckle with an air of triumph at the adroitness he had displayed in some of the knavish tricks he had practised. He looked upon this world as one vast stage, crowded with empirics and jugglers; and that he who could practise his deceptions with the greatest skill was entitled to the greatest applause.

I asked him to give me an account of Natchez and his adventures there, and I would put it in the book I intended to write, when he gave me the following, which betrays that his feelings were somewhat irritated at being obliged to give them leg bail when Judge Lynch made his appearance. I give it in his own words:

"Natchez is a land of fevers, alligators, niggers, and cotton bales: where the sun shines with force sufficient to melt the diamond, and the word ice is expunged from the dictionary, for its definition cannot be comprehended by the natives: where to refuse grog before breakfast would degrade you below the brute creation; and where a good dinner is looked upon as an angel's visit, and voted a miracle: where the evergreen and majestic magnolia tree, with its superb flower, unknown to the north-

ern climes, and its fragrance unsurpassed, calls forth the
admiration of every beholder; and the dark moss hangs in
festoons from the forest trees, like the drapery of a funeral
pall: where bears, the size of young jackasses, are fondled
in lieu of pet dogs; and knives, the length of a barber's
pole, usurp the place of toothpicks: where the filth
of the town is carried off by buzzards, and the inhabitants
are carried off by fevers: where nigger women are knocked
down by the auctioneer, and knocked up by the purchaser;
where the poorest slave has plenty of yellow boys, but not
of Benton's mintage; and indeed the shades of colour are
so varied and mixed, that a nigger is frequently seen black
and blue at the same time. And such is Natchez.

"The town is divided into two parts, as distinct in
character as they are in appearance. Natchez on the
hill, situated upon a high bluff overlooking the Mississippi, is a pretty little town with streets regularly laid
out, and ornamented with divers handsome public buildings. Natchez under the hill,—where, oh! where shall
I find words suitable to describe the peculiarities of that
unholy spot? 'Tis, in fact, the jumping off place. Satan
looks on it with glee, and chuckles as he beholds the orgies
of his votaries. The buildings are for the most part
brothels, taverns, or gambling houses, and frequently
the whole three may be found under the same roof.
Obscene songs are sung at the top of the voice in all
quarters. I have repeatedly seen the strumpets tear a
man's clothes from his back, and leave his body beauti-
fied with all the colors of the rainbow.

"One of the most popular tricks is called the 'Spanish
burial.' When a greenhorn makes his appearance among
them, one who is in the plot announces the death of a

resident, and that all strangers must subscribe to the custom of the place upon such an occasion. They forthwith arrange a procession; each person, as he passes the departed, kneels down and pretends to kiss the treacherous corpse. When the unsophisticated attempts this ceremony the dead man clinches him, and the mourners beat the fellow so entrapped until he consents to treat all hands; but should he be penniless, his life will be endangered by the severity of the castigation. And such is Natchez under the hill.

"An odd affair occurred while I was last there," continued Thimblerig. "A steamboat stopped at the landing, and one of the hands went ashore under the hill to purchase provisions, and the adroit citizens of that delectable retreat contrived to rob him of all his money. The captain of the boat, a determined fellow, went ashore in the hope of persuading them to refund, but that cock wouldn't fight. Without farther ceremony, assisted by his crew and passengers, some three or four hundred in number, he made fast an immense cable to the frame tenement where the theft had been perpetrated, and allowed fifteen minutes for the money to be forthcoming; vowed if it was not produced within that time, to put steam to his boat, and drag the house into the river. The money was instantly produced.

"I witnessed a sight during my stay there," continued the thimble conjuror, "that almost froze my blood with horror, and will serve as a specimen of the customs of the far south. A planter, of the name of Foster, connected with the best families of the state, unprovoked, in cold blood, murdered his young and beautiful wife, a few months after marriage. He beat her deliberately to death in a walk

adjoining his dwelling, carried the body to the hut of one
of his slaves, washed the dirt from her person, and assisted
by his negroes, buried her upon his plantation. Suspicion
was awakened, the body disinterred, and the villain's
guilt established. He fled, was overtaken and secured in
prison. His trial was, by some device of the law, delayed
until the third term of the court. At length it came on,
and so clear and indisputable was the evidence that not a
doubt was entertained of the result; when, by an oversight
on the part of the sheriff, who neglected swearing into
office his deputy who summoned the jurors, the trial was
abruptly discontinued, and all proceedings against Foster
were suspended, or rather ended.

"There exist throughout the extreme south, bodies of
men who style themselves Lynchers. When an individual
escapes punishment by some technicality of the law, or
perpetrates an offence not recognized in courts of justice,
they seize him, and inflict such chastisement as they conceive adequate to the offence. They usually act at night
and disguise their persons. This society at Natchez em-
braces all the lawyers, physicians, and principal merchants
of the place. Foster, whom all good men loathed as a
monster unfit to live, was called into court, and formally
dismissed. But the Lynchers were at hand. The moment
he stept from the court-house he was knocked down, his
arms bound behind him, his eyes bandaged, and in this
condition was marched to the rear of the town, where a
deep ravine afforded a fit place for his punishment. His
clothes were torn from his back, his head partially scalped,
they next bound him to a tree; each Lyncher was supplied
with a cow-skin, and they took turns at the flogging until
the flesh hung in ribands from his body. A quantity of

heated tar was then poured over his head, and made to cover every part of his person; they finally showered a sack of feathers on him, and in this horrid guise, with no other apparel than a miserable pair of breeches, with a drummer at his heels, he was paraded through the principal streets at midday. No disguise was assumed by the Lynchers; the very lawyers employed upon his trial took part in his punishment.

"Owing to long confinement his gait had become cramped, and his movements were very faltering. By the time the procession reached the most public part of the town, Foster fell down from exhaustion, and was allowed to lie there for a time, without exciting the sympathies of any one, an object of universal detestation. The blood oozing from his stripes had become mixed with the feathers and tar, and rendered his aspect still more horrible and loathsome. Finding him unable to proceed further, a common dray was brought, and with his back to the horse's tail, the drummer standing over him playing the rogue's march, he was reconducted to prison, the only place at which he would be received.

"A guard was placed outside of the jail to give notice to the body of Lynchers when Foster might attempt to escape, for they had determined on branding him on the forehead and cutting his ears off. At two o'clock in the morning of the second subsequent day, two horsemen with a led horse stopped at the prison, and Foster was with difficulty placed astride.

"The Lynchers wished to secure him; he put spurs to his beast, and passed them. As he rode by they fired at him; a ball struck his hat, which was thrown to the ground, and he escaped; but if ever found within the limits of the state, he will be shot down as if a price was set on his head.

"Sights of this kind," continued Thimblerig, "are by no means unfrequent. I once saw a gambler, a sort of friend of mine by-the-way, detected cheating at faro, at a time when the bets were running pretty high. They flogged him almost to death, added the tar and feathers, and placed him aboard a dug-out, a sort of canoe, at twelve at night; and with no other instrument of navigation than a bottle of whisky and a paddle, set him adrift in the Mississippi. He has never been heard of since, and the presumption is, that he either died of his wounds or was run down in the night by a steamer. And this is what we call Lynching in Natchez."

Thimblerig had also been at Vicksburg in his time, and entertained as little liking for that place as he did for Natchez. He had luckily made his escape a short time before the recent clearing-out of the sleight-of-hand gentry; and he reckoned some time would elapse before he would pay them another visit. He said they must become more civilized first. All the time he was talking to me he was seated on a chest, and playing mechanically with his pea and thimbles, as if he was afraid that he would lose the sleight unless he kept his hand in constant practice. Nothing of any consequence occurred in our passage down the river, and I arrived at Natchitoches in perfect health, and in good spirits.*

* Thimblerig's account of Natchez under the hill some twenty years since is only too true. It was a notoriously bad place. Life and property were so unsafe there that few decent persons were willing to run the risk of visiting the place. Of late years it seems to have lost its former bad eminence. We hear no more of riots, murders, lynchings, and gambling broils at Natchez under the hill; and the next generation will probably doubt the credibility of the stories related of this den of infamy. [Footnote in 1880 edition]

CHAPTER TWENTY-NINE

A Tussle at Natchitoches

Natchitoches is a post town and seat of justice for the parish of Natchitoches, Louisiana, and is situated on the right bank of the Red river. The houses are chiefly contained in one street, running parallel to the river; and the population I should reckon at about eight hundred. The soil in this parish is generally sterile, and covered with pine timber, except near the margin of Red river, where the greatest part of the inhabitants are settled on the alluvial banks. Some other, though comparatively small, tracts of productive soil skirt the streams. An extensive body of low ground, subject to annual submersion, extends along the Red river, which, it is said, will produce forty bushels of frogs to the acre, and alligators enough to fence it.

I stayed two days at Natchitoches, during which time I procured a horse to carry me across Texas to the seat of war. Thimblerig remained with me, and I found his conversation very amusing; for he is possessed of humor and observation, and has seen something of the world. Between whiles he would amuse himself with his thimbles, to which he appeared greatly attached, and occasionally he would pick up a few shillings from the tavern loungers. He no longer asked me to play with him, for he felt somewhat ashamed to do so, and he knew it would be no go.

I took him to task in a friendly manner, and tried to shame him out of his evil practices. I told him that it was a burlesque on human nature, that an able-bodied man, possessed of his full share of good sense, should voluntarily debase himself, and be indebted for subsistence to such pitiful artifice.

"But what's to be done, Colonel?" says he. "I'm in the slough of despond, up to the very chin. A miry and slippery path to travel."

"Then hold your head up," says I, "before the slough reaches your lips."

"But what's the use?" says he: "it's utterly impossible for me to wade through; and even if I could, I should be in such a dirty plight, that it would defy all the waters in the Mississippi to wash me clean again. No," he added, in a desponding tone, "I should be like a live eel in a frying pan, Colonel; sort of out of my element, if I attempted to live like an honest man at this time o'day."

"That I deny. It is never too late to become honest," said I. "But even admit what you say to be true—that you cannot live like an honest man, you have at least the next best thing in your power, and no one can say nay to it."

"And what is that?"

"Die like a brave one. And I know not whether, in the eyes of the world, a brilliant death is not preferred to an obscure life of rectitude. Most men are remembered as they died, and not as they lived. We gaze with admiration upon the glories of the setting sun, yet scarcely bestow a passing glance upon its noonday splendor."

"You are right; but how is this to be done?"

"Accompany me to Texas. Cut aloof from your degrading habits and associates here, and in fighting for their freedom, regain your own."

He started from the table, and hastily gathering up the thimbles with which he had been playing all the time I was talking to him, he thrust them into his pocket, and after striding two or three times across the room, suddenly stopped, his leaden eye kindled, and grasping me by the hand violently, he exclaimed with an oath, "By ——, I'll be a man again. Live honestly, or die bravely. I go with you to Texas."

I said what I could to confirm him in his resolution, and finding that the idea had taken fast hold of his mind, I asked him to liquor, which he did not decline, notwithstanding the temperance habits that he boasted of; we then took a walk on the banks of the river.

The evening preceding my departure from Natchitoches, a gentleman, with a good horse and a light wagon, drove up to the tavern where I lodged. He was accompanied by a lady who carried an infant in her arms. As they alighted I recognized the gentleman to be the politician at whom I had discharged my last political speech, on board the boat coming down the Red river. We had let him out in our passage down, as he said he had some business to transact some distance above Natchitoches. He entered the tavern, and seemed to be rather shy of me, so I let him go, as I had no idea of firing two shots at such small game.

The gentleman had a private room, and called for supper; but the lady, who used every precaution to keep the child concealed from the view of any one refused to eat supper, saying she was unwell. However, the gentleman made a hearty meal, and excused the woman, saying, "My wife is subject to a pain in the stomach, which had deprived her of her food." Soon after supper the gentleman desired a bed to be prepared, which being done, they immediately retired to rest.

About an hour before daybreak, next morning, the repose of the whole inn was disturbed by the screams of the child. This continued for some time, and at length the landlady got up to see what it was ailed the noisy bantling. She entered the chamber without a light, and discovered the gentleman seated in the bed alone, rocking the infant in his arms, and endeavoring to quiet it by saying, "Hush, my dear—mamma will soon return." However the child still squalled on, and the long absence of the mother rendered it necessary that something should be done to quiet it.

The landlady proposed taking up the child, to see what was the reason of its incessant cries. She approached the bed, and requested the man to give her the infant, and tell her whether it was a son or daughter; but this question redoubled his consternation, for he was entirely ignorant which sex the child belonged to; however, with some difficulty, he made the discovery, and informed the landlady it was a son.

She immediately called for a light, which was no sooner

brought than the landlady began to unfold the wrapper from the child, and exclaim, "O, what a fine big son you have got!" But on a more minute examination they found to their great astonishment, and to the mortification and vexation of the supposed father, that the child was a mulatto.

The wretched man, having no excuse to offer, immediately divulged the whole matter without reserve. He stated that he had fell in with her on the road to Natchitoches the day before, and had offered her a seat in his vehicle. Soon perceiving that she possessed an uncommon degree of assurance, induced him to propose that they should pass as man and wife. No doubt she had left her own home in order to rid herself of the stigma which she had brought on herself by her lewd conduct; and at midnight she had eloped from the bed, leaving the infant to the paternal care of her pretended husband.

Immediate search was made for the mother of the child, but in vain. And, as the song says, "Single misfortunes ne'er come alone," to his great consternation and grief, she had taken his horse, and left the poor politician destitute of everything except a fine *yellow boy*, but of a widely different description from those which Benton put in circulation.

By this time all the lodgers in the tavern had got up and dressed themselves, from curiosity to know the occasion of the disturbance. I descended to the street in front of the inn. The stars were faintly glimmering in the heavens, and the first beams of the morning sun were struggling through the dim clouds that skirted the eastern horizon. I thought myself alone in the street, when the hush of morning was suddenly broken by a clear, joyful, and musical voice, which sang, as near as I could catch it, the following scrap of a song:—

> "Oh, what is the time of the merry round year,
> That is fittest and sweetest for love?
> Ere sucks the bee, ere buds the tree;
> And primroses by two, by three,
> Faintly shine in the path of the lonely deer,
> Like the few stars of twilight above."

I turned towards the spot whence the sounds proceeded, and discovered a tall figure leaning against the sign post. His eyes were fixed on the streaks of light in the east; his mind was absorbed, and he was clearly unconscious of any one being near him. He continued his song in so full and clear a tone that the street re-echoed—

> "When the blackbird and thrush, at early dawn,
> Prelude from leafy spray—
> Amid dewy scents and blandishments,
> Like a choir attuning their instruments,
> Ere the curtain of nature aside be drawn
> For the concert the live long day."

I now drew nigh enough to see him distinctly. He was a young man, not more than twenty-two. His figure was light and graceful, and at the same time it indicated strength and activity. He was dressed in a hunting shirt, which was made with uncommon neatness, and ornamented tastily with fringe. He held a highly finished rifle in his right hand, and a hunting pouch covered with Indian ornaments, was slung across his shoulders. His clean shirt collar was open, secured only by a black riband around his neck. His boots were polished without a soil upon them; and on his head was a neat fur cap, tossed on in a manner which said, "I don't care a d——n," just as plainly as any cap could speak it. I thought it must be some popinjay of a lark, until I took a look at his countenance. It was handsome, bright, and manly. There was no mistake in that face. From the eyes down to his breast he was sunburnt as dark as mahogany, while the upper part of his high forehead was as white and polished as marble. Thick clusters of black hair curled from under his cap. I passed on unperceived, and he continued his song:—

> "In the green spring-tide, all tender and bright,
> When the sun sheds a kindlier gleam
> O'er the velvet bank, that sweet flowers prank,
> That have fresh dews and sunbeams drank—
> Softest and most chaste, as enchanted light
> In the visions of maiden's dream."

The poor politician, whose misfortunes had roused up the inmates of the tavern at such an unusual hour, now returned from the stable, where he had been in search of his horse and his woman; but they were both among the missing. He held a whip in his hand, and about a dozen men followed him, some from curiosity to see the result of the adventure, and others from better feelings. As he drew nigh to the front of the tavern, chafing with mortification at both his shame and his loss, his rage increasing to a flame as his windy exclamations became louder and louder, he chanced to espy the fantastic personage I have just described, still leaning against the sign post, carelessly humming his song, but in a lower tone, as he perceived he was not alone.

The irritated politician no sooner saw the stranger against the sign post, whose self-satisfied air was in striking contrast with the excited feelings of the other, than he paused for a moment, appeared to recognize him; then coming up in a blustering manner, and assuming a threatening attitude, he exclaimed fiercely,

"You're an infernal scoundrel, do you hear? an infernal scoundrel, sir!"

"I do; but it's news to me," replied the other quietly.

"News, you scoundrel! do you call it news?"

"Entirely so."

"You needn't think to carry it off so quietly. I say, you're an infernal scoundrel, and I'll prove it."

"I beg you will not; I shouldn't like to be proved a scoundrel," replied the other, smiling with the most provoking indifference.

"No, I dare say you wouldn't. But answer me directly —did you, or did you not say, in the presence of certain ladies of my acquaintance, that I was a mere—"

"Calf?—O, no, sir; the truth is not to be spoken at all times."

"The truth! Do you presume to call me a calf, sir?"

"O, no, sir; I call you —— nothing," replied the stranger, just as cool and as pleasant as a morning in spring.

"It's well you do; for if you had presumed to call me ——"

"A man, I should have been grossly mistaken."

"Do you mean to say I am not a man, sir?"

"That depends upon circumstances."

"What circumstances?" demanded the other fiercely.

"If I should be called as an evidence in a court of justice, I should be bound to speak the truth."

"And you would say I was not a man, hey? Do you see this cow-skin?"

"Yes; and I have seen it with surprise ever since you came up," replied the stranger, calmly, at the same time handing me his rifle to take care of.

"With surprise!" exclaimed the politician, who saw that his antagonist had voluntarily disarmed himself. "Why, did you suppose that I was such a coward that I dare not use the article when I thought it was demanded?"

"Shall I tell you what I thought?"

"Do, if you dare."

"I thought to myself what use has a calf for a cow-skin?" He turned to me, and said, "I had forgot, Colonel, shall I trouble you to take care of this also?" Saying which he drew a long hunting knife from his belt, and placed it in my hand. He then resumed his careless attitude against the sign post.

"You distinctly call me a calf, then?"

"If you insist upon it, you may."

"You hear, gentlemen," said he, speaking to the by-standers. "Do you hear the insult? What shall I do with the scoundrel?"

"Dress him, dress him!" exclaimed twenty voices, with shouts and laughter.

"That I'll do at once!" Then, turning to the stranger, he cried out fiercely, "Come one step this way, you rascal, and I'll flog you within an inch of your life."

"I've no occasion."

"You're a coward."

"Not on your word."

"I'll prove it by flogging you out of your skin."

"I doubt it."

"I am a liar, then, am I?"

"Just as you please."

"Do you hear that, gentlemen?"

"Ay, we hear," was the unanimous response. "You can't avoid dressing him now."

"O heavens! grant me patience! I shall fly out of my skin."

"It will be so much the better for your pocket; calf-skins are in good demand."

"I shall burst."

"Not here in the street, I beg of you. It would be disgusting."

"Gentlemen, can I any longer avoid flogging him?"

"Not if you are able," was the reply. "Go at him."

Thus provoked, thus stirred up, and enraged, the fierce politician went like lightning at his provoking antagonist. But before he could strike a blow he found himself disarmed of his cow-skin, and lying on his back under the spout of a neighboring pump, whither the young man had carried him to cool his rage, and before he could recover from his astonishment at such unexpected handling, he was as wet as a thrice drowned rat, from the cataracts of water which his laughing antagonist had liberally pumped upon him. His courage, by this time, had fairly oozed out; and he declared, as he arose and went dripping away from the pump, that he would never again trust to quiet appearances, and that the devil himself might, the next time, undertake to cowskin such a cucumber-blooded scoundrel for him. The bystanders laughed heartily. The politician now went in pursuit of his horse and his woman, taking his yellow boy with him; and the landlady declared that he richly deserved what he had got, even if he had been guilty of no other offence than the dirty imposition he had practiced on her.

The stranger now came to me, and calling me by name, asked for his rifle and knife, which I returned to him. I expressed some astonishment at being known to him, and he said that he had heard of my being in the village, and had sought me out for the purpose of accompanying me to Texas. He told me that he was a bee hunter: that he had travelled pretty much over that country in the way of his business, and that I would find him of considerable use in navigating through the ocean of prairies.

He told me that honey-trees are abundant in Texas, and that honey of an excellent quality, and in any quantity, may be obtained from them. There are persons who have a peculiar tact in coursing the bee, and thus discovering their deposits of the luscious food. This employment is not a mere pastime, but is profitable. The wax alone, thus obtained, is a valuable article of commerce in Mexico, and commands a high price. It is much used in churches, where some of the candles made use of are as long as a man's arm. It often happens that the hunters throw away the honey, and save only the wax.

"It is a curious fact," said the bee hunter, "in the natural history of the bee, that it is never found in a wild country, but always precedes civilization, forming a kind of advance guard between the white man and the savage. The Indians, at least, are perfectly convinced of this fact, for it is a common remark among them, when they observe these insects, 'There come the white men.' "

Thimblerig came up, and the bee hunter spoke to him, calling him by name, for he had met with him in New

Orleans. I told him that the conjurer had determined to accompany me also, at which he seemed well pleased, and encouraged the poor fellow to adhere to that resolution; for he would be a man among men in Texas, and no one would be very particular in inquiring about his fortunes in the States. If once there, he might boldly stand up and feed out of the same rack with the rest.

I asked him what was his cause of quarrel with the politician, and he told me that he had met him a few weeks before down at Baton Rouge, where the fellow was going the big figure, and that he had exposed him to some ladies, which completely cut his comb, and he took wing; that this was the first time they had met since, and being determined to have his revenge, he had attacked him without first calculating consequences.

With the assistance of our new friend, who was a generous, pleasant fellow, we procured a horse and rifle for Thimblerig, and we started for Nacogdoches, which is about one hundred and twenty miles west of Natchitoches, under the guidance of the bee hunter.

CHAPTER THIRTY

The Bee Hunter and His Lady-Love

Our route, which lay along what is called the old Spanish road, I found to be much better defined on the map than upon the face of the country. We had, in many instances, no other guide to the path than the blazes on the trees. The Bee hunter was a cheerful, communicative companion, and by his pleasant conversation, rendered our journey anything but fatiguing. He knew all about the country, had undergone a variety of adventure, and described what he had witnessed with such freshness, and so graphically, that if I could only remember one half he told me about the droves of wild horses, buffalo, various birds, beautiful scenery of the wide-spreading and fertile prairies, and his adventures with the roving tribes of Indians, I should fill my book, I am sure, much more agreeably than I shall be able to do on my own hook. When he'd get tired of talking, he'd commence singing, and his list of songs seemed to be as long as a rainy Sunday. He had a fine, clear voice, and though I have heard the Woods sing at the Park Theatre, in New York, I must give the Bee hunter the preference over all I have ever heard, except my friend Jim Crow, who, it must be allowed, is a real steamboat at the business, and goes a leetle ahead of anything that will come after him.

He gave me, among other matters, the following account of a rencounter between one of the early settlers and the Indians:—

"Andrew Tumlinson," said he, "belonged to a family which the colonists of De Witt will long remember as one of their chief stays in the dangers of settling those wilds trod only by the children of the forest. This indefatigable champion of revenge for his father's death, who had fallen some years before by Indian treachery, had vowed never to rest until he had received satisfaction. In order the better to accomplish his end, he was one of the foremost, if possible, in every skirmish with the Indians; and that he might be enabled to do so without restraint, he placed his wife under the care of his brother-in-law, shouldered his rifle and headed a ranging party, who were resolved to secure peace to those who followed them, though purchased by their own death.

"He had been frequently victorious in the most desperate fights, where the odds were greatly against him, and at last fell a victim to his own imprudence. A Caddo had been seized as a spy, and threatened with death, in order to compel him to deliver up his knife. The fellow never moved a muscle, or even winked, as he beheld the rifles pointed at him. He had been found lurking in the yard attached to the house of a solitary and unprotected family, and he knew that the whites were exasperated at his tribe for injuries that they had committed. When discovered he was accompanied by his little son.

"Tumlinson spoke to him in Spanish, to learn what had brought him there at such a time, but instead of giving any satisfaction, he sprung to his feet, from the log where he was seated, at the same time seizing his rifle, which was lying beside him. The owner of the house, with whom the Indian had been on a friendly footing, expostulated with him, and got him to surrender the gun, telling him that the whites only wished to be satisfied of his friendly intentions, and had no desire to injure one who might be useful in conciliating his red brethren.

"He appeared to acquiesce, and wrapping his blanket more closely around his body, moved on in silence ahead of the whites. Tumlinson approached him, and though the rest of the party privately cautioned him not to go too nigh, as they believed the Indian had a knife under his blanket, he disregarded the warning, trusting for safety to his rifle and dexterity.

"He continued to interrogate the captive until he awakened his suspicions that his life was not safe. The Indian returned no answer but a short caustic laugh at the end of every question. Tumlinson at length beheld his countenance become more savage, which was followed by a sudden movement of the right hand beneath his blanket. He fired, and the next instant the Caddo's knife was in his heart, for the savage sprung with the quickness of the wild cat upon his prey. The rifle ball had passed through the Indian's body, yet his victim appeared to be no more in his grasp than a sparrow in the talons of an eagle, for he was a man of gigantic frame, and he knew that not only his own life, but that of his little son, would be taken on the spot. He called to the boy to fly, while he continued to plunge his knife into the bosom of his prostrate victim. The rest of the party leveled their rifles, and the victor shouted, with an air of triumph,—'Do your worst. I have sacrificed another pale-face to the spirits of my fathers.' They fired, and he fell dead across the body of the unfortunate Tumlinson. The poor boy fell also. He had sprung forward some distance, when his father was shot, and was running in a zigzag manner, taught them in their youth, to avoid the balls of their enemies, by rendering it difficult for the best marksman to draw a sight upon them."

In order to afford me some idea of the state of society in the more thickly settled parts of Texas, the Bee hunter told me that he had set down to the breakfast table one morning, at an inn, at San Felipe, and among the small party around the board were eleven who had fled from the States charged with having committed murder. So accustomed are the inhabitants to the appearance of fugitives from justice, that they are particularly careful to make inquiries of the characters of new-comers, and generally obtain early and circumstantial information concerning strangers. "Indeed," said he, "it is very common to hear the inquiry made, 'What did he do that made him leave home?' or 'What have you come to Texas for?' intimating almost an assurance of one's being a criminal. Notwithstanding this state of things, however, the good of the public, and of each individual, is so evidently dependent on the public morals, that all appear ready to discountenance and punish crime. Even men who have been expatriated by fear of justice, are here among the last who would be disposed to shield a culprit guilty of a crime against life or property."

Thimblerig was delighted at this favorable account of the state of society, and said that it would be the very place for him to flourish in; he liked their liberal way of thinking, for it did not at all tally with his ideas of natural law, that a man who happened to give offence to the straight laced rules of action established by a set of people contracted in their notions, should be hunted out of all society, even though willing to conform to their regulations. He was lawyer enough, he said, to know that every offence should be tried on the spot where it was committed; and if he had stolen the pennies from his grandmother's eyes in Louisiana, the people in Texas would have nothing to do with that affair, nohow they could fix it. The dejected conjurer pricked up his ears, and from that moment was as gay and cheerful as a blue bird in spring.

As we approached Nacogdoches, the first object that struck our view, was a flag flying at the top of a high liberty pole. Drums were beating, and fifes playing, giving an indication, not to be misunderstood, of the spirit that had been awakened in a comparative desert. The people of the town no sooner saw us than many came out to meet us. The Bee hunter, who was known to them, introduced me; and it seems that they had already received the news of my intended visit, and its object, and I met with a cordial and friendly reception.

Nacogdoches is the capitol of the department of that name, and it is situated about sixty miles west of the river Sabine, in a romantic dell, surrounded by woody bluffs of considerable eminence, within whose inner borders, in a semicircle embracing the town, flow the two forks of the Nana, a branch of the Naches. It is a flourishing town, containing about one thousand actual citizens, although it generally presents twice that number on account of its extensive inland trade, one-half of which is supported by the friendly Indians. The healthiness of this town yields to none in the province, except Bexar, and to none whatsoever south of the same latitude, between the Sabine and the Mississippi. There was a fort established here, by the French, as far back as the year 1717, in order to overawe the wandering tribes of red men, between their borders and the colonists of Great Britain. The soil around it is of an easy nature and well adapted to cultivation.

I passed the day at Nacogdoches in getting information from the principal patriots as to the grievances imposed upon them by the Mexican government; and I passed the time very pleasantly, but I rather reckon not quite so much as my friend the Bee hunter. In the evening, as I had missed him for several hours, while I was attending the affairs of the patriots, I inquired for my companion, and was directed by the landlord, to an apartment appropriated to his family, and accordingly I pushed ahead. Before I reached the door, I heard the joyous and musical voice of the young rover singing as usual.

> "I'd like to have a little farm,
>   And leave such scenes as these,
> Where I could live, without a care,
>   Completely at my ease.
> I'd like to have a pleasant house
>   Upon my little farm,
> Airy and cool in summer time,
>   In winter close and warm."

"And is there nothing else you'd like to have to make you happy, Edward?" demanded a gentle voice, which sounded even more musical in my ear than that of the Bee hunter.

"Yes, in good faith there is, my gentle Kate; and I'll tell you what it is," he exclaimed, and resumed his song:—

> "I'd like to have a little wife—
>   I reckon I know who;
> I'd like to have a little son—
>   A little daughter too;
> And when they'd climb upon my knee,
>   I'd like a little toy
> To give my pretty little girl,
>   Another for my boy."

"O, fie, for shame of you to talk so, Edward!" exclaimed the same gentle voice.

"Well, my pretty Kate, if you'll only listen, now I'll tell you what I wouldn't like."

"Let me hear that, by all means."

> "I should not like my wife to shake
>   A broomstick at my head—
> For then I might begin to think
>   She did not love her Ned;
> But I should always like to see
>   Her gentle as a dove;
> I should not like to have her scold—
>   But be all joy and love."

"And there is not much danger, Edward, of her ever being otherwise."

"Bless your sweet lips, that I am certain of," exclaimed the Bee hunter, and I heard something that sounded marvelously like a kiss. But he resumed his song:—

"If I had these I would not ask
   For anything beside;
I'd be content thus smoothly through
   The tedious world to glide.
My little wife and I would then
   No earthly troubles see—
Surrounded by our little ones,
   How happy we would be!"

I have always endeavored to act up to the golden rule of doing as I would be done by, and as I never liked to be interrupted on such occasions, I returned to the barroom, where I found Thimblerig seated on a table practicing with his thimbles, his large white Vicksburg hat stuck up in a most independent manner on the side of his head. About half a dozen men were looking on with amazement at his skill, but he got no bets. When he caught my eye, his countenance became sort of confused, and he hastily thrust the thimbles into his pocket, saying, as he jumped from the table, "Just amusing myself a little, Colonel, to kill time, and show the natives that some things can be done as well as others. Let us take an ideer." So he walked up to the bar, took a nip, and let the matter drop.

My horse had become lame, and I found I would not be able to proceed with him, so I concluded to sell him and get another. A gentleman offered to give me a mustang in exchange, and I gladly accepted of his kindness. The mustangs are the wild horses, that are to be seen in droves of thousands pasturing on the prairies. They are taken by means of a lasso, a long rope with a noose, which is thrown around their necks, and they are dragged to the ground with violence, and then secured. These horses, which are considerably smaller than those in the States, are very cheap, and are in such numbers that in times of scarcity of game the settlers and the Indians have made use of them as food. Thousands have been destroyed for this purpose.

I saw nothing of the Bee hunter until bed-time, and then I said nothing to him about what I had overheard. The next morning, as we were preparing for an early start, I went into the private apartment where my companion was, but he did not appear quite as cheerful as usual. Shortly afterward, a young woman, about eighteen, entered the room. She was as healthy and blooming as the wild flowers of the prairie. My companion introduced me, she courtesied modestly, and turning to the Bee hunter, said, "Edward, I have made you a new deer-skin sack since you were last here. Will you take it with you? Your old one is so soiled."

"No, no, dear Kate, I shall not have leisure to gather wax this time."

"I have not yet shown you the fine large gourd that I have slung for you. It will hold near a gallon of water." She went to a closet, and producing it, suspended it around his shoulders.

"My own kind Kate!" he exclaimed, and looked as if he would devour her with his eyes.

"Have I forgotten any thing? Ah! yes, your books." She ran to a closet, and brought out two small volumes.

"One is sufficient this time, Kate—my Bible. I will leave the poet with you." She placed it in his hunting bag, saying,

"You will find here some biscuit and deer sinews, in case you should get bewildered in the prairies. You know you lost your way the last time, and were nearly famished."

"Kind and considerate Kate."

I began to find out that I was a sort of fifth wheel to the wagon, so I went to the front of the tavern to see about starting. There was a considerable crowd there, and I made them a short address on the occasion. I told them, among other things, that "I will die with my Betsey in my arms. No, I will not die—I'll grin down the walls of the Alamo, and the Americans will lick up the Mexicans like fine salt."

I mounted my little mustang, and my legs nearly reached the ground. The thimble conjurer was also ready; at length the Bee hunter made his appearance, followed by his sweetheart, whose eyes looked as though she had been weeping. He took a cordial leave of all his friends, for he appeared to be a general favorite; he then approached Kate, kissed her, and leaped upon his horse. He tried to conceal his emotion by singing, carelessly,

"Saddled and bridled, and booted rode he,
A plume in his helmet, a sword at his knee."

The tremulous and plaintive voice of Kate took up the next two lines of the song, which sounded like a prophecy:

"But toom cam' the saddle, all bluidy to see,
And hame cam' the steed, but hame never cam' he."

We started off rapidly, and left Nacogdoches amid the cheering of true patriots and kind friends.*

* The story of the Bee hunter and his lady love forms one of the most agreeable episodes in this portion of the Colonel's narrative. The Bee hunter is a very original and spirited character, of whom the reader is destined to meet with still more interesting particulars in the sequel. [Footnote in 1880 edition.]

CHAPTER THIRTY-ONE

I Chase a Great Herd of Buffaloes

An hour or two elapsed before the Bee hunter recovered his usual spirits, after parting from his kind little Kate of Nacogdoches. The conjurer rallied him good-humoredly, and had become quite a different man from what he was on the west side of the Sabine. He sat erect in his saddle, stuck his large white Vicksburger conceitedly on his bushy head, carried his rifle with as much ease and grace as if he had been used to the weapon, and altogether he assumed an air of impudence and independence which showed that he had now a soul above thimbles. The Bee hunter at length recovered his spirits, and commenced talking very pleasantly, for the matters he related were for the most part new to me.

My companions, by way of beguiling the tediousness of our journey, repeatedly played tricks upon each other, which were taken in good part. One of them I will relate.

We had observed that the Bee hunter always disappeared on stopping at a house, running in to talk with the inhabitants and ingratiate himself with the women, leaving us to take care of the horses. On reaching our stopping place at night he left us as usual, and while we were rubbing down our mustangs, and hobbling them, a negro boy came out of the house with orders from our companion within to see to his horse. Thimblerig, who possessed a good share of roguish ingenuity, after some inquiries about the gentleman in the house, how he looked and what he was doing, told the boy, in rather a low voice, that he had better not come nearer to him than was necessary, for it was possible he might hurt him, though still he didn't think he would. The boy asked why he need be afraid of him. He replied he did not certainly know that there was any reason—he hoped there was none—but the man had been bitten by a mad dog, and it was rather uncertain whether he was not growing mad himself. Still, he would not alarm the boy, but cautioned him not to be afraid, for there might be no danger, though there was something rather strange in the conduct of his poor friend. This was enough for the boy; he was almost afraid to touch the horse of such a man, and when, a moment afterward, our companion came out of the house, he slunk away behind the horse, and though he was in a great hurry to get him unsaddled, kept his eyes fixed steadily on the owner, closely watching his motions.

"Take off that bridle," exclaimed the impatient Bee hunter, in a stern voice: and the black boy sprung off, and darted away as fast as his feet could carry him, much to the vexation and surprise of our companion, who ran after him a little distance, but could in no way account for his singular and provoking conduct. When we entered the house, things appeared a great deal more strange; for the negro had rushed hastily into the midst of the family, and in his terrified state communicated the alarming tale, that the gentleman had been bitten by a mad dog. He, unconscious all the time of the trick that was playing off, endeavored, as usual, to render himself as agreeable as possible, especially to the females with whom he had already formed a partial acquaintance. We could see that they looked on him with apprehension, and retreated whenever he approached them. One of them took an opportunity to inquire of Thimblerig the truth of the charge; and his answer confirmed their fears, and redoubled their caution; though, after confessing with apparent candor, that his friend had been bitten, he stated that there was no certainty of evil consequences, and it was a thing which of course could not be mentioned to the sufferer.

As bed time approached the mistress of the house expressed her fears, lest trouble should arise in the night, for the house, according to custom, contained but two rooms, and was not built for security. She therefore urged us to sleep between him and the door, and by no means to let him pass us. It so happened, however, that he chose to sleep next the door, and it was with great difficulty that we could keep their fears within bounds. The ill-disguised alarm of the whole family was not less a source of merriment to him who had been the cause, than of surprise and wonder to the subject of it. Whatever member of the household he approached promptly withdrew, and as for the negro, whenever he was spoken to by him, he would jump and roll his eyes. In the morning, when we were about to depart, we commissioned our belied companion to pay our bill; but as he approached the hostess she fled from him, and shut the door in his face. "I want to pay our bill," said he. "Oh! if you will only leave the house," cried she, in terror, "you are welcome to your lodging."

The jest, however, did not end here. The Bee hunter found out the trick that had been played upon him, and determined to retaliate. As we were about mounting, the conjurer's big white Vicksburger was unaccountably missing, and nowhere to be found. He was not altogether pleased with the liberty that had been taken with him, and after searching some time in vain, he tied a handkerchief around his head, sprung upon his horse, and rode off with more gravity than usual. We had rode about two miles, the Bee hunter bantering the other with a story of his hat lying in pawn at the house we had left, and urged upon him to return and redeem it; but finding Thimblerig out of humor, and resolved not to return, he began to repent of his jest, and offered to go back and bring it, on condition that the past should be forgotten and there should be no more retaliation. The other consented to the terms, so lighting a cigar with his sun glass, he set off at a rapid rate on his return. He had not been gone long before I presented Thimblerig with his hat for I had seen the Bee hunter conceal it, and had secretly brought it along with me. It was some time before our absent friend overtook us, having frightened all the family away by his sudden return, and searched the whole house without success. When he perceived the object of his ride upon the head of the conjurer, and recollected the promise by which he had bound himself not to have any more jesting, he could only exclaim, "Well, it's hard, but it's fair." We all laughed heartily, and good humor was once again restored.

Cane brakes are common in some parts of Texas. Our way led us through one of considerable extent. The frequent passage of men and horses had kept open a narrow path not wide enough for two mustangs to pass with convenience. The reeds, the same as are used in the northern states as fishing rods, had grown to the height of about twenty feet, and were so slender, that having no support directly over the path, they drooped a little inward, and intermingled their tops, forming a complete covering overhead. We rode about a quarter of a mile along this singular arched avenue with the view of the sky completely shut out. The Bee hunter told me that the largest brake is that which lines the banks of Caney Creek, and is seventy miles in length, with scarcely a tree to be seen the whole distance. The reeds are eaten by cattle and horses in the winter when the prairies yield little or no other food.

When we came out of the brake we saw three black wolves jogging like dogs ahead of us, but at too great a distance to reach them with a rifle. Wild turkeys and deer repeatedly crossed our path, and we saw several droves of wild horses pasturing in the prairies. These sights awakened the ruling passion strong within me, and I longed to have a hunt upon a large scale; for though I had killed many bears and deer in my time, I had never brought down a buffalo in all my life, and so I told my friends; but they tried to dissuade me from it, by telling me that I would certainly lose my way, and perhaps perish; for though it appeared as a cultivated garden to the eye, it was still a wilderness. I said little more on the subject until we crossed the Trinidad river, but every mile we traveled I found the temptation grow stronger and stronger.

The night after we crossed the river we fortunately found shelter in the house of a poor woman, who had little but the barest necessaries to offer us. While we were securing our horses for the night we beheld two men approaching the house on foot. They were both armed with rifles and hunting-knives, and though I have been accustomed to the sight of men who have not stepped far over the line of civilization, I must say these were just about the roughest samples I had seen any where. One was a man of about fifty years old, tall and rawboned. He was dressed in a sailor's round jacket, with a tarpaulin on his head. His whiskers nearly covered his face; his hair was coal black and long, and there was a deep scar across his forehead, and another on the back on his right hand. His companion, who was considerably younger, was bareheaded, and clad in a deer-skin dress made after our fashion. Though he was not much darker than the old man, I perceived that he was an Indian. They spoke friendly to the Bee hunter, for they both knew him, and said they were on their way to join the Texan forces, at that time near the San Antonio river. Though they had started without horses, they reckoned they would come across a couple before they went much farther. The right of ownership to horse flesh is not much regarded in Texas, for those that have been taken from the wild droves are soon after turned out to graze on the prairies, the owner having first branded them with his mark, and hobbled them by tying their fore feet together, which will enable another to capture them just as readily as himself.

The old woman set about preparing our supper, and

apologized for the homely fare, which consisted of bacon and fried onions, when the Indian went to a bag and produced a number of eggs of wild fowls, and a brace of fat rabbits, which were speedily dressed, and we made as good a meal as a hungry man need wish to set down to. The old man spoke very little: but the Indian, who had lived much among the whites, was talkative, and manifested much impatience to arrive at the army. The first opportunity that occurred I inquired of the Bee hunter who our new friends were, and he told me that the old man had been for many years a pirate with the famous Lafitte, and that the Indian was a hunter belonging to a settler near Galveston Bay. I had seen enough of land rats at Washington, but this was the first time that I was ever in company with a water rat to my knowledge; however, baiting that black spot on his escutcheon, he was a well-behaved and inoffensive man. Vice does not appear so shocking when we are familiar with the perpetrator of it.

Thimblerig was for taking airs upon himself after learning who our companions were, and protested to me, that he would not sit down at the same table with a man who had outraged the laws in such a manner;—for it was due to society that honest men should discountenance such unprincipled characters, and much more to the same effect; when the old man speedily dissipated the gambler's indignant feelings by calmly saying, "Stranger, you had better take a seat at the table, I think," at the same time drawing a long hunting-knife from his belt, and laying it on the table. "I think you had better take some supper with us," he added, in a mild tone, but fixing his eye sternly upon Thimblerig. The conjurer first eyed the knife, and then the fierce whiskers of the pirate, and, unlike some politicians, he wasn't long in making up his mind what course to pursue, but he determined to vote as the pirate voted, and said, "I second that motion, stranger," at the same time seating himself on the bench beside me. The old man then commenced cutting up the meat, for which purpose he had drawn his hunting-knife, though the gambler had thought it was for a different purpose; and being relieved from his fears, everything passed off quite sociable.

Early the following morning we compensated the old woman for the trouble she had been at, and we mounted our horses and pursued our journey, our new friends following on foot, but promising to arrive at the Alamo as soon as we should. About noon we stopped to refresh our horses beneath a cluster of trees that stood in the open prairie, and I again spoke of my longing for a buffalo hunt. We were all seated on the grass, and they strived hard to dissuade me from the folly of allowing a ruling passion to lead me into such imminent danger and difficulty as I must necessarily encounter. At this time, while they were running down my weakness, as they called it, Thimblerig was amusing himself with his eternal thimbles and pea upon the crown of his big white hat. I could not refrain from laughing outright to see with what gravity and apparent interest he slipped the pea from one thimble to another while in the midst of a desert. Man is a queer animal, and Colonel Dick Johnson is disposed to make him even queerer than Dame Nature originally intended.

The Bee hunter told me, that if I was determined to leave them, he had in his bag a paper of ground coffee, and biscuit, which little Kate of Nacogdoches had desired him to carry for my use, which he handed to me, and proposed drinking to her health, saying that she was one of the kindest and purest of God's creatures. We drank her health, and wished him all happiness when she should be his own, which time he looked forward to with impatience. He still continued to dissuade me from leaving them, and all the time he was talking his eyes were wandering above, when suddenly he stopped, sprang to his feet, looked around for a moment, then leaped on his mustang, and without saying a word, started off like mad, and scoured along the prairie. We watched him, gradually diminishing in size, until he seemed no larger than a rat, and finally disappeared in the distance. I was amazed, and thought to be sure the man was crazy; and Thimblerig, who continued his game, responded that he was unquestionably out of his head.

Shortly after the Bee hunter had disappeared, we heard a noise like the rumbling of distant thunder. The sky was clear, there were no signs of a storm, and we concluded it could not proceed from that cause. On turning to the west, we saw an immense cloud of dust in the distance, but could perceive no object distinctly, and still the roaring continued. "What can all this mean?" said I. "Burn my old shoes if I know," said the conjurer, gathering up his thimbles, and at the same time cocking his large Vicksburger fiercely on his head. We continued looking in the direction whence the sound proceeded, the cloud of dust became thicker and thicker, and the roaring more distinct—much louder than was ever heard in the White House at Washington.

We at first imagined that it was a tornado, but whatever it was, it was coming directly toward the spot where we

stood. Our mustangs had ceased to graze, and cocked up
their ears in evident alarm. We ran and caught them, took
off the hobbles, and rode into the grove of trees;—still the
noise grew louder and louder. We had scarcely got under
the shelter of the grove before the object approached near
enough for us to ascertain what it was. It was a herd of
buffalo, at least four or five hundred in number, dashing
along as swift as the wind, and roaring as if so many devils
had broke loose. They passed near the grove, and if we
had not taken shelter there, we should have been in great
danger of being trampled to death. My poor little mustang
shook worse than a politician about to be turned out of
office, as the drove came sweeping by. At their head, apart
from the rest, was a black bull, who appeared to be their
leader; he came roaring along, his tail straight on an end,
and at times tossing up the earth with his horns. I never
felt such a desire to have a crack at anything in all my
life. He drew nigh the place where I was standing; I
raised my beautiful Betsey to my shoulder, took deliberate
aim, blazed away, and he roared and suddenly stopped.
Those that were near him did so likewise, and the con-
cussion occasioned by the impetus of those in the rear
was such, that it was a miracle that some of them did not
break their legs or necks. The black bull stood for a few
moments pawing the ground after he was shot, then darted
off around the cluster of trees, and made for the uplands
of the prairies. The whole herd followed, sweeping by
like a tornado, and I do say, I never witnessed a more
beautiful sight to the eye of a hunter in all my life. Bear
hunting is no more to be compared to it than Colonel
Benton is to Henry Clay. I watched them for a few mo-

ments, then clapped spurs to my mustang and followed in their wake, leaving Thimblerig behind me.

I followed on the trail of the herd for at least two hours, by which time the moving mass appeared like a small cloud in the distant horizon. Still, I followed, my whole mind absorbed by the excitement of the chase, until the object was entirely lost in the distance. I now paused to allow my mustang to breathe, who did not altogether fancy the rapidity of my movements, and to consider which course I would have to take to regain the path I had abandoned. I might have retraced my steps by following the trail of the buffaloes, but it had always been my principle to go ahead, and so I turned to the west and pushed forward.

I had not rode more than an hour before I found I was as completely bewildered as "the Government" was when he entered upon an examination of the post-office accounts. I looked around, and there was, as far as the eye could reach, spread before me a country apparently in the highest state of cultivation. Extended fields, beautiful and productive, groves of trees cleared from the underwood, and whose margins were as regular as if the art and taste of man had been employed upon them. But there was no other evidence that the sound of the axe, or the voice of man, had ever here disturbed the solitude of nature. My eyes would have cheated my senses into the belief that I was in an earthly paradise, but my fears told me that I was in a wilderness.

I pushed along, following the sun, for I had no compass to guide me, and there was no other path than that which my mustang made. Indeed, if I had found a beaten track, I should have been almost afraid to have followed it; for my friend the Bee hunter had told me, that once, when he had been lost in the prairies, he had accidentally struck into his own path, and had traveled around and around for a whole day before he discovered his error. This I thought was a poor way of going ahead; so I determined to make for the first large stream, and follow its course.

I had traveled several hours without seeing the trace of a human being, and even game was almost as scarce as Benton's mint drops, except just about election time, and I began to wish that I had followed the advice of my companions. I was a good deal bothered to account for the abrupt manner in which the Bee hunter had absconded; and I felt concerned for the poor thimble conjurer, who was left alone, and altogether unaccustomed to the difficulties that he would have to encounter. While my mind was occupied with these unpleasant reflections, I was suddenly startled by another novelty quite as great as that I have just described.

I had just emerged from a beautiful grove of trees, and was entering upon an extended prairie, which looked like the luxuriant meadows of a thrifty farmer; and as if nothing should be wanting to complete the delusion, but a short distance before me, there was a drove of about one hundred beautiful horses quietly pasturing. It required some effort to convince my mind that man had no agency in this. But when I looked around, and fully realized it all, I thought of him who had preached to me in the wilds of the Arkansas, and involuntarily exclaimed, "God, what hast thou not done for man, and yet how little he does for thee! Not even repays thee with gratitude!"

I entered upon the prairie. The mustangs no sooner espied me than they raised their heads, whinnied, and began coursing around me in an extended circle, which gradually became smaller and smaller, until they closely surrounded me. My little rascally mustang enjoyed the sport, and felt disposed to renew his acquaintance with his wild companions; first turning his head to one, then to another, playfully biting the neck of this one, rubbing noses with that one, and kicking up his heels at a third. I began to feel rather uncomfortable, and plied the spur pretty briskly to get out of the mess, but he was as obstinate as the "old Roman" himself, who will neither be led nor driven. I kicked, and he kicked, but fortunately he became tired first, and he made one start, intending to escape from the annoyance if possible. As I had an annoyance to escape from likewise, I beat the devil's tattoo on his ribs, that he might have some music to dance to, and we went ahead right merrily, the whole drove following in our wake, head up, and tail and manes streaming. My little critter, who was both blood and bottom, seemed delighted at being at the head of the heap; and having once got fairly started, I wish I may be shot if I did not find it impossible to stop him. He kept along, tossing his head proudly, and occasionally neighing, as much as to say, "Come on, my hearties, you see I ha'n't forgot our old amusement yet." And they did come on with a vengeance, clatter, clatter, clatter, as if so many fiends had broke loose. The prairie lay extended before me as far as the eye could reach, and I began to think that there would be no end to the race.

My little animal was full of fire and mettle, and as it was the first bit of genuine sport that he had had for some time, he appeared determined to make the most of it. He kept the lead for full half an hour, frequently neighing as if in triumph and derision. I thought of John Gilpin's celebrated ride, but that was child's play to this. The proverb says, "The race is not always to the swift, nor the battle to the strong," and so it proved in the present instance. My mustang was obliged to carry weight, while his competitors were as free as nature had made them. A beautiful bay, who had trod close upon my heels the whole way, now came side by side with my mustang, and we had it hip and thigh for about ten minutes, in such style as would have delighted the heart of a true lover of the turf. I now felt an interest in the race myself, and for the credit of my bit of blood, determined to win it if it was at all in the nature of things. I plied the lash and spur, and the little critter took it quite kindly, and tossed his head, and neighed, as much as to say, "Colonel, I know what you're after—Go ahead!"—and he cut dirt in beautiful style, I tell you.

This could not last for ever. At length my competitor dashed ahead, somewhat the same way that Adam Huntsman served me last election, except that there was no gouging; and my little fellow was compelled to clatter after his tail, like a needy politician after an office holder when he wants his influence, and which my mustang found it quite as difficult to reach. He hung on like grim death for some time longer, but at last his ambition began to flag; and having lost his ground, others seemed to think that he was not the mighty critter he was cracked up to be, no how, and they tried to outstrip him also. A second shot ahead, and he kicked up his heels in derision as he passed us; then a third, a fourth, and so on, and even the

scrubbiest little rascal in the whole drove was disposed
to have a fling at their broken down leader. A true picture
of politicians and their truckling followers, thought I. We
now followed among the last of the drove until we came
to the banks of the Navasola river. The foremost leaped
from the margin into the rushing stream, the others, politician like, followed him, though he would lead them to
destruction; but my wearied animal fell on the banks,
completely exhausted with fatigue. It was a beautiful sight
to see them stemming the torrent, ascend the opposite
bank and scour over the plain, having been refreshed by
the water. I relieved my wearied animal from the saddle,
and employed what means were in my power to restore
him.

CHAPTER THIRTY-TWO

I Wrestle with a Cougar

After toiling for more than an hour to get my mustang upon his feet again, I gave it up as a bad job, as little Van did when he attempted to raise himself to the moon by the waistband of his breeches. Night was fast closing in, and as I began to think that I had just about sport enough for one day, I might as well look around for a place of shelter for the night, and take a fresh start in the morning, by which time I was in hopes my horse would be recruited. Near the margin of the river a large tree had been blown down, and I thought of making my lair in its top, and approached it for that purpose. While beating among the branches I heard a low growl, as much as to say, "Stranger, the apartments are already taken." Looking about to see what sort of a bed-fellow I was likely to have, I discovered, not more than five or six paces from me, an enormous Mexican Cougar, eyeing me as an epicure surveys the table before he selects his dish, for I have no doubt the cougar looked upon me as the subject of a future supper. Rays of light darted from his large eyes, he showed his teeth like a negro in hysterics, and he was crouching on his haunches ready for a spring; all of which convinced me that unless I was pretty quick upon the trigger, posterity would know little of the termination of my eventful career, and it would be far less glorious and useful than I intend to make it.

One glance satisfied me that there was no time to be lost, as Pat thought when falling from a church steeple, and exclaimed, "This would be mighty pleasant, now, if it would only last,"—but there was no retreat either for me or the cougar, so I leveled my Betsey and blazed away. The report was followed by a furious growl, (which is sometimes the case in Congress,) and the next moment, when I expected to find the tarnal critter struggling with death, I beheld him shaking his head as if nothing more than a bee had stung him. The ball had struck him on the forehead and glanced off, doing no other injury than stunning him for an instant, and tearing off the skin, which tended to infuriate him the more. The cougar wasn't long in making up his mind what to do, nor was I neither; but he would have it all his own way, and vetoed my motion to back out. I had not retreated three steps before he sprang at me like a steamboat; I stepped aside, and as he lit upon the ground, I struck him violently with the barrel of my rifle, but he didn't mind that, but wheeled around and made at me again. The gun was now of no use, so I threw it away, and drew my hunting knife, for I knew we should come to close quarters before the fight would be over. This time he succeeded in fastening on my left arm, and was just beginning to amuse himself by tearing the flesh off with his fangs, when I ripped my knife into his side, and he let go his hold much to my satisfaction.

He wheeled about and came at me with increased fury, occasioned by the smarting of his wounds. I now tried to blind him, knowing that if I succeeded he would become an easy prey; so as he approached me I watched my opportunity, and aimed a blow at his eyes with my knife, but unfortunately it struck him on the nose, and he paid no other attention to it than by a shake of the head and a low growl. He pressed me close, and as I was stepping backward my foot tripped in a vine, and I fell to the ground. He was down upon me like a nighthawk upon a June bug. He seized hold of the outer part of my right thigh, which afforded him considerable amusement; the hinder part of his body was towards my face; I grasped his tail with my left hand, and tickled his ribs with my hunting knife, which I held in my right. Still the critter wouldn't let go his hold; and as I found that he would lacerate my leg dreadfully, unless he was speedily shaken off, I tried to hurl him down the bank into the river, for our scuffle had already brought us to the edge of the bank. I stuck my knife into his side, and summoned all my strength to throw him over. He resisted, was desperate heavy; but at last I got him so far down the declivity that he lost his balance, and he rolled over and over till he landed on the margin of the river; but in his fall he dragged me along with him. Fortunately, I fell uppermost, and his neck presented a fair mark for my hunting knife. Without allowing myself time even to draw breath, I aimed one desperate blow at his neck, and the knife entered his gullet up to the handle, and reached his heart. He struggled for a few moments, and died. I have had many fights with bears, but that was mere child's play; this was the first fight ever I had with a cougar, and I hope it may be the last.

I now returned to the tree-top to see if any one else would dispute my lodging; but now I could take peaceable and quiet possession. I parted some of the branches, and cut away others to make a bed in the opening; I then gathered a quantity of moss, which hung in festoons from the trees, which I spread on the litter, and over this I spread my horse blanket; and I had as comfortable a bed as a weary man need ask for. I now took another look at my mustang, and from all appearances, he would not live until morning. I ate some of the cakes that little Kate of Nacogdoches had made for me, and then carried my saddle into my tree top, and threw myself down upon my bed with no very pleasant reflections at the prospect before me.

I was weary, and soon fell asleep, and did not awake until daybreak the next day. I felt somewhat stiff and sore from the wounds I had received in the conflict with the cougar; but I considered myself as having made a lucky escape. I looked over the bank, and as I saw the carcass of the cougar lying there, I thought that it was an even chance that we had not exchanged conditions; and I felt grateful that the fight had ended as it did. I now went to look after my mustang, fully expecting to find him as dead as the cougar; but what was my astonishment to find that he had disappeared without leaving trace of hair or hide of him! I first supposed that some beasts of prey had consumed the poor critter; but then they wouldn't have eaten his bones, and he had vanished as effectually as the deposites, without leaving any mark of the course they had taken. This bothered me amazing; I couldn't figure it out by any rule that I had ever heard of, so I concluded to think no more about it.

I felt a craving for something to eat, and looking around for some game, I saw a flock of geese on the shore of the river. I shot a fine, fat gander, and soon stripped him of his feathers: and gathering some light wood, I kindled a fire, run a long stick through my goose for a spit, and put it down to roast, supported by two sticks with prongs. I had a desire for some coffee; and having a tin cup with me, I poured the paper of ground coffee that I had received from the bee hunter into it, and made a strong cup, which was very refreshing. Off of my goose and biscuit I made a hearty meal, and was preparing to depart without clearing up the breakfast things, or knowing which direction to pursue, when I was somewhat taken aback by another of the wild scenes of the west. I heard a sound like the trampling of many horses, and I thought to be sure the mustangs or buffaloes were coming upon me again; but, on raising my head, I beheld in the distance about fifty mounted Camanches, with their spears glittering in the morning sun, dashing toward the spot where I stood at full speed. As the column advanced, it divided, according to their usual practice, into two semicircles, and in an instant I was surrounded. Quicker than thought I sprang to my rifle, but as my hand grasped it, I felt that resistance against so many would be of as little use as pumping for thunder in dry weather.

The chief was for making love to my beautiful Betsey, but I clung fast to her, and assuming an air of composure,

I demanded whether their nation was at war with the Americans. "No," was the reply. "Do you like the Americans?" "Yes; they are our friends." "Where do you get your spear heads, your rifles, your blankets, and your knives from?" "Get them from our friends, the Americans." "Well, do you think, if you were passing through their nation, as I am passing through yours, they would attempt to rob you of your property?" "No, they would feed me, and protect me; and the Camanche will do the same by his white brother."

I now asked him what it was had directed him to the spot where I was, and he told me, that they had seen the smoke from a great distance, and had come to see the cause of it. He inquired what had brought me there alone; and I told him that I had come to hunt, and that my mustang had become exhausted, and though I thought he was about to die, that he had escaped from me; at which the chief gave a low chuckling laugh, and said it was all a trick of the mustang, which is the most wily and cunning of all animals. But he said, that as I was a brave hunter, he would furnish me with another; he gave orders, and a fine young horse was immediately brought forward.

When the party approached there were three old squaws at their head, who made a noise with their mouths, and served as trumpeters. I now told the chief that, as I now had a horse, I would go for my saddle, which was in the place where I had slept. As I approached the spot I discovered one of the squaws devouring the remains of my roasted goose, but my saddle and bridle were nowhere to be found. Almost in despair of seeing them again, I observed, in a thicket at a little distance, one of the trumpeters kicking and belaboring her horse to make him

move off, while the sagacious beast would not move a step
from the troop. I followed her, and, thanks to her restive
mustang, secured my property, which the chief made her
restore to me. Some of the warriors had by this time discovered the body of the cougar, and had already commenced skinning it; and seeing how many stabs were
about it, I related to the chief the desperate struggle I had
had; he said, "Brave hunter, brave man," and wished me
to be adopted into his tribe, but I respectfully declined
the honor. He then offered to see me on my way; and I
asked him to accompany me to the Colorado river, if he
was going in that direction, which he agreed to do. I
put my saddle on my fresh horse, mounted, and we darted
off, at a rate not much slower than I had rode the day
previous with the wild herd, the old squaws at the head
of the troop braying like young jackasses the whole way.

About three hours after starting we saw a drove of mustangs quietly pasturing in the prairie at a distance. One
of the Indians immediately got his lasso ready, which was
a long rope made of hide plaited like whip cord, with an
iron ring at one end, through which the rope was passed
so as to form a noose; and thus prepared, he darted ahead
of the troop to make a capture. They allowed him to
approach pretty nigh, he all the time flourishing his lasso;
but before he got within reaching distance, they started
off at a brisk canter, made two or three wide circuits
around him, as if they would spy out what he was after,
then abruptly changed their course and disappeared. One
mustang out of all the drove remained standing quietly;
the Indian made up to him, threw the lasso, but the
mustang dodged his head between his fore legs, and escaped the noose, but did not attempt to escape. The

Indian then rode up to him, and the horse very patiently submitted while he put a bridle on him, and secured him. When I approached, I immediately recognized in the captive the pestilent little animal that had shammed sickness and escaped from me the day before; and when he caught my eye he cast down his head and looked rather sheepish, as if he were sensible and ashamed of the dirty trick he had played me. I expressed my astonishment to the Indian chief at the mustang's allowing himself to be captured without an effort to escape; and he told me, that they are generally hurled to the ground with such violence when first taken with the lasso, that they remember it ever after, and that the sight of it will subdue them to submission, though they may have run wild for years. Just so with an office-holder, who, being kicked out, turns patriot—shake a commission at him, and the fire of his patriotism usually escapes in smoke.

We traveled all day, and toward evening we came across a small drove of buffaloes; and it was a beautiful sight to behold with what skill the Indians hunted down this noble game. There are no horsemen who ride more gracefully than the Camanches; and they sit so closely, and hold such absolute control over the horse, that he seems to be part of their own person. I had the good fortune to bring down a young heifer, and as it was the only beef that we killed, the chief again complimented me as being a brave hunter; and while they were preparing the heifer for our supper, I related to him many of my hunting exploits, at which he manifested pleasure and much astonishment for an Indian. He again urged upon me to become one of the tribe.

We made a hearty supper, hobbled our mustangs, which

we turned into the prairie to graze, and then encamped
for the night. I awoke about two hours before daybreak,
and looking over the tract of country through which we
had traveled, the sky was as bright and clear as if the sun
had already risen. I watched it for some time without
being able to account for it, and asked my friend, the
chief, to explain, who told me that the prairie was on
fire, and that it must have caught when we cooked our
dinner. I have seen hundreds of acres of mountain timber
on fire in my time, but this is the first time that I ever
saw a prairie burning.

Nothing of interest occurred until we reached the Colorado, and were following the river to the place where it
crosses the road to Bexar, which place the Indians promised to conduct me to. We saw a light column of smoke
ascending in the clear sky, and hastened toward it. It proceeded from a small cluster of trees near the river. When
we came within five hundred yards of it, the warriors
extended their line around the object, and the chief and
myself cautiously approached it. When we came within
eyeshot, what was my astonishment to discover a solitary
man seated on the ground near the fire, so intent upon
some pursuit that he did not perceive our approach. We
drew nigh to him, and still he was unconscious of our
approach. It was poor Thimblerig, practicing his game of
thimbles upon the crown of his white Vicksburger. This
is what I call the ruling passion most amazing strong. The
chief shouted the war whoop, and suddenly the warriors
came rushing in from all quarters, preceded by the old
squaw trumpeters squalling like mad. The conjurer
sprang to his feet, and was ready to sink into the earth
when he beheld the ferocious looking fellows that sur-

rounded him. I stepped up, took him by the hand, and quieted his fears. I told the chief that he was a friend of mine, and I was very glad to have found him, for I was afraid that he had perished. I now thanked him for his kindness in guiding me over the prairies, and gave him a large Bowie knife, which he said he would keep for the sake of the brave hunter. The whole squadron then wheeled off, and I saw them no more. I have met with many polite men in my time, but no one who possessed in a greater degree what may be called true spontaneous politeness than this Camanche chief, always excepting Philip Hone, Esq., of New York, whom I look upon as the politest man I ever did see; for when he asked me to take a drink at his own sideboard he turned his back upon me, that I mightn't be ashamed to fill as much as I wanted. That was what I call doing the fair thing.

Thimblerig was delighted at meeting me again, but it was some time before he recovered sufficiently from the cold sweat into which the sudden appearance of the Indians had thrown him to recount his adventures to me. He said that he felt rather down-hearted when he found himself abandoned both by the Bee hunter and myself, and he knew not which course to pursue; but after thinking about the matter for two hours, he had made up his mind to retrace the road we had traveled over, and had mounted his mustang for that purpose, when he spied the Bee hunter laden with honey. The mystery of his abrupt departure was now fully accounted for; he had spied a solitary bee shaping its course to its hive, and at the moment he couldn't control the ruling passion, but followed the bee without reflecting for a moment upon the difficulties and dangers that his thoughtlessness might occasion his friends.

I now asked him what had become of the Bee hunter, and he said that he had gone out in pursuit of game for their supper, and he expected that he would return shortly, as he had been absent at least an hour. While we were still speaking our friend appeared, bending under the weight of a wild turkey. He manifested great joy at meeting with me so unexpectedly; and desiring the conjurer to pluck the feathers of the bird, which he cheerfully undertook, for he said he had been accustomed to plucking pigeons, we set about preparing our supper.

The position we occupied was directly on the route leading to Bexar, and at the crossings of the Colorado. We were about to commence our supper, for the turkey was done in beautiful style, when the sound of a horse neighing startled us. We looked over the prairie, and beheld two men approaching on horseback, and both armed with rifles and knives. The Bee hunter said that it was time for us to be on our guard, for we should meet, perhaps, more enemies than friends as soon as we crossed the river, and the new comers were making directly for the spot we occupied; but, as they were only two, it occasioned no uneasiness.

As they drew nigh we recognized the strangers; they turned out to be the old pirate and the Indian hunter who had lodged with us a few nights before. We hailed them, and on seeing us they alighted and asked permission to join our party, which we gladly agreed to, as our journey was becoming rather more perilous every mile we advanced. They partook of our turkey, and as they had some small cakes of bread, which they threw into the general stock, we made a hearty supper: and, after a battle song from the Bee hunter, we prepared to rest for the night.

Early next morning we crossed the river and pushed forward for the fortress of Alamo. The old pirate was taciturn as ever, but his companion was talkative and in good spirits. I asked him where he had procured their mustangs, and he said he had found them hobbled in Burnet's Grant, just at a time that he felt very tired; and as he believed that no one would lay claim to them at Bexar, he couldn't resist mounting one, and persuading his friend to mount the other.

Nothing of interest occurred until we came within about twenty miles of San Antonio. We were in the open prairie, and beheld a band of about fifteen or twenty armed men approaching us at full speed. "Look out for squalls," said the old pirate, who had not spoken for an hour; "they are a scouting party of Mexicans." "And are three or four times our number," said Thimblerig. "No matter," replied the old man; "they are convicts, jail birds, and cowardly ruffians, no doubt, who would tremble at a loud word as much as a mustang at the sight of a lasso. Let us spread ourselves, dismount, and trust to our arms."

We followed his orders, and stood beside our horses, which served to protect our persons, and we awaited the approach of the enemy. When they perceived this movement of ours, they checked their speed, appeared to consult together for a few minutes, then spread their line, and came within rifle shot of us. The leader called out to us in Spanish, but as I did not understand him, I asked the old man what it was, who said he called upon us to surrender.

"There will be a brush with those blackguards," continued the pirate. "Now each of you single out your man for the first fire, and they are greater fools than I take them for if they give us a chance at a second. Colonel, as you are a good shot, just settle the business for that talking fellow with the red feather; he's worth any three of the party."

"Surrender, or we fire," shouted the fellow with the red feather, in Spanish.

"Fire, and be d——d," returned the pirate at the top of his voice, in plain English.

And sure enough they took his advice, for the next minute we were saluted with a discharge of musketry, the report of which was so loud that we were convinced they all had fired. Before the smoke had cleared away we had each selected our man, fired, and I never did see such a scattering among their ranks as followed. We beheld several mustangs running wild without their riders over the prairie, and the balance of the company were already retreating at a more rapid gait than they approached. We hastily mounted, and commenced pursuit, which we kept up until we beheld the independent flag flying from the battlements of the fortress of Alamo, our place of destination. The fugitives succeeded in evading our pursuit, and we rode up to the gates of the fortress, announced to the sentinel who we were, and the gates were thrown open; and we entered amid shouts of welcome bestowed upon us by the patriots.

CHAPTER THIRTY-THREE

The Alamo at Last!

The fortress of Alamo is at the town of Bexar, on the San Antonio river, which flows through the town. Bexar is about one hundred and forty miles from the coast, and contains upward of twelve hundred citizens, all native Mexicans, with the exception of a few American families who have settled there. Besides these there is a garrison of soldiers, and trading pedlars of every description, who resort to it from the borders of the Rio Grande, as their nearest depot of American goods. A military outpost was established at this spot by the Spanish government in 1718. In 1721 the town was settled by emigrants sent out from the Canary Islands by the King of Spain. It became a flourishing settlement, and so continued until the revolution in 1812, since which period the Cumanche and other Indians have greatly harassed the inhabitants, producing much individual suffering, and totally destroying, for a season at least, the prospects of the town. Its site is one of the most beautiful in the western world. The air is salubrious, the water delightful, especially when mixed with a little of the ardent, and the health of the citizens is proverbial. The soil around it is highly fertile, and well calculated for cotton and grain.

The gallant young Colonel Travis, who commands the Texian forces in the fortress of Alamo, received me like a man; and though he can barely muster one hundred and fifty efficient men, should Santa Anna make an attack upon us, with the whole host of ruffians that the Mexican prisons can disgorge, he will have snakes to eat before he gets over the wall, I tell you. But one spirit appeared to animate this little band of patriots—and that is liberty, or death. To worship God according to the dictates of their own conscience, and govern themselves as freemen should be governed.

All the world knows by this time, that the town of Bexar, or, as some call it, San Antonio, was captured from the Mexicans by General Burlison on the 10th day of December, 1835,* after a severe struggle of five days and five nights, during which he sustained a loss of four men only, but the brave old Colonel Milam was among them. There were seventeen hundred men in the town, and the Texian forces consisted of but two hundred and sixteen. The Mexicans had walled up the streets leading from the public square, intending to make a desperate resistance; the Texians however made an entrance, and valiantly drove them from house to house, until General

* On October 2, 1835, the first pitched battle broke out between the Texans and the Mexicans. By December, the Mexican towns of Gonzales, Goliad, and San Antonio had fallen to the Texans.

Cos retreated to the castle of Alamo, without the city, and there hoisted the white flag, and sent out the terms of capitulation, which were as follows:

General Cos is to retire within six days, with his officers, arms, and private property, on parole of honor. He is not to oppose the re-establishment of the constitution of 1824.

The infantry and the cavalry, the remnant of Morale's battalion, and the convicts, to return, taking with them ten rounds of cartridge for safety against the Indians.

All public property, money, arms, and ammunition, to be delivered to General Burlison, of the Texian army, with some other stipulation in relation to the sick and wounded, private property, and prisoners of war. The Texians would not have acceded to them, preferring to storm him in his stronghold, but at this critical juncture they hadn't a single round of ammunition left, having fought from the 5th to the 9th of the month. General Ugartechea had arrived but the day before with three hundred troops, and the four hundred convicts mentioned above, making a reinforcement of seven hundred men; but such rubbish was no great obstacle to the march of freedom. The Mexicans lost about three hundred men during the siege, and the Texians had only four killed and twenty wounded. The articles of capitulation being signed, we marched into the town, took possession of the fortress, hoisted the independent flag, and told the late proprietors to pack up their moveables and clear out in the snapping of a trigger, as we did not think our pockets quite safe with so many jail birds around us. And this is the way the Alamo came into our possession; but the way we shall maintain our possession of it will be a subject for the future historian to record, or my name's not

Crockett. I wish I may be shot if I don't go ahead to the last.

I found Colonel Bowie, of Louisiana, in the fortress, a man celebrated for having been in more desperate personal conflicts than any other in the country, and whose name has been given to a knife of a peculiar construction, which is now in general use in the south-west. I was introduced to him by Colonel Travis, and he gave me a friendly welcome, and appeared to be mightily pleased that I had arrived safe. While we were conversing, he had occasion to draw his famous knife to cut a strap, and I wish I may be shot if the bare sight of it wasn't enough to give a man of a squeamish stomach the cholic, especially before breakfast. He saw I was admiring it, and, said he, "Colonel, you might tickle a fellows ribs a long time with this little instrument before you'd make him laugh; and many a time have I seen a man puke at the idea of the point touching the pit of his stomach."

My companions, the Bee hunter and the conjurer, joined us, and the colonel appeared to know them both very well. He had a high opinion of the Bee hunter, for turning to me, he said, "Colonel, you could not have had a braver, better, or more pleasant fellow for a companion than honest Ned here. With fifteen hundred such men I would undertake to march to the city of Mexico, and occupy the seat of Santa Anna myself before three months should elapse."

The colonel's life has been marked by constant peril, and deeds of daring. A few years ago, he went on a hunting excursion into the prairies of Texas, with nine companions. They were attacked by a roving party of Cumanches, about two hundred strong, and such was the science of the colonel in this sort of wild warfare, that after killing a considerable number of the enemy, he fairly frightened the remainder from the field of action, and they fled in utter dismay. The fight took place among the high grass in the open prairie. He ordered his men to dismount from their horses and scatter; to take deliberate aim before they fired, but as soon as they had discharged their rifles to fall flat on the ground, and crawl away from the spot, and reload their pieces. By this scheme, they not only escaped the fire of the Indians, but by suddenly discharging their guns from another quarter, they created the impression that their party was a numerous one; and the Indians, finding that they were fighting against an invisible enemy, after losing about thirty of their men, took to flight, believing themselves lucky in having escaped with no greater loss. But one of the colonel's party was slightly wounded, and that was owing to his remaining to reload his rifle without having first shifted his position.

Santa Anna, it is said, roars like an angry lion at the disgraceful defeat that his brother-in-law, General Cos, lately met with at this place. It is rumored that he has recruited a large force, and commenced his march to San Louis de Potosi, and he is determined to carry on a war of extermination. He is liberal in applying his epithets to our countrymen in Texas, and denounces them as a set of perfidious wretches, whom the compassion of the generous Mexicans has permitted to take refuge in their country; and who, like the serpent in the fable, no sooner warmed themselves, than they stung their benefactors. This is a good joke. By what title does Mexico lay claim to all the territory which belonged to Spain in North America? Each province or state of New Spain contended separately or jointly, just as it happened, for their independence, as we did, and were not united under a general government representing the whole of the Spanish possessions, which was only done afterward by mutual agreement or federation. Let it be remembered that the Spanish authorities were first expelled from Texas by the American settlers, who, from the treachery of their Mexican associates, were unable to retain it; but the second time they were more successful. They certainly had as good a right to the soil thus conquered by them, as the inhabitants of other provinces who succeeded against Spain. The Mexicans talk of the ingratitude of the Americans; the truth is, that the ingratitude has been on the other side. What was the war of Texas, in 1813, when the revolutionary spark was almost extinguished in Mexico? What was the expedition of Mina, and his three hundred American Spartans, who perished heroically in the very heart of Mexico, in the vain attempt to resuscitate and keep alive the spark of independence which has at this time kindled such an ungrateful blaze? If a just estimate could be made of the lives and the treasures contributed by American enterprise in that cause, it would appear incredible. How did the Mexicans obtain their independence at last? Was it by their own virtue and courage? No, it was by the treachery of one of the king's generals, who established himself by successful treason, and they have been in constant commotion ever since, which proves they are unfit to govern themselves, much less a free and enlightened people at a distance of twelve hundred miles from them.

The Mexican government, by its colonization laws, invited and induced the Anglo-American population of

Texas to colonize its wilderness, under the pledged faith of a written constitution, that they should continue to enjoy that constitutional liberty and republican government to which they had been habituated in the land of their birth, the United States of America. In this expectation they have been cruelly disappointed, as the Mexican nation has acquiesced in the late changes made in the government by Santa Anna, who, having overturned the constitution of his country, now offers the settlers the cruel alternative, either to abandon their homes acquired by so many privations, or submit to the most intolerable of all tyranny, the combined despotism of the sword and the priesthood.

But Santa Anna charges the Americans with ingratitude! This is something like Satan reviling sin. I have gathered some particulars of the life of this moral personage from a gentleman at present in the Alamo, and who is intimately acquainted with him, which I will copy into my book exactly as he wrote it.

Santa Anna is about forty-two years of age, and was born in the city of Vera Cruz. His father was a Spaniard, of old Spain, of respectable standing, though poor; his mother was a Mexican. He received a common education, and at the age of thirteen or fourteen was taken into the military family of the then Intendant of Vera Cruz, General Davila, who took a great fancy to him, and brought him up. He remained with General Davila until about the year 1820. While with Davila he was made a major, and when installed he took the honors very coolly, and on some of his friends congratulating him, he said, "If you were to make me a god, I should desire to be something greater." This trait, developed at so early a period of his life, indicated the existence of that vaulting ambition which has ever since characterized his life.

After serving the Spanish royal cause until 1821, he left Vera Cruz, turned against his old master and benefactor, and placed himself at the head of some irregular troops which he raised on the sea-coast near Vera Cruz, and which are called Jarochos in their language, and which were denominated by him his Cossacks, as they were all mounted and armed with spears. With this rude cavalry he besieged Vera Cruz, drove Davila into the castle of San Juan d'Ulloa, and after having been repulsed again entered at a subsequent period, and got entire possession of the city, expelling therefrom the old Spanish troops, and reducing the power of the mother country in Mexico to the walls of the castle.

Subsequent to this, Davila is said to have obtained an interview with Santa Anna, and told him he was destined to act a prominent part in the history of his country. "And now," says he, "I will give you some advice: always go with the strongest party." He always acted up to this motto until he raised the *grito,* (or cry,) in other words, took up the cudgels for the friars and church. He then overturned the federal government, and established a central despotism, of which the priests and the military were the two privileged orders. His life has been, from the first, of the most romantic kind, constantly in revolutions, constantly victorious.

His manners are extremely affable; he is full of anecdote and humor, and makes himself exceedingly fascinating and agreeable to all who come into his company; he is about five feet ten, rather spare, has a moderately high forehead, with black hair, short black whiskers, without mustaches, and an eye large, black, and expressive of a lurking devil in his look; he is a man of genteel and dignified deportment, but of a disposition perfectly heartless. He married a Spanish lady of property, a native of Alvarado, and through that marriage obtained the first part of his estate, called Manga de Clavo, six leagues from Vera Cruz. He has three fine children, yet quite young.

The following striking anecdote of Santa Anna illustrates his peculiar quickness and management: During the revolution of 1829, while he was shut up in Oaxaca, and surrounded by the government troops, and reduced to the utmost straits for the want of money and provisions; having a very small force, there had been, in consequence of the siege and firing every day through the streets, no mass for several weeks. He had no money, and hit upon the following expedient to get it: he took possession of one of the convents, got hold of the wardrobe of the friars, dressed his officers and some of his soldiers in it, and early in the morning had the bells rung for the mass. The people, delighted at having again an opportunity of adoring the Supreme Being, flocked to the church where he was; and after the house was pretty well-filled, his friars showed their side-arms and bayonets from beneath the cowls, and closed the doors upon the assembled multitude.

At this unexpected denouement there was a tremendous shrieking, when one of his officers ascended the pulpit, and told the people that he wanted ten thousand dollars, and must have it. He finally succeeded in getting about thirty-six hundred dollars, when he dismissed the congregation.

As a sample of Santa Anna's pious whims we relate the following:

In the same campaign of Oaxaca, Santa Anna and his officers were there besieged by Rincon, who commanded the government troops. Santa Anna was in a convent surrounded by a small breastwork. Some of the officers one night, to amuse themselves, took the wooden saints out of the church and placed them as sentries, dressed in uniforms, on the breastwork. Rincon, alarmed on the morning at this apparent boldness, began to fire away at the wooden images, supposing them to be flesh and blood, and it was not until some of the officers who were not in the secret had implored Santa Anna to prevent this desecration that the firing ceased.

Many similar facts are related of him. He is, in fact, all things to all men; and yet, after his treachery to Davila, he has the impudence to talk about ingratitude. He never was out of Mexico. If I only live to tree him, and take him prisoner, I shall ask for no more glory in this life.

CHAPTER THIRTY-FOUR

The Siege of the Alamo

I write this on the nineteenth of February, 1836, at San Antonio. We are all in high spirits, though we are rather short of provisions, for men who have appetites that could digest any thing but oppression; but no matter, we have a prospect of soon getting our bellies full of fighting, and that is victuals and drink to a true patriot any day. We had a little sort of convivial party last evening: just about a dozen of us set to work, most patriotically, to see whether we could not get rid of that curse of the land, whiskey, and we made considerable progress; but my poor friend, Thimblerig, got sewed up just about as tight as the eyelet-hole in a lady's corset, and a little tighter too. I reckon; for when he went to bed he called for a bootjack, which was brought to him, and he bent down on his hands and knees, and very gravely pulled off his hat with it, for the darned critter was so thoroughly swiped that he didn't know his head from his heels. But this wasn't all the folly he committed; he pulled off his coat and laid it on the bed, and then hung himself over the back of a chair; and I wish I may be shot if he didn't go to sleep in that position, thinking every thing had been done according to Gunter's late scale. Seeing the poor fellow completely used up, I carried him to bed, though he did belong to the Temperance society; and he knew nothing about what had occurred until I told him the next morning. The Bee hunter didn't join us in this blow-out. Indeed, he will seldom drink more than just enough to prevent his being called a total abstinence man. But then he is the most jovial fellow for a water drinker I ever did see.

This morning I saw a caravan of about fifty mules passing by Bexar, and bound for Santa Fe. They were loaded with different articles to such a degree that it was astonishing how they could travel at all, and they were nearly worn out by their labors. They were without bridle or halter, and yet proceeded with perfect regularity in a single line; and the owners of the caravan rode their mustangs with their enormous spurs, weighing at least a pound a piece, with rowels an inch and a half in length, and lever bits of the harshest description, able to break the jaws of their animals under a very gentle pressure. The men were dressed in the costume of Mexicans. Colonel Travis sent out a guard to see that they were not laden with munitions of war for the enemy. I went out with the party. The poor mules were bending under a burden of more than three hundred pounds, without including the panniers, which were bound so tight as almost to stop the breath of the poor animal. Each of the sorrowful line came up, spontaneously, in turn to have his girth unbound and his load removed. They seemed scarcely able to keep upon their feet, and as they successively obtained relief, one after another heaved a long deep sigh, which it was painful to hear, because it proved that the poor brutes had been worked beyond their strength. What a world of misery man inflicts upon the rest of creation in his brief passage through life!

Finding that the caravan contained nothing intended for the enemy, we assisted the owners to replace the heavy burdens on the backs of the patient but dejected mules, and allowed them to pursue their weary and lonely way. For full two hours we could see them slowly winding along the narrow path, a faint line that ran like a thread through the extended prairie; and finally they were whittled down to the little end of nothing in the distance, and were blotted out from the horizon.

The caravan had no sooner disappeared than one of the hunters, who had been absent several days, came in. He was one of those gentleman who don't pride themselves much upon their costume, and reminded me of a covey who came into a tavern in New York when I was last in that city. He was dressed in five jackets, all of which failed to conceal his raggedness, and as he bolted in, he exclaimed,

"Worse than I look, by ——. But no matter, I've let myself for fourteen dollars a month, and find my own grog and lodging."

"To do what?" demanded the barkeeper.

"To stand at the corner for a paper-mill sign—'cash for rags'—that's all. I'm about to enter upon the stationary business, you see." He tossed off his grog, and bustled out to begin his day's work.

But to return to the hunter. He stated that he had met some Indians on the banks of the Rio Frio, who informed him that Santa Anna, with a large force, had already crossed the Neuces, and might be expected to arrive before San Antonio in a few days. We immediately set about preparing to give him a warm reception, for we are all well aware, if our little band is overwhelmed by numbers, there is little mercy to be expected from the cowardly Mexicans—it is war to the knife.

I jocosely asked the ragged hunter, who was a smart, active young fellow, of the steamboat and alligator breed, whether he was a rhinoceros or a hyena, as he was so eager for a fight with the invaders. "Neither the one, nor t'other, Colonel," says he, "but a whole menagerie in myself. I'm shaggy as a bear, wolfish about the head, active as a cougar, and can grin like a hyena, until the bark will curl off a gum log. There's a sprinkling of all sorts in me, from the lion down to the skunk; and before the war is over you'll pronounce me an entire zoological institute, or I miss a figure in my calculation. I promise to swallow Santa Anna without gagging, if you will only skewer back his ears, and grease his head a little."

He told me that he was one in the fatal expedition fitted out from New Orleans, in November last, to join the contemplated attack upon Tampico by Mehia and Peraza. They were, in all, about one hundred and thirty men, who embarked as emigrants to Texas; and the terms agreed upon were, that it was optional whether the party took up arms in defence of Texas, or not, on landing. They were at full liberty to act as they pleased. But the truth was, Tampico was their destination, and an attack on that city the covert design, which was not made known before land was in sight. The emigrants were landed, some fifty, who doubtless had a previous understanding, joined the standard of General Mehia, and the following day a formidable fort surrendered without an attack.

The whole party were now tendered arms and ammunition, which even those who had been decoyed accepted; and, the line being formed, they commenced the attack upon the city. The hunter continued: "On the 15th of November our little army, consisting of one hundred and fifty men, marched into Tampico, garrisoned by two thousand Mexicans, who were drawn up in battle array in the public square of the city. We charged them at the point of the bayonet, and although they so greatly outnumbered us, *in two minutes* we completely routed them; and they fled, taking refuge on the house tops, from which they poured a destructive fire upon our gallant little band. We fought them until daylight, when we found our number decreased to fifty or sixty broken down and disheartened men. Without ammunition, and deserted by the officers, twenty-eight immediately surrendered. But a few of us cut our way through, and fortunately escaped to the mouth of the river, where we got on board a vessel and sailed for Texas.

"The twenty-eight prisoners wished to be considered as prisoners of war; they made known the manner in which they had been deceived, but they were tried by a court-martial of Mexican soldiers, and condemned to be shot on the 14th day of December, 1835, which sentence was carried into execution."

After receiving this account from my new friend, the old pirate and the Indian hunter came up, and they went off to liquor together, and I went to see a wild Mexican hog, which one of the hunters had brought in. These animals have become scarce, which circumstance is not to be deplored, for their flesh is of little value; and there will still be hogs enough left in Mexico, from all that I can learn, even though these should be extirpated.

CHAPTER THIRTY-FIVE

Last Days at the Alamo

February 22. The Mexicans, about sixteen hundred strong, with their President Santa Anna at their head, aided by Generals Almonte, Cos, Sesma, and Castrillon, are within two leagues of Bexar. General Cos, it seems, has already forgot his parole of honor, and is come back to retrieve the credit he lost in this place in December last. If he is captured a second time, I don't think he can have the impudence to ask to go at large again without giving better bail than on the former occasion. Some of the scouts came in, and bring reports that Santa Anna has been endeavoring to excite the Indians to hostilities against the Texians, but so far without effect. The Cumanches, in particular, entertain such hatred for the Mexicans, and at the same time hold them in such contempt, that they would rather turn their tomahawks against them, and drive them from the land, than lend a helping hand. We are up and doing, and as lively as Dutch cheese in the dog-days. The two hunters that I have already introduced to the reader left the town this afternoon, for the purpose of reconnoitring.

February 23. Early this morning the enemy came in sight, marching in regular order, and displaying their strength to the greatest advantage, in order to strike us with terror. But that was no go; they'll find that they have to do with men who will never lay down their arms as long as they can stand on their legs. We held a short council of war, and, finding that we should be completely surrounded, and overwhelmed by numbers, if we remained in the town, we concluded to withdraw to the fortress of Alamo, and defend it to the last extremity. We accordingly filed off, in good order, having some days before placed all the surplus provisions, arms, and ammunition in the fortress. We have had a large national flag made; it is composed of thirteen stripes, red and white, alternately, on a blue ground, with a large white star, of five points, in the centre, and between the points the letters TEXAS. As soon as all our little band, about one hundred and fifty in number, had entered and secured the fortress in the best possible manner, we set about raising our flag on the battlements; on which occasion there was no one more active than my young friend, the Bee hunter. He had been all along sprightly, cheerful, and spirited, but now, notwithstanding the control that he usually maintained over himself, it was with difficulty that he kept his enthusiasm within bounds. As soon as we commenced raising the flag he burst forth, in a clear, full tone of voice, that made the blood tingle in the veins of all who heard him:—

"Up with your banner, Freedom,
    Thy champions cling to thee;
They'll follow where'er you lead 'em,
    To death, or victory;—
Up with your banner, Freedom.

Tyrants and slaves are rushing
    To tread thee in the dust;
Their blood will soon be gushing,
    And stain our knives with rust;—
But not thy banner Freedom.

While stars and stripes are flying,
    Our blood we'll freely shed;
No groan will 'scape the dying,
    Seeing thee o'er his head;—
Up with your banner, Freedom."

This song was followed by three cheers from all within the fortress, and the drums and trumpets commenced playing. The enemy marched into Bexar, and took possession of the town, a blood-red flag flying at their head, to indicate that we need not expect quarters if we should fall into their clutches. In the afternoon a messenger was sent from the enemy to Colonel Travis, demanding an unconditional and absolute surrender of the garrison, threatening to put every man to the sword in case of refusal. The only answer he received was a cannon shot, so the messenger left us with a flea in his ear, and the Mexicans commenced firing grenades at us, but without doing any mischief. At night Colonel Travis sent an express to Colonel Fanning, at Goliad, about three or four days' march from this place, to let him know that we are besieged. The old pirate volunteered to go on this expedition, and accordingly left the fort after nightfall.

February 24. Very early this morning the enemy commenced a new battery on the banks of the river, about three hundred and fifty yards from the fort, and by afternoon they amused themselves by firing at us from that quarter. Our Indian scout came in this evening, and with him a reinforcement of thirty men from Gonzales, who are just in the nick of time to reap a harvest of glory; but there is some prospect of sweating blood before we gather it in. An accident happened to my friend Thimblerig this afternoon. He was intent on his eternal game of thimbles, in a somewhat exposed position, while the enemy were bombarding us from the new redoubt. A three-ounce ball glanced from the parapet and struck him on the breast, inflicting a painful, but not dangerous wound. I extracted the ball, which was of lead, and recommended to him to drill a hole through it, and carry it for a watch seal. "No," he replied, with energy, "may I be shot six times if I do: that would be making a bauble for an idle boast. No, Colonel, lead is getting scarce, and I'll lend it out at compound interest. Curse the thimbles!" he muttered, and went his way, and I saw no more of him that evening.

February 25. The firing commenced early this morning, but the Mexicans are poor engineers, for we haven't lost a single man, and our outworks have sustained no injury. Our sharpshooters have brought down a considerable number of stragglers at a long shot. I got up before the peep of day, hearing an occasional discharge of a rifle just over the place where I was sleeping, and I was somewhat amazed to see Thimblerig mounted alone on the battlement, no one being on duty at the time but the sentries. "What are you doing there?" says I. "Paying my debts," says he, "interest and all." "And how do you make out?" says I. "I've nearly got through," says he; "stop a moment, Colonel, and I'll close the account." He clapped his rifle to his shoulder, and blazed away, then jumped down from his perch, and said, "That account's settled; them chaps will let me play out my game in quiet next time." I looked over the wall, and saw four Mexicans lying dead on the plain. I asked him to explain what he meant by paying his debts, and he told me that he had run the grape shot into four rifle balls, and that he had taken an early stand to have a chance of picking off stragglers. "Now, Colonel, let's go take our bitters," said he;—and so we did. The enemy have been busy during the night, and have thrown up two batteries on the opposite side of the river. The battalion of Matamoras is posted there, and cavalry occupy the hills to the east and on the road to Gonzales. They are determined to surround us, and cut us off from reinforcement, or the possibility of escape by a sortie. Well, there's one thing they cannot prevent; we'll still go ahead, and sell our lives at a high price.

February 26. Colonel Bowie has been taken sick from overexertion and exposure. He did not leave his bed to-day until twelve o'clock. He is worth a dozen common men in a situation like ours. The Bee hunter keeps the whole garrison in good heart with his songs and his jests, and his daring and determined spirit. He is about the quickest on the trigger, and the best rifle shot we have in the fort. I have already seen him bring down eleven of the enemy, and at such a distance that we all thought it would be a waste of ammunition to attempt it. His gun is first rate, quite equal to my Betsey, though she has not quite as many trinkets about her. This day a small party sallied out of the fort for wood and water, and had a slight skirmish with three times their number from the division under General Sesma. The Bee hunter headed them, and beat the enemy off, after killing three. On opening his Bible at night, of which he always reads a portion before going to rest, he found a musket ball in the middle of it. "See here, Colonel," said he, "how they have treated the valued present of my dear little Kate of Nacogdoches." "It has saved your life," said I. "True," replied he, more seriously than usual, "and I am not the first sinner whose life has been saved by this book." He prepared for bed, and before retiring he prayed, and returned thanks for his providential escape; and I heard the name of Catherine mingled in his prayer.

February 27. The cannonading began early this morning, and ten bombs were thrown into the fort, but fortunately exploded without doing any mischief. So far it has been a sort of tempest in a tea-pot, not unlike a pitched battle in the Hall of Congress, where the parties array their forces, make fearful demonstrations on both sides, then fire away with loud-sounding speeches, which contain about as much meaning as the report of a howitzer charged with a blank cartridge. Provisions are becoming scarce, and the enemy are endeavoring to cut off our water. If they attempt to stop our grog in that manner, let them look out, for we shall become too wrathy for our shirts to hold us. We are not prepared to submit to an excise of that nature, and they'll find it out. This discovery has created considerable excitement in the fort.

February 28. Last night our hunters brought in some corn, and had a brush with a scout from the enemy beyond gun-shot of the fort. They put the scout to flight, and got in without injury. They bring accounts that the settlers are flying in all quarters, in dismay, leaving their possessions to the mercy of the ruthless invader, who is literally engaged in a war of extermination more brutal than the untutored savage of the desert could be guilty of. Slaughter is indiscriminate, sparing neither sex, age, nor condition. Buildings have been burnt down, farms laid waste, and Santa Anna appears determined to verify his threat, and convert the blooming paradise into a howling wilderness. For just one fair crack at that rascal, even at a hundred yards' distance, I would bargain to break my Betsey, and never pull trigger again. My name's not Crockett if I wouldn't get glory enough to appease my stomach for the remainder of my life. The scouts report that a settler by the name of Johnson, flying with his wife and three little children, when they reached the Colorado, left his family on the shore, and waded into the river to see whether it would be safe to ford with his wagon. When about the middle of the river he was seized by an alligator, and after a struggle, was dragged under the water, and perished. The helpless woman and her babes were discovered, gazing in agony on the spot, by other fugitives, who happily passed that way, and relieved them. Those who fight the battles experience but a small part of the privation, suffering, and anguish that follow in the train of ruthless war. The cannonading continued at intervals throughout the day, and all hands were kept up to their work. The enemy, somewhat emboldened, draws nigher to the fort. So much the better. There was a move in General Sesma's division toward evening.

February 29. Before daybreak, we saw General Sesma leave his camp with a large body of cavalry and infantry, and move off in the direction of Goliad. We think that he must have received news of Colonel Fanning's coming to our relief. We are all in high spirits at the prospect of being able to give the rascals a fair shake on the plain. This business of being shut up makes a man wolfish. I had a little sport this morning before breakfast. The enemy had planted a piece of ordnance within gun-shot of the fort during the night, and the first thing in the morning they commenced a brisked cannonade, point blank, against the spot where I was snoring. I turned out pretty smart and mounted the rampart. The gun was charged again, a fellow stepped forth to touch her off, but before he could apply the match, I let him have it, and he keeled over. A second stepped up, snatched the match from the hand of the dying man, but Thimblerig, who had followed me, handed me his rifle, and the next instant the Mexican was stretched on the earth beside the first. A third came up to the cannon, my companion handed me another gun, and I fixed him off in like manner. A fourth, then a fifth, seized the match, who both met with the same fate, and then the whole party gave it up as a bad job, and hurried off to the camp, leaving the cannon ready charged where they had planted it. I came down, took my bitters, and went to breakfast. Thimblerig told me that the place from which I had been firing was one of the snuggest stands in the whole fort, for he never failed picking off two or three stragglers before breakfast, when perched up there.

And I recollect, now, having seen him there, ever since he was wounded, the first thing in the morning, and the last at night, and at times, thoughtlessly playing at his eternal game.

March 1. The enemy's forces have been increasing in

numbers daily, notwithstanding they have already lost about three hundred men in the several assaults they have made upon us. I neglected to mention in the proper place, that when the enemy came in sight we had but three bushels of corn in the garrison, but have since found eighty bushels in a deserted house. Colonel Bowie's illness still continues, but he manages to crawl from his bed every day, that his comrades may see him. His presence alone is a tower of strength. The enemy becomes more daring as his numbers increase.

March 2. This day the delegates meet in general convention at the town of Washington, to frame our Declaration of Independence. That the sacred instrument may never be trampled on by the children of those who have freely shed their blood to establish it, is the sincere wish of David Crockett. Universal independence is an almighty idea, far too extensive for some brains to comprehend. It is a beautiful seed that germinates rapidly, and brings forth a large and vigorous tree, but like the deadly Upas, we sometimes find the smaller plants wither and die in its shades. Its blooming branches spread far and wide, offering a perch of safety to all alike, but even among its protecting branches we find the eagle, the kite, and the owl preying upon the helpless dove and sparrow. Beneath its shades myriads congregate in goodly fellowship; but the lamb and the fawn find but frail security from the lion and the jackal, though the tree of independence waves over them. Some imagine independence to be a natural charter, to exercise without restraint, and to their fullest extent, all the energies, both physical and mental, with which they have been endowed; and for their individual aggrandizement alone, without regard to the rights of others, provided they extend to all the same privilege and freedom of action. Such independence is the worst of tyranny.

March 3. We have given over all hopes of receiving assistance from Goliad or Refugio. Colonel Travis harangued the garrison, and concluded by exhorting them, in case the enemy should carry the fort, to fight to the last gasp, and render their victory even more serious to them than to us. This was followed by three cheers.

March 4. Shells have been falling into the fort like hail during the day, but without effect. About dusk, in the evening, we observed a man running toward the fort, pursued by about half a dozen of the Mexican cavalry. The Bee hunter immediately knew him to be the old pirate who had gone to Goliad, and, calling to the two hunters, he sallied out of the fort to the relief of the old man who was hard pressed. I followed close after. Before we reached the spot the Mexicans were close on the heel of the old man, who stopped suddenly, turned short upon his pursuers, discharged his rifle and one of the enemy fell from his horse. The chase was renewed, but finding that he would be overtaken and cut to pieces, he now turned again, and, to the amazement of the enemy, became the assailant in his turn. He clubbed his gun, and dashed among them like a wounded tiger, and they fled like sparrows. By this time we reached the spot, and, in the ardor of the moment, followed some distance before we saw that our retreat to the fort was cut off by another detachment of cavalry. Nothing was to be done but to fight our way through. We were all of the same mind. "Go ahead!" cried I, and they shouted, "Go ahead, Colonel!" We dashed among them, and a bloody conflict ensued. They were about twenty in number, and they stood their ground. After the fight had continued about five minutes, a detachment was seen issuing from the fort to our relief, and the Mexicans scampered off, leaving eight of their comrades dead upon the field. But we did not escape unscathed, for both the pirate and the Bee hunter were mortally wounded, and I received a sabre cut across the forehead. The old man died, with out speaking, as soon as we entered the fort. We bore my young friend to his bed, dressed his wounds, and I watched beside him. He lay, without complaint or manifesting pain, until about midnight, when he spoke, and I asked him if he wanted any thing. "Nothing," he replied, but drew a sigh that seemed to rend his heart, as he added, "Poor Kate of Nacogdoches!" His eyes were filled with tears, as he continued, "Her words were prophetic, Colonel;" and then he sang in a low voice that resembled the sweet notes of his own devoted Kate,

> "But toom cam' the saddle, all bluidy to see,
> And hame cam' the steed, but hame never cam' he."

He spoke no more, and a few minutes after, died. Poor Kate, who will tell this to thee!"

March 5. Pop, pop, pop! Bom, bom, bom! throughout the day. No time for memorandums now. Go ahead! Liberty and independence forever!

[*Here ends Davy Crockett's Own Story.*]

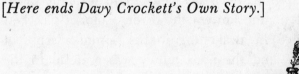

The following was added to the above manuscript by Charles T. Beale for inclusion in the 1880 edition.

The hand is cold that wrote the foregoing pages, and it devolves upon another to record the subsequent events. Before daybreak, on the 6th of March, the Alamo was assaulted by the whole force of the Mexican army, commanded by Santa Anna in person. The battle was desperate until daylight, when only six men belonging to the Texian garrison were found alive. They were instantly surrounded, and ordered by General Castrillon to surrender, which they did, under a promise of his protection, finding that resistance any longer would be madness. Colonel Crockett was of the number. He stood alone in an angle of the fort, the barrel of his shattered rifle in his right hand, in his left his huge Bowie knife dripping blood. There was a frightful gash across his forehead, while around him there was a complete barrier of about twenty Mexicans, lying pell mell, dead, and dying. At his feet lay the dead body of that well known character, designated in the Colonel's narrative by the assumed name of Thimblerig, his knife driven to the haft in the throat of a Mexican, and his left hand clenched in his hair. Poor fellow, I knew him well, at a time when he was possessed of many virtues, but of late years the weeds had choked up the flowers; however, Colonel Crockett had succeeded in awakening in his bosom a sense of better things, and the poor fellow was grateful to the last, and stood beside his friend throughout the desperate havoc.

General Castrillon was brave and not cruel, and disposed to save the prisoners. He marched them up to that part of the fort where stood Santa Anna and his murderous crew. The steady fearless step and undaunted tread of Colonel Crockett, on this occasion, together with the bold demeanor of the hardy veteran, had a powerful effect on all present. Nothing daunted he marched up boldly in front of Santa Anna, and looked him sternly in the face, while Castrillon addressed "his excellency,"— "Sir, here are six prisoners I have taken alive; how shall I dispose of them?" Santa Anna looked at Castrillon fiercely, flew into a violent rage, and replied, "Have I not told you before how to dispose of them? Why do you bring them to me?" At the same time his brave officers plunged their swords into the bosoms of their defenceless prisoners. Colonel Crockett, seeing the act of treachery, instantly sprang like a tiger at the ruffian chief, but before he could reach him a dozen swords were sheathed in his indomitable heart; and he fell and died without a groan, a frown on his brow, and a smile of scorn and defiance on his lips. Castrillon rushed from the scene, apparently horror-struck, sought his quarters, and did not leave them for several days, and hardly spoke to Santa Anna after.

The conduct of Colonel Bowie was characteristic to the last. When the fort was carried he was sick in bed. He had also one of the murderous butcher knives which bears his name. Lying in bed, he discharged his pistols and gun, and with each discharge brought down an enemy. So intimidated were the Mexicans by this act of desperate and cool bravery, that they dared not approach him, but shot him from the door; and as the cowards approached his bed, over the dead bodies of their companions, the dying Bowie, nerving himself for a last blow, plunged his knife into the heart of his nearest foe at the same instant that he expired.

The gallant Colonel Travis fought as if determined to verify his prediction, that he would make a victory more serious than a defeat to the enemy. He fell from the rampart, mortally wounded, into the fort; and his musket fell forward among the foe, who were scaling the wall. After a few minutes he recovered sufficiently to sit up, when the Mexican officer who led that party attempted to cut his head off with a sabre. The dying hero, with a death grasp, drew his sword and plunged it into the body of his antagonist and both together sank into the arms of death. General Cos, who had commanded this fortress while in the possession of the Mexicans, and from whom it was captured, on entering the fort after the battle, ordered the servant of Colonel Travis to point out the body of his master; he did so, when Cos drew his sword, waved it triumphantly over the corpse, and then mangled the face and limbs with the malignant feelings of a Cumanche savage. One woman, Mrs. Dickinson, and a negro of Colonel Travis, were the only persons whose lives were spared. The bodies of the slain were then thrown into a mass in the centre of the Alamo, and burned. The loss of the Mexicans in storming the place was not less than eight hundred killed and mortally wounded, making their losses since the first assault more than fifteen hundred. This immense slaughter, by so small a number, can only be accounted for by the fact of the Texians having five or six guns to each man in the fort. Immediately after the capture Santa Anna sent Mrs. Dickinson and the servant to General Houston, accompanied by a Mexican with a flag, offering the Texians peace and general amnesty, if they would lay down their arms, and submit to his government. General Houston's reply was, "True, sir, you have succeeded in killing some of our brave men, but the Texians are not yet conquered."

★   ★   ★

A Texan force of 400 was captured by the Mexicans near Goliad, but in April, 1836, a reorganized Texas army under General Sam Houston decisively defeated Santa Anna, who was captured. A convention declared Texas to be independent on March 2, 1836. Texas entered the Union on December 29, 1845 as the 28th state.